CHYŽHEVS'KYÏ, Dmytro.   History of nineteenth-century Russian literature, tr. by Richard Noel Porter. Vanderbilt, 1974. 2v bibl 72-2878. 15.00, 5.95 pa. ea. v.1, ISBN 0-8265-1187-2; v.2, ISBN 0-8265-1189-9.   C.I.P.

Contents — v.1: *The Romantic period;* v.2: *The Realistic period.* Each volume of this history contains a foreword by Serge A. Zenkovsky, who is also the editor. The volume on Romanticism was first published in 1964 in German and was translated from that language by Richard Porter, who, like Zenkovsky, is a professor at Vanderbilt. The two volumes are actually v.2 and 3 of a three-part series starting with *History of Russian literature from the eleventh century to the end of the Baroque,* which appeared in 1960. A bibliography on Russian Romanticism (shorter than that in the German edition) is included, but not one on Realism, because there is actually yet to come another (fourth) volume which will treat late Realism, Symbolism, and Futurism, and to which a bibliography will be affixed. A definitive study. Recommended for all libraries, undergraduate and graduate.

History of
Nineteenth-Century Russian Literature

Volume I. The Romantic Period

History of Nineteenth-Century Russian Literature

Volume I. The Romantic Period

by

Dmitrij Čiževskij

Translated by

Richard Noel Porter

Edited, with a Foreword, by

Serge A. Zenkovsky

1974
Vanderbilt University Press
Nashville

English-language edition
COPYRIGHT © 1974 BY VANDERBILT UNIVERSITY PRESS
All rights reserved

German-language edition
Originally published in 1964 as
Russische Literaturgeschichte des 19. Jahrhunderts
(I. Die Romantik)
Copyright © 1964 Eidos Verlag München

English translation Copyright © 1974 by Vanderbilt University Press
All rights reserved. Published in 1973.

The bibliography for the English-language edition has been
revised and enlarged by Serge A. Zenkovsky to include
recent publications.

Library of Congress Cataloguing-in-Publication Data

Chyzhevs'kyĭ, Dmytro, 1894-
History of nineteenth-century Russian literature.

Translation of Russische Literaturgeschichte des 19. Jahrhunderts.
Includes bibliographies.
CONTENTS: v. 1. Romantic period.
1. Russian literature—19th cent.—History and criticism. I. Title.
PG3012.C513   891.7'09'003   72-2878
ISBN 0-8265-1187-2 (cloth)
ISBN 0-8265-1188-0 (paper)

Printed in the United States of America

Contents

Editor's Foreword

The Romantic era has a particularly prominent place in Russian literature. It was during the Romantic era that Russian poetry and prose first achieved a substantially high level and became an important part of the literature of the Western world. Actually, most of Russia's great names in nineteenth-century literature were associated with this "Golden Age" in Russian poetry and extremely significant age in Russian prose. Puškin, Tjutčev, Lermontov, and Gogol' all wrote and attained the acme of their creativity in the decades from 1810 to 1850, while Turgenev, Dostoevskij, and L. Tolstoj, founders of the later great age of the Russian novel, also won their earliest recognition toward the end of the Romantic period.

It should not be forgotten that when the Russians produced their first literary works in the eleventh century, their country, despite increasing political, dynastic, and economic contacts with Western Europe, was still outside the main stream of European life. Having received their religion and basic elements of culture from the Eastern Christian Byzantines, the Russians remained for more than half a millennium part of the Byzantine spiritual and artistic world. Even after the fall of Byzantium in 1453, the Russians perpetuated for two more centuries their own version of the Byzantine tradition and remained strictly a part of Eastern Christian civilization. Certainly, from the eleventh to the seventeenth centuries, they were able to make considerable and lasting contributions to the visual arts and letters; but due to geographical factors and external political pressures, they remained unaware of the Western achievements of the late Middle Ages and the Renaissance among the peoples speaking Romance and Germanic languages.

In the early seventeenth century, however—a time of fiercely cruel religious struggles in the West—Russia began to become involved in these spiritual confrontations and her people experienced the expansionist assault of revived, post-Trentian Roman Catholicism. Thereafter, military or friendly encounters with Catholic and Protestant Europe grew more frequent and lasting, and the seventeenth century became the age of the penetration into Russia of the Baroque, the first *Western* artistic and literary movement directly to influence and even to alter the destinies of Russian culture and literature. The following hundred years were dominated by the culturally revolutionary and dynamic reigns of Peter I (1682–1725) and Catherine II (1763–1796). They were years primarily of imitation of the newly discovered West European patterns, themes, genres, and poetics. From the point of view of Russian literary development, the most lasting eighteenth-century achievements were the introduction of the syllabo-tonic metric poetic system, and the rise of poetry, for Russia produced in the eighteenth century at least two native poets of majestic stature, Mixail Lomonosov and Gavriil R. Deržavin. In the West, this century was the time of Enlightenment and of classicism, which followed in the footsteps of the previously dominant school there of the Baroque. Russia, however, was ill prepared for these two movements. In most other European countries, the phenomenon of Enlightenment was the result of prolonged philosophical and other cultural trends which had their roots in the Renaissance. Russia had never experienced the latter and could hardly then catch up with more advanced Western Europe or contribute significantly to this movement. Moreover, having never undergone the effects either of the Renaissance or of the Reformation or of the entire sumptuous blooming of the Baroque, Russians in the eighteenth century borrowed from the West—primarily, a new system of education, secularized ways of thought, and, at a more slackened pace, the latest fashions in the arts. Therefore, as Professor Dmitrij Čiževskij points out in his new introduction, written especially for this edition, classicism never developed any really deep roots in Russia. At the same time, the Russian eighteenth-century Enlightenment, being only imitative and much more shallow than that of the West, could not produce as rapidly the same intense reaction as was observed in England, Germany, and France.

Classicism, which was founded on Horatian ideas of proportion and the strict teaching of Aristotle on the various categories of drama, strengthened by the severe Cartesian rationalist philosophy, began to consume itself in Western Europe. Disappointment with the teachings of the Philosophes and the lessons of the French revolution accelerated this process; and by the turn of the century, romanticism manifested itself, primarily as a reaction to classicism and the Enlightenment, especially in England and Germany.

Russia, which had not developed a strong attachment to classicism, as noted above, therefore had little reason immediately to develop or to adopt the romantic approach in literature. The earliest works of Russian romanticists coincide, consequently, with the War of 1812—when Napoleon invaded Russia and was then driven out—and with the Russian campaign in Western Europe, which was undertaken to pursue the Corsican conqueror. The rediscovery of the Russian past— different from that of the West but nonetheless significant—the rise of national, philosophical, and mystical ideas, and the impact of Western literature hastened the rise of romanticism in Russia in the second part of the reign of Alexander I, who ruled from 1801 to 1825. The Decembrist movement and revolt of 1825 further contributed to the strengthening of romantic ideas and to the appearance of Russia's own romantic hero, the "superfluous man," misunderstood by society. The true blooming of the romantic literary school, however, came, as the reader will find from this book, only in the reign of Nicolas I, from 1825 to the early 1840s.

This latest book on Russian romanticism is not a separate investigation in this era of Russian literature. Professor Dmitrij Čiževskij, the West's most outstanding specialist in Russian letters, wrote it largely as a sequel to his *History of Russian Literature from the Eleventh Century to the End of the Baroque* (The Hague: Mouton and Co., 1960). The present volume, in turn, is to be followed by yet another, devoted to Russian realism, and it is expected that a further work covering the period from the 1890s to 1917 will soon become available to readers.

Čiževskij's *History of Russian Literature of the Nineteenth Century, Part One: Romanticism*, was first published in 1964 in German and its author had in mind primarily the German student and reader. This new edition, in English, has required some explanations of facts, literary trends, and names not readily identifiable by American students and lovers of Russian literature, as well as a different bibliography for English-language readers. I have therefore provided the book with some additional footnotes, have radically reworked the bibliography of the original edition and, together with the translator, Richard N. Porter, and Martha I. Strayhorn, editor, Vanderbilt University Press, have eliminated some errata and misprints in the original German edition. I should also like to express my gratitude to my American colleagues who helped me bring the bibliography up to date with works published on Russian romanticism in this country.

SERGE A. ZENKOVSKY

Preface

The question of Russian romanticism is one of many debatable ones in the history of Russian literature. At his first glance into the innumerable works of the Russian poets of the nineteenth century, every person well-read in Western literature can notice features of romantic style and themes familiar to him. If he looks into a standard textbook on the history of Russian literature published in the USSR, however, or even at a specialized Soviet study of these poets in whom he has recognized typical romantic features, he will be faced with a puzzle: all these romanticists turn out, from the contemporary Russian point of view, to be realists; or, if there are unmistakable traits of literary romanticism in their works, it is always pointed out that such romantic stylistic characteristics and themes were accidental, insignificant, merely preparing the way for the advent of triumphant Russian realism. In some cases, the fact is particularly emphasized that Russian romanticism actually belonged to a special type of romanticism—revolutionary romanticism (or, at least, "progressive"), to be contrasted, it would seem, to some "reactionary" romanticism.

The question arises, who is right?—Western criticism and the history of literature as reflected in the impressions of European and American readers, or the unshakable dogmas of contemporary Soviet theses about Russian realism, the insignificance of Russian romanticism and its minimal role in the development of Russian literature?

I wish to say a few words about these questions to the readers of my book on Russian romanticism.

First of all, in what historical situation does romanticism arise in Russian literature? Then, what are the characteristic

Translated from the Russian by Betty J. Zenkovsky.

features of this literary trend? What are the basic stages of its development? And what is its end? The reader will also find material answering these questions in my book.

1. How and in what context does romanticism appear in Russian literature? It comes in the wake of classicism, but orthodox classicism is represented rather weakly in Russia. M. V. Lomonosov is not a classicist, but the admirer and follower of the late poets of the German Baroque, G. C. Günther and B. H. Brockes. Lomonosov knew something about the German representatives of classicism and of their theoretician, Johann Christoph Gottsched, but at the writing of his theoretical works on poetics, he did not draw upon Gottsched. Gavriil R. Deržavin, likewise, was not a classicist. Not knowing French, he was under the influence of German poetry and, partially, of the representatives of the later Baroque. Aleksandr P. Sumarokov and Mixail M. Xeraskov, certainly, were classicists and their generally boring and colorless works, of course, were read, but they called up no great enthusiasm on the part of readers, who turned more eagerly to French models. Far more success was enjoyed at the end of the eighteenth and beginning of the nineteenth centuries by the works of Karamzin and his "school": foremost, I. Dmitriev and V. Kapnist. The works of these writers were lighter, more alive, and more "sensitive." Theoretically, they were all practitioners of the poetics of classicism, but there were already visible threads leading from their poetry to a new poetics of feeling and imagination. Moreover, one of the late classicists, Konstantin N. Batjuškov, found it possible to write,

o pamjat' serdca, ty sil'nej
rassudka pamjati pečal'noj.

O memory of the heart, you are stronger than the sad memory of reason.

Of the Russian romanticists, V. Žukovskij and Prince I. Vjazemskij were the first to break with the poetic traditions of classicism. They denied the bases of its poetics—particularly, the teaching of literary genres—and the odes, epistles, and satires typical of classicism disappear from their works. The didactic element vanishes, as well, but, most importantly, there appear *new* genres: ballads, mysteries, and fairy tales (imitating folk tales), while of the old genres only the elegy, speaking the "language of the heart," comes to the fore.

In general, romantic poetry loses those *external* aspects of classical poetics which, in the poetry of classicism, themselves designated works as classical; that is, a poem of the school of classicism would begin with the stating of its theme, an ode would "sing" of some person or event announced at the beginning, and the poet-singer would "sing" and accompany his "singing" on the lyre. Before the classical poet, or over his shoulders, stood a muse, a pagan goddess who was admitted into Christian literature for her virtues. All this retreated to the background or completely disappeared in the *new* literary style. The romantic poet stopped singing and playing on the lyre. Everything was changed.

2. Romantic works recommended themselves also as the representatives of a new trend, a new literature, and they already bear the distinctive features of the romantic style. This style is one of those representing a direct antithesis of the classical and related style of the Renaissance. Works of romantic style characterized themselves, first of all, as works not bound by any strict rules, being *free* both stylistically and compositionally. For this reason, they do not usually bear the names of the traditional literary genre to which they belong and it is for this reason, also, that they often destroy the basic rules of classical poetics. In *Evgenij Onegin*, Puškin points out the theme of the work— *"poju prijatelja mladogo"* [I sing my young friend]—at the *end* of one of the last chapters. Romantic works combine or mix features of various genres (Puškin's *Evgenij Onegin* is a novel in the tradition of that prose genre but is written in verse; in *Boris Godunov*, there are combined features of tragedy and of comedy, as there are in Shakespeare, etc.). In every possible way, romantic works emphasize deliberately the absolutely free character of the author's creation. Therefore, works sometimes appear in the form of fragments or are published with intentional

deletions (for example, the deletion of several stanzas in *Evgenij Onegin*; or of lines in verses; or of whole chapters in novels or stories, as in Puškin's *Kapitanskaja dočka*). The author combines or puts together works of separate, almost independent, components, as in Lermontov's *Geroj našego vremeni*. He lends a work, partially, the character of private conversation with friends—mentioning their names or hinting at their and his own personal lives, entering into conversation with the readers or giving a verse the form of an answer to someone's remarks. Examples are Tjutčev's *"Ty skažeš'..."* [You would say ...]; and Gogol's *Revizor*, in which the governor addresses the public from the stage. The author converses with his heroes or with himself, asking about the further course of the work or hinting at a theme (Puškin: *"Skaži, kuda ž nam plyt'?"* ["Say, where should we move to now?"]) and declares his literary intentions (Gogol': *"Priprjažem i podleca"* [Let's include the scoundrel]). All these are the symptoms of *free creativity*.

All norms of a work's unity are destroyed, most clearly, of course, in theatrical works, which disintegrate into a series of short scenes; but the unity of language is also destroyed—hence, the sea of Ukrainianisms in Gogol', words of various linguistic strata in Dal's stories, the multicolored adornment of Vel'tman's works. In many cases, it is even unclear whether to take the author himself seriously, and everything he says (Vel'tman's hero "travels" on a geographical map; in Gogol' there are such communications as *"Eto byla ta samaja koljaska, v kotoroj ezdil Adam"* [It was the same carriage in which Adam used to ride.]). The *grotesque* is permitted and is especially popular. Plots and separate motifs should not be true to life. For instance, there is an improbable concurrence of coincidences in Puškin's *Metel'*; and in Gogol's stories, the *sjužety* are often almost hidden from the reader and have to be guessed. (Puškin's *Stancionnyj smotritel'* did not believe in the possibility of a happy fate for his daughter, who, by the way, at the end of the story appears at her father's grave as a wealthy and, apparently, married, woman with children —her "seducer," it would seem, married her.) All sorts of improbabilities are permitted. In *Revizor*, the officials believe Xlestakov's wild lies; in *Mërtvye duši*, Čičikov's fantastic scheme isn't noticed by the officials even at the execution of official acts regarding the purchase of peasants for a *groš* (half a penny), although later those same officials believe rumors that Čičikov is a counterfeiter, bandit, and even Napoleon! And in Mirgorod, one citizen goes around in a blue frockcoat with sky-blue sleeves, the police search a year in the square for the mayor's button, while a brown pig successfully interferes with a court trial. Gogol' himself called his play *Ženit'ba* "A completely improbable occurrence in three acts."

The fantastic element plays no less a role in the improbabilities of romantic composition than does the grotesque, which knows no limitations. The romanticists could believe or not in real spirits, witches, and devils (by the way, it should be noted that the greatest successes of spiritism in Russia coincided with the epoch of the ascendancy of the realistic world view!) but fantastic and mysterious creatures and events were the best means for enlivening and "freshening" the narrative material. In addition, the fantastic was favored by its close ties with the popular world view and with folklore.

In short, *all* the poetics of romanticism were built on the idea of *free* poetic creativity, and this freedom was emphasized by all the minutiae of literary device.

3. In romanticism, the *world view* was especially important for writers. Even it was free (it may be said, from a deep faith in God to atheism and struggle with God), but in it were especially clear features of the denial of rationalism. True, in classicism, rationalism (and enlightment) *were not the exclusive* currents of that era; along with rationalism there were also, in the eighteenth century, numerous antirationalistic and mystical currents. Romanticism knew no such varied convictions and beliefs. For a romanticist most important was the conviction that the world, history, and the individual man were mysterious—not at all simple, not divisible into simple elements, and still largely unknown.

The romantic world view is one of "many worlds": in reality are depth and mysteries, in the world are unknown forces, forces perhaps impossible for man to know. In their search for such powers and elements, the romantic naturalists encountered a few real mysteries and made some discoveries (for example, in the fields of history, natural science, physics, and chemistry). Even more vital than the external world for romanticism is history: in it function not only individual people but also "collective personalities"—peoples and states, all subject not merely to understandable causes lying "on the surface" of reality but also to the mysterious destinies of states and peoples. Therefore, in the past are often revealed the "mysterious designs" of destiny and precisely in these collective, still subconscious ("preconscious") personalities appear the images of future peoples and men.

Probably the most important was the discovering of the depths of the individual personality. Man's consciousness is not a simple spiritual life formed by individual experiences and subject to primitive laws resembling mechanical ones. The romanticists saw the depth and height of the psychic life, its "underground and exalted" strata and roots, the unique destinies of the individual, and those experiences which are unusual, exceptional. (To these belong various forms of ecstasy, love, dreams, premonition, and insight into the depth of one's own and another's soul—in other words, everything the romanticists designated by the term "the 'night' side of the soul"—parallel to the "dark side of life," the "dark side of the world" which they saw beyond everyday reality.) It is of importance that all these positive and negative (sometimes even criminal) depths of the soul are in some way contiguous with each other: poetry is ecstasy, but akin to dreams; ecstasy is close to madness; and psychic deviations should be not only the objects of serious study but also the ways to individual self-perception.

All this complex interweaving of motifs becomes the source of the romanticists' poetical creativity and opens the way to a renewal of the linguistic means. (Compare, for instance, the romanticists' new semantics of the words *dream* and *sight*.) The poet ceases to be a singer but is raised above the human norm: he is the seer of the depths of existence and of the soul; therefore, he becomes a preacher, an oracle, a teacher, the leader of mankind and, as a creator, even "God" (i.e., Baratynskij's words regarding Mickiewicz).

Such was the *beginning* of Russian romanticism, wholly bound up with these themes. And even if they later pale or weaken in the works of individual romanticists, there still remains in all its strength the heroic self-awareness of the creator-poet. A poet is not always the victor and leader of the crowd; he is also a victim of its persecution, of its repudiation; he is a martyr, an exile, and the object of scorn (compare Puškin's poem, *The Prophet*, with Lermontov's of the same title). Or he sees and speaks altogether differently from what the crowd would like to hear. Already at the very beginning of the romantic movement there appears a caricaturized, satirical depiction of the internally unfree, tradition-bound, "ordinary," everyday man—particularly, as he imagines himself to be superior. Such are the recognized "leaders"—the rulers, the self-assured scholars who ostensibly know "the world and man's soul." Satirical tones in their depictions strengthen from year to year. Along with the portrayal of the "upper world," there appear clear pictures of prosaic life, deprived of everything "nocturnal" or "dark."

In the poetry of the epoch of the romanticists' "reign" (in Russia, the end of the 1820s and the beginning of the 1830s) can be heard precisely this *double* tonality of passion—rapture and desperation, or hopelessness. Incidentally, contemporary man begins to be understood as torn away, uprooted, from his real depths and heights: this is, for the most part, the "average," gray citizen of the vain world. But man not only can still mount the heights to which the romanticists summon him; he still basically carries within him all the instincts of such an upward evolution (*razvitie k vys'jam*). These potentialities once (before the baleful influence of civilization) alive in man were now discovered. His "instinctual" life (as Vladimir Odoevskij used to write) stood in live contact with the depths of the world. Forbearings, premonition, penetration into the world's mysteries were natural characteristics of primordial man and, possibly, of contemporary man even now. Hence, the particular interest of romanticists for popular superstitions, prejudices and all the ancient folk wisdom preserved by folk poetry. Gogol', who observed such elements in the Ukrainian folk song, not only depicts the ecstasy at contemplation of nature in no other than Ivan Fedorovič Špon'ka, he not only shows—perhaps albeit vulgarized—the love of Čičikov, but he portrays completely seriously the strength of real love in the unfortunate son of Taras Bul'ba, Andrij, and he expects spiritual rebirth from the heroes of *Dead Souls*—even from *Pljuškin* ("if he wants . . ."). The end of Russian romanticism, too, is precisely in the victory of the depiction of the Philistine or the vulgar (*pošlost'*), of man fallen into some sort of nonexistence in the style of the "natural school" (whose foundation Gogol' laid), in that style which begins with his portrayal of the idyllic, almost vegetable, life of Afanasij Ivanovič and Pul'xerija Ivanovna—in whom, however, a love which conquers death is alive in the depth of her soul—and in the depiction of the almost prehuman being of Akakij Akakievič, who, nonetheless, is seized by a passion, the love for such an "unfit" object as an overcoat, a love which ruined his life.

The final stage of romanticism is, namely, the natural school (not to be confused with "naturalism"). This is a literary current which depicted only the "unworthy"—life in its inglorious manifestations. The authors' purpose is the contrast of the depths of spiritual life with its heights. This current attracted a number of talented poets and prose writers who at bottom were still romanticists: the young Turgenev and young Dostoevskij (who, however, in the long stories *Poor Folk* and *The House Lady* succeeded in showing in almost unfit subjects a bright and strong luminescence of soul); Gončarov and the young Nekrasov; P. Kuliš, a Ukrainian—forgotten as the author of Russian stories; and a number of less important writers (Jakov Butkov, Ivan Kokorev, and Ivan Panaev, whose further paths are unclear); as well as even partially the young Lev Tolstoj. True, after the decade 1845–1855, all of them gradually departed from the path of the "natural school," which led to horrifying examples and the propaganda of high ideals. But all of them learned much on this road and some, especially Turgenev ("a romanticist of realism," as his researcher, S. Rodzevič, called him fifty years ago) preserved even longer a great deal of those romantic motifs which conquered their inspiration in the early years of their lives.

The "natural school" died in an unusual guise which seems

to many investigators to be a "realistic" mask of Russian romanticism. Romanticism, however, had not died. Tjutčev wrote before the 1870s (he died in 1873); Vjazemskij wrote in the latter years of his life (he died in 1878); there were some echoes of romanticism in the musical articles of Vladimir Odoevskij, who died in 1869; and there were still the "late romanticists": A. K. Tolstoj, who died in 1875 and who wrote almost entirely after the end of the romantic epoch; the great lyricist A. Fet, who experienced in his youth only the last flames of romanticism (he was born in 1820), but who carried its traditions to the end of the century (he died in 1892). From them extend numerous threads to the "new romanticism" of Russian symbolism.

Why did Russian romanticism die? It was extinguished under the influence of a number of factors. First of all, the majority of literary trends come to an end by consuming their artistic means. The rapid extinction of Russian romanticism, however, was not compulsory. Within a few years, moreover, romanticists in Russia became some sort of bugbear of the Russian intelligentsia. This was not death, but worse: the mortification of a still vital current which should have only retreated to the background. Political trends and social reasons played the primary role: the morose era of Emperor Nikolaj I, spanning the years 1825 to 1855, ended in the complete ruin of his internal and external policies. Although romanticism, in particular that of the Slavophiles, was not at all connected with the politics of the Emperor and some romantic writers were even persecuted by him, it seemed unexpectedly in the eyes of contemporaries to be in a paradoxically mistaken connection with this past reign. After 1855, reforms were begun by Alexander II, especially emancipation of the serfs in 1861, but his efforts were too insufficient. As it often happens, maximalist programs (even up to socialism) pushed the programs of the possible out of the minds of part of society, and any conservatism began to seem the "vilest reaction."

Romanticism was a Utopian trend, but its Utopia lay outside any political-social programs. When this Utopia appeared superfluous, leading away from the essential problems of the day, its ideology was declared not merely erroneous, but harmful, even odious. The majority of the undoubted successes and "conquests" of romanticism, even the great literature created by it, with Puškin at the head (Gogol' was overinterpreted in the spirit of the time, but important elements of his world view were forgotten) turned out superfluous—not even a luxury, but a *whim* of a generation dead and gone. Even the science which arose in the romantic milieu—not deprived of merit—remained outside the attention of society. Despite their undoubted scholarly achievements, the fate of scholar-romanticists was sad: they were not even forgotten because they were never well-known, but simply were passed by, sometimes even with a sardonic smile! Only the music of romanticism had more lasting success: it knew no words and therefore could be accepted without hesitation, although it would seem that even it was often not excluded from the sphere of art considered unnecessary and fruitless.

Let us not, however, forget something else: the influence of the West, with its strengthening ideas of positivism, of materialism, and of a brand of literary realism. In Western Europe, however, literary realism was not torn off from the literary tradition to such a degree as was demanded in Russian circles. Russian literary realism (Dostoevskij, L. Tolstoj, Turgenev), likewise, was not recognized unhesitatingly. Part of the intelligentsia preferred to these great writers the "lesser" ones: Nikolaj Pomjalovskij, Rešetnikov and even the microscopic Nikolaj Uspenskij. The followers of romanticism (A. K. Tolstoj, Fet) as well as Nikolaj Leskov (for different and accidental reasons but little connected with romanticism) altogether disappeared from the sphere of influence of cultural, so-called progressive Russian society. (The worst boycott is that by progressives!)

The history of realism is not our concern here. It, too, was somewhat tragic and ended at first with a crisis, in the form of symbolism, then later reemerged in various forms—in which romanticism had a certain significance and was here renamed (and partially reinterpreted) as realism. Realism became some sort of sacred word which began to designate everything majestic in literature, beginning with Homer, Sophocles, and including Shakespeare and Goethe. This infinite broadening of the concept of realism was just as illegitimate as the narrowing of the concept of romanticism. My book is directed against this narrowing.

DMITRIJ ČIŽEVSKIJ

Heidelberg
October 1972

Preface to German Edition

This first volume of my history of nineteenth-century Russian literature deals with Russian romanticism and begins with the particular form of late classicism that Russian literary historians usually call sentimentalism. In their early work, many romanticists belonged to or were close to a current that we call the School of Karamzin. Although the Karamzin School is not now interpreted as it has been until recently, the fact remains that it laid the foundation for the modern Russian literary language, broke with the poetic tradition of Russian classicism—at least in some matters—and prepared the way for romantic poetics.

The Karamzin School, which is treated at the beginning of this volume, should not be equated exactly with Western European "sensibility." Although it was influenced by Western European bourgeois sensibility, there was little connection between the two currents in their view of the world.

The *Natural'naja škola* is a special current in Russian literature and it should be regarded, I feel, as a variant of late romanticism, even though it prepared the way for Russian realism and included nonromanticists as well as romanticists. We shall call this current the Natural School. The characteristic stylistic features of this school are appreciably different from those of the later realism. One should not refer to the Natural School as "naturalism," a term that has acquired another meaning (see chapter IV, sec. 16).

I shall deal with the crisis in Russian romanticism along with realism, which evolved from this crisis.

A few remarks on terminology and transliteration:

Poetic tradition in Russia has created a number of terms that one should retain in a foreign-language history of Russian literature. First, there is the expression *poèma*, which we shall call "poem." In English, a poem is any composition in verse; but in Russian, the word designates specifically a long epic or epic-lyric work, for instance, the Homeric epics and the *Aeneid*, the classicist epics, and, later, the epics of George Gordon Byron and the Russian "Byronic poems" written in imitation of them.[1]

The Russian term *povest'* is sometimes translated "novella" (Russian *rasskaz*) and sometimes "novel." It is a long novella and, in contrast to a novel, focuses on one person or on a closely connected group, such as two lovers.[2]

I shall not try to preserve in this book the distinction that is tenaciously held to in Russian between a poet (*poèt*) and a prose writer (*pisatel'*).

The system of transliteration used here[3] is the one normally used in Slavistic publications and enables the reader to reconstruct the Cyrillic spelling of a word from the Latin spelling. I shall explain here the features of this system of transliteration that might be unfamiliar to a non-Slavist:

1. Consonants followed by the sign ' or by an *e, i,* or *j* are palatalized. For example, the Russian *n'* is analagous to the French or Italian *gn*. Other examples are Karamzin, *mysl',* *žizn', volnenie*—these words should be pronounced Karamz'in, *voln'en'ie,* etc.

2. The letter *ž* corresponds to the English *zh* in the transliteration of the Library of Congress or to *s* in such words as *pleasure* or *leisure*. The Russian letter is ж.

The letter *č* corresponds to the English *ch*. The Russian letter is ч.

The letter *š* corresponds to the English *sh*. The Russian letter is ш.

---

1. A more detailed definition of the Russian term *poema* may be found in *Literaturnaia Entsiklopediia* (Moscow: OGIZ RSFSR, 1935) IX, col. 203–215, and *Kratkaja Literaturnaia Entsiklopediia* (1968) V, p. 934 ff.

2. *Povest* is also more completely defined in *Literaturnaia Entsiklopediia* (1935) IX, pp. 17–27, and *Kratkaja Literaturnaia* (1968) V, p. 814.

3. With the exception of bibliographic references in the footnotes and the bibliographic lists at the end of this book, where the transliteration of the Library of Congress is used.

The letter *c* corresponds to the English *ts*. The Russian letter is ц.

The letter *x* corresponds to the German *ch* after *a, o,* or *u* but is "less vigorous" (O. Broch) and is formed farther back in the mouth, and the accoustic effect is different.

3. Initially and after a vowel, *e* is pronounced like the English sound *ye*. It is also pronounced *ye* after a palatalized consonant (*nje-n' je*). When *e* is pronounced without *y*, it is transliterated *è*.

4. *y* represents the Russian ы, a peculiar back vowel pronounced with the tongue in position for the vowel of *boot* and the lips in position for the vowel of *beet*.

5. *j* is used to palatalize the following vowels (thus *ja, ju* are equivalents of the Russian я, ю).

DMITRIJ ČIŽEVSKIJ

Heidelberg
Summer 1963

History of
Nineteenth-Century Russian Literature

The Romantic Period

I
Russian Literature in the Nineteenth Century

1. Nineteenth-century Russian literature can be thought of as unified. It is distinctly different from the literature of the eighteenth century. In his history of Russian literature, the German literary historian Arthur Luther calls the language of eighteenth-century literature "almost unintelligible." This may be an exaggeration, but it is a fair statement of the view that most readers in 1900 had of the eighteenth century. On the other hand, the theoreticians of socialist realism were not the first to draw a dividing line between themselves and nineteenth-century Russian classical literature. As early as 1910, the futurists began issuing manifestoes in which they rejected all previous literature. The slogan "To throw Puškin overboard from the steamer of the present" stood for the complete denial of nineteenth-century literature, of which Aleksandr Puškin was representative. Later, Vladimir Majakovskij referred more pointedly to "Puškin and other classical generals." Although the chronological dividing line has now moved forward and the futurists themselves have become part of the past, the fact remains that, in the nineteenth century, Russian literature was unified.

2. Of course, the literary limits of the nineteenth century can no more be set at 1800 and 1900 than can political or cultural limits. It would be better, actually, to think of 1790 and 1920 as the limiting years, although there are individuals and events beyond these bounds that should be included in the nineteenth century. Some writers of this period, such as Fedor Dostoevskij, belong not only

to Russian, but to world literature, even though as early as the eighteenth century, Russian works were being translated into Western European languages: Antiox Dmitrievič Kantemir's satires, for example, and the odes of Gavriil Romanovič Deržavin. Not all important Russian writers of the nineteenth century are well known abroad. On the other hand, some writers have been translated and popularized by chance, without any apparent reason, as was the case with the novels of F. V. Bulgarin in the first half of the nineteenth century. It is even more regrettable that an appraisal of Russian writers abroad has been hampered by bad translations—or by translations that were too good of works that were insignificant, a frequent occurrence in poetry; by a bias in nineteenth-century Russian criticism and literature, as a result of which social and political values were virtually the only ones considered, even into the twentieth century; and by attempts to-day to make all Russian literature of the past subservient to con-temporary needs. In addition to the harm done by Communist interpreters of the Stalin era and of the more moderate present and that of "revisionists," such as Georg Lukács, damage is also done by the far less numerous but often equally biased émigres and by the inventors of such fundamentally false slogans as "boundless Russia" and "East minus West equals nothing."

3. When one considers the rapid pace of political, social, and in-tellectual change in the nineteenth century, it is understandable that there were differences in the literature of this generally unified period. Many forces were at work, some of which drew writers together, while others divided them. Several periods with-in the nineteenth century are readily discernible.

The first of these periods began in 1790 with the appearance of young Nikolaj Mixajlovič Karamzin (1766–1826). He was an inno-vator, although within the limits of the then prevalent classicism, which until Karamzin's time had produced few writers of real distinction. Writers, some of whom had already been pursuing the same literary goals, gathered around Karamzin; in time, younger writers joined ranks with them. This "Karamzin School," which is often called "sentimentalism" or "sensibility," would un-questionably have dominated Russian literature, had it not been for a much more powerful literary movement—romanticism—that began to make itself felt through Western influence around 1810 and that attracted several members of the Karamzin School. Many adherents of romanticism had been more or less faithful classicists. Romanticism introduced a new style and new ways of looking at the world.

The central figures in Russian romanticism were two towering writers who do not fit easily into any literary school: Aleksandr Puškin and Nikolaj Gogol'. But apart from them, there were perhaps more important poets than Russia would ever again have at one time. Russian poets of this period—from about 1815 to 1845 —were, first of all, dedicated foes of classicist poetics and of the Enlightenment, which was not, of course, the only important current within classicism.

In contrast to classicist poetics—which required strict adherence to certain norms, stood for the ideal of harmonious beauty and transparent clarity, and preferred formally complete works (the prevalent view in Russia from about 1760 on)—the romantics stood for freedom of form and loved open horizons and endless perspectives. They countered the rationalistic view of man and the world with a belief in the great diversity of life. More important to them than reason was depth of soul, in which they believed above all else. In contrast to the Enlightenment's optimistic belief in progress, they viewed history as a game of destiny played by various forces capable of causing men to fall as well as to rise. As a result, they were able to perceive worthwhile qualities in the past and in the "lower strata" of the present, among the common people with their superstitions and "primitive" art.

Classicism was by no means ideologically unified. Not all classicists were Enlighteners; and they were divided on philosophical, religious, and—especially—political issues. Within classicism were all shades of political sentiment, from faithful, unquestioning monarchists to those who radically rejected the Russian monarchic tradition, as did A. N. Radiščev. The romanticists, on the contrary, were more unified in their view of the world. Although they were divided on political issues, the frequently made distinction between romanticists who were "reactionaries" and those who were "progressives" misses the essence of their movement. In their philosophical and religious view of the world, the romanticists were, above all, "anti-Enlighteners" and, as such, in contrast to the unhistorical Enlightenment, they were traditionalists. They expected to find tradition, or something ontologically concrete that corresponded to tradition, in the depths of the human soul, in the depths of the rich and meaningful past (although the Russians turned less often to the Middle Ages than did Western Europeans), in the "spirit" or "soul" of the people, and in the secrets of art. Essentially, all romanticists believed that secret, hidden forces and destinies were stronger than those that were clear and obvious.

In time, the ardor of the romanticists began to give way; their principles proved less attractive and influential. Later on we shall deal with the external and internal causes of this change. In any event, a late form of romanticism appeared, one that was probably stronger in Russia than in Western Europe and that led to a new, "realistic" literature by way of the so-called Natural School (*Natural'naja škola*), which should not be confused with naturalism.

Russian realism prevailed almost without competition from 1850 to 1890. Afterward, it was carried on and stubbornly defended by a number of epigones, some of them important, up to the time of socialist realism, which has nothing in common with nineteenth-century realism but the name. Realism had no developed system of poetics and required of its practitioners no particular view of the world, least of all a political view. A great many realists were political radicals, to be sure; but none of the great writers—Turgenev, Tolstoj, Nikolaj S. Leskov—identified himself with their views. Dostoevskij even protested modestly against having his works called realistic, but stylistically he is as realistic as are various political reactionaries who, as writers, were unimportant.

It is pointless to define realism as "the portrayal of reality as it actually is." First of all, this raises the question of what reality actually is. To romanticists, reality was what *they saw* in the world and in their own souls in accordance with their view of the world. In this respect, Dostoevskij was much closer to the romanticists than to authoritative realist theoreticians, such as the critics Nikolaj Černyševskij, Nikolaj Dobroljubov, and Dmitrij Pisarev, who in turn did not agree among themselves. Turgenev was called, not unjustly, "a romanticist of realism." To Tolstoj and Leskov, the religious sphere was a reality, which many other realists relegated to the sphere of illusion. A writer can portray only that reality that is accessible to him. What reality meant to Dostoevskij can best be seen in the *Brothers Karamazov*.

Realism can be characterized much better on the basis of its particular stylistic features, among which the most conspicuous are the varieties of metonymy, as suggested by Professor Roman Jakobson. In romanticism, and even in classicism, metaphor played a prominent part, representing a kind of game between various levels of being, a bringing together of different spheres of reality. Hyperbole, personification, and plays on words (such as etymological figures of speech, oxymoron, and zeugma) also conceal the danger of divergence into other levels of being. Realism, however, seeks to portray the world on a single level. Even writers of this period who preserve the romantic belief in the variety of life, such as Dostoevskij, succumb to the metonymical stylistics of realism. As a result, one cultivates long forms and presents the entire biography and surroundings of one's hero, even if one does not believe in the decisive role of external influences on a man's life. Formally, parallel and antithetical structures are used; but everything must remain on the same plane, as in the comparison of two or more characters or their environments. Long novels are the most appropriate form of realistic literature.

Like all previous literary styles, realism passed out of fashion. The generation that had given impetus to this literary movement died out, and the way was left open for a new school that proceeded from impulses inherent in the development of Russian literature—that is, for symbolism, which began around 1895.

For polemic purposes, symbolism was first called "decadence," but it is best termed neoromanticism, since in it many elements of the romantic style and view of the world returned in a new guise. As a defensive gesture toward all too political realism, symbolism was at first deliberately unpolitical. The philosophical foundation on which the symbolist aesthetic rested was less obvious than in romanticism, which was based on the great systems of German idealism. The early philosophical basis of symbolism was a matter of chance and merely appeared to be a new line of approach. The works of Schopenhauer and Nietzsche were influential. The second generation of symbolists thought that they had found deeper and sounder principles in the ancients, in Kant, and in the Russian philosopher Vladimir Solov'ev; but one still cannot speak of commonly accepted principles and aims, as had been the case in romanticism; at best, there is only a seeming unity among symbolists. During the great upheaval in Russia in 1905, it became clear that symbolism was faced with problems that were alien to poetry, problems that this primarily aesthetic movement was not able to cope with; and a crisis arose.

Various smaller groups of poets may be considered to constitute a new phase in the neoromantic movement, in particular the futurists, who proposed radical solutions to the problems of poetry. And here we shall close our survey. Literature must continue to develop. One cannot predict whether the present stagnation will persist, even though it is under pressure from extraliterary forces. One is rather inclined to expect an unproductive period of silence, as was the case in Russia for two decades after Ivan the Terrible and for thirty years after the reforms of Peter the Great.

II

The Karamzin School

1. Nikolaj Mixajlovič Karamzin (1766–1826) came from a family of lesser nobility on the Volga. When he was fourteen, he went to Moscow to board at the private school of Professor Schaden, where he received a good education and was trained for society life. After a short period of duty in the guards, he returned home to Simbirsk, where he was discovered by the educated Freemason, I. P. Turgenev. Karamzin was taken back to Moscow by Turgenev and put in a sort of cloister for Freemasons, where, along with other young men, he was given further instruction (1785–1789) and where he also took an interest in literature. In 1789, he left Moscow to take a trip to Europe that was to affect the cultural history of Russia. He traveled through Germany and Switzerland and visited Paris and London. After fifteen months, he returned, to dedicate himself to journalism and literature.

His first major work was *Letters of a Russian Traveler*. In the *Moskovskij žurnal*, which he had founded, Karamzin also published his novellas, the best known of which, *Poor Liza* (1792), was even more successful than his account of his travels.

The next few years were a time of great political unrest. The French Revolution ran its course, the persecution of the Russian Freemasons began, Empress Catherine II died in 1796. Her successor, Paul I, was murdered by conspirators in 1801 after four years of turbulent rule. Finally, Alexander I drew up plans for reform in the first years of his reign. None of these events deterred Karamzin from his pursuit of literature, although he was forced at times to forgo publishing periodicals and put out almanacs instead. These appeared at irregular intervals and were filled mostly with Karamzin's own novellas and poetry.

In 1803, a new phase in Karamzin's life began when he became the official historiographer of the Russian empire. From this time on, he devoted himself exclusively to work on *The History of the Russian State*. Significantly, he left in fragmentary form several poetic works that he had already begun. In 1818, the first eight volumes of Karamzin's history appeared and brought new fame to the author, who was still very much remembered as a literary innovator. The work was, in fact, a considerable scholarly achievement. Karamzin was later able to finish three more volumes, and a nearly completed twelfth volume appeared after his death.

In addition to his literary and scholarly work, Karamzin presented a *Zapiska* [Mémoire] to Alexander I in 1811 on the subject of "the old and new Russia," to warn the Tsar against carrying out his liberal reforms.

2. Karamzin became the center of a group of poets who later emerged as a school. Among the poets were his friend Ivan Ivanovič Dmitriev (1760–1837), Aleksandr Puškin's uncle Vasilij L'vovič Puškin (1770–1830), Mixail Vasil'evič Milonov (1792–1821), and Jurij Aleksandrovič Neledinskij-Meleckij (1752–1829). There were other poets in the group who later went over to the romanticists: Nikolaj Ivanovič Gnedič (1784–1833), Vasilij Andreevič Žukovskij (1783–1852), and Prince Petr Andreevič Vjazemskij (1792–1878). Žukovskij's youthful friend Andrej Ivanovič Turgenev (1781–1803) also displayed a notable poetic talent. The last playwright of the classicist period, Vladislav Aleksandrovič Ozerov (1769–1816), had some connections with the school. So did Konstantin Nikolaevič Batjuškov (1787–1855), the most significant poet of the early nineteenth century. (Batjuškov, who was insane from 1821 on, would be unthinkable without Karamzin's reforms.)

3. Karamzin is remembered primarily for his part in transforming the Russian literary language. One can even speak of "Karamzin's linguistic reforms," although it has been recently

demonstrated that as a linguistic innovator he was much more limited than contemporary and later historians thought. Most of his neologisms (which were largely loan translations from French or German) were already in use in Russian; Karamzin simply transplanted them from official or school-book language to the language of literature. Even words that he appears to have coined are "weak" neologisms and were naturally derived from words already present in the language. Karamzin first used the words *vljublennost'* ("being in love") and *promyšlennost'* ("industry," "economic activity"); but Sumarokov used the verb *vljubit'sja*, and Kotošixin spoke of a *promyšlennyj narod* in the seventeenth century.[1]

Karamzin's contribution to renewing the language consisted of setting aside to a large extent the Church Slavonic elements and of orienting literary style toward the spoken language of polite society. Even here he was not really an innovator. One finds the same vocabulary that he used in the private correspondence and diaries of educated Russians in the second half of the eighteenth century. Primarily, Karamzin rejected the theory of the "three styles," which had sharply divided the literary and spoken languages. Otherwise he simply made use of classical poetics with its demand for clarity of language, although he did not always follow the precepts of school-book grammar (as in his use of short and long adjectival forms).

It is a mark of Karamzin's style that he prefers to express himself in paraphrase, a predilection that Aleksandr S. Puškin criticizes. Karamzin cannot avoid circumlocution; simple statements are replaced by paraphrase or images. Of the onset of winter he says, "Oak and birch are blazing in our fireplace. Let the wind rage and pelt our windows with white snow." "To live," for Karamzin, is "to drink of the cup of life," and so on. He places great stress on sentence construction and vocabulary. The various editions of his works show how he constantly revised his vocabulary, simplified and Russified it, and how he sought to express himself more precisely. (Two critics who have pointed that

1. [In the seventeenth century, however, the word *promyšlennik* meant generally an enterpriser, very often one engaged in the fur trade, and not specifically an industrialist, as it is used today.—EDITOR]

out are V. Sipovskij and V. Vinogradov.) His aim in writing is always to create even, consistent language in accordance with good taste.

In an early poem, Karamzin names those poets whom he considers most important. They are the Englishmen Shakespeare, Milton, Edward Young, and James Thomson, and the Swiss idyllist Salomon Gessner. It is surprising that Shakespeare should come first, but Karamzin had already translated him before he went abroad. After J. G. Herder chided him in Weimar for his old-fashioned taste in poetry, Karamzin did read Goethe and Schiller but apparently understood them only on his own terms. It was the pious Johann Kaspar Lavater who impressed him most as an intellect.

4. Karamzin's poems are the least important part of his work and added little to the language. There is a new tone in his poetry, but one not entirely absent from the older classicists, such as M. M. Xeraskov and V. V. Kapnist, the tone of subjective feeling and sad resignation. Karamzin calls this mood "melancholy." (As early as 1788, he wrote *Spring Song of a Melancholiac*.) The words "sadness" (*pečal', toska*), "melancholy" (*unynie*), "dejected," "touching," "languishing" (*tomno*), and especially "sigh," "tears," "cry" and its synonyms occur in almost every poem. Less often, one finds "boredom," "bitterness," "torment," and other words expressing stronger feelings.

For descriptions of nature, love, and friendship, Karamzin resorts to the same vocabulary. One does not find much force or depth in his other poems, his hymns, his pure descriptions of nature, his verse narratives (he translated a Spanish romance and left an incomplete poem on the Russian epic hero Il'ja Muromec), or even in his military songs; and these shortcomings are not offset by an attitude of sympathy on the part of the poet. Karamzin appears not to have recognized his limitations. He tried his hand at various literary forms but wrote always in the same way.

5. Karamzin's strong point is his prose. His well-known novella *Poor Liza* (1792) is particularly outstanding. His other novellas are *Flor Silin, the Charitable Man, Natal'ja, Daughter of a Boyar,*

Liodor, and *Julija* (1794).[2] One should mention his narratives on Western European themes, *The Island of Bornholm* and *Sierra-Morena*, both written in 1793; and, from a later period, a novel, *A Knight of Our Time* (1803) (*rycar'* means "knight," but is better translated "hero"), which was unfortunately left unfinished.

In all Karamzin's novellas, his subjectivity is evident; and, as in his poems, there is much sentiment and melancholy. Karamzin was influenced by the "bourgeois novels" of such writers as Richardson, as well as by Rousseau's *Nouvelle Héloise*, and he was inspired by them to write his own novellas. One does not find in Karamzin, however, the same psychological power as is found in his Western European models. As a consequence, his novellas are merely touching pictures of misfortune or of human kindness and do no more than awaken our sympathy and pity. From his choice of a virtuous peasant (Flor Silin) as the hero of one novella and of the peasant girl (*poseljanka*) Lisa as the heroine of another, we know something of Karamzin's humaneness; but he does not succeed in penetrating into the inner lives of his characters. The virtuous Lisa falls in love with a young nobleman, is seduced by him, and commits sucide; but the aphorisms with which Karamzin portrays Lisa (such as "Peasant girls are also capable of having feelings") seem inadequate. In *The Island of Bornholm*, the hero's tragic love that is "condemned by laws"—we assume that he is in love with his sister—is not developed, but is only mentioned. Even in the later fragment, *A Knight of Our Time*, Karamzin merely hints at the feelings of his hero and speaks of feelings in almost the same vocabulary as in his poems. But everything is told clearly and smoothly and is framed with pretty descriptions of nature, with which Karamzin usually begins his stories, as in *Poor Lisa*. The treatment of the Nordic landscape in *The Island of Bornholm* is particularly impressive. Such descriptions of nature were something new to the Russian reader, who was not really accustomed to pretty writing.

Poor Lisa begins with a description of the view of Moscow from the rise on which the Simonov monastery stands.

2. [Not to be confused with another work by Karamzin, *Evgenij i Julija*, published in 1787.—EDITOR]

I come to this place and almost always welcome spring here. I come here too on dark fall days to grieve with nature. The wind howls dreadfully in the walls of the abandoned monastery, between the graves overgrown with tall grass, and in the dark passageways between the cells. There, as I rest on the ruins of tombstones, I hear the dull groan of times devoured by the abyss of the past—a groan that shakes my heart and makes it tremble. Sometimes I go into the cells and imagine the men who lived there—sad pictures!

Here I see a gray old man kneeling before the crucifix and praying for a speedy release from his mortal fetters—because for him all pleasures in life have passed, all his feelings have died, except for his awareness of being sick and weak. There a young monk with pale face looks piningly through the bars of his window into the field and sees the happy birds swimming freely in the sea of air—sees them and bitter tears flow from his eyes. He languishes, withers, desiccates—and the sad sound of the bell tolls his early death.

This may have sounded pretty at the time, but it could easily have been the description of a Western European monastery; it is not Russian (crucifixes, for example, are not customary among Russians) and not at all concrete.

Here is another example from Lisa's experiences: "Night fell— the mother blessed her daughter and wished her a restful sleep; this time her wish was not realized; Lisa slept poorly. The new guest in her soul, the image of Erast, appeared so vividly before her that she woke up almost every minute and sighed . . . " In the morning, as Lisa was sitting on the river bank, "she heard oars stroking—she looked out into the river, saw a boat and in it Erast. All her veins began to throb, of course not from fear. She stood up and was about to leave but could not. Erast jumped onto the bank, came up to Lisa, looked at her amiably, and took her hand." And Lisa? "Lisa stood with her eyes lowered, with burning cheeks, with pounding heart—she could not take her hand away, could not turn away from him . . . " And finally when Erast had left her: "Memories shook her soul; the terrible pain in her heart showed in her face. But a few minutes later she was sunk in thought"— she intended to take her life, but this decision is not even hinted at. A few lines later we read: "She plunged into the water." This is not concrete, and the country in which the action is supposed to have taken place is unrecognizable. The author is not one of those who were later called "Westernizers"—he is simply a Western European in Russia. At the same time, he is a stranger in Western Europe, since the real essence of Western Europe remained unintelligible to him, as we know from his principal work, the account of his travels.

6. Karamzin developed his style considerably in his greatest literary work, his description of his travels; and the content of this work is of great importance from the point of view of cultural history. He was the first Russian to attempt to acquaint his reader with European culture and not merely to entertain him by describing amusing sights. His account of his visits to Kant, J. G. Herder, C. M. Wieland, Charles Bonnet, and Friedrich von Matthisson are therefore important, as is his acquaintance with Johann Kaspar Lavater, with whom he spent several weeks. Karamzin also visited such literary authorities of the day as Christoph Friedrich Nicolai, Karl Wilhelm Ramler, and Ernst Platner; and he gives detailed appraisals of older writers such as Christian F. Gellert, Ewald von Kleist, and especially Rousseau, Voltaire, Rabelais, and Shakespeare.

At the theater, he saw Schiller's *Don Carlos*, which was foreign to him; he read *Fiesco* and attended the French theater.

He also reports on his conversations with traveling companions and other guests at hotels and describes, often in rather unpoetic language, cities and their monuments, especially Paris and London, and the collections of pictures in Dresden, Basel, and Paris. He never fails to try to acquaint the reader with the cultural history of Europe as he understands it.

His descriptions of nature, on the other hand, are poetic; he finds nature more beautiful in Western Europe than in Russia. On the bank of the Rhine Falls at Schaffhausen, Karamzin drops to his knees, kisses the earth, and cries, "Fortunate Swiss!" Europe is, for Karamzin, as for so many Russians before and after him, a promised land. In Mainz, he is "as happy as a child" that he "can drink Rhine wine on the banks of the Rhine." Much of the work is devoted to pure reportage and is often a rather dry, simple compendium of the travel literature that Karamzin collected as he went. This is particularly true of the chapters on France, where he stops during critical days of the Revolution without reporting on events. In his account of England, too, he seems unaware of what is going on.

Nevertheless, Karamzin achieved what he had hoped to do: he conveyed to the Russian reader an idea, at least, of Western culture. He was quite right in suggesting several times that he was like the legendary Scythian Anacharsis, who is supposed to have visited ancient Greece. But like Anacharsis, he too was unable to understand many things in the countries that he visited.

These brief comments on this particular work of Karamzin have shown that *The Letters of a Russian Traveler*, which he did not set down completely and polish until after his return to Russia, does not have much in common with the *Sentimental Journey* of Laurence Sterne, although it was probably Sterne's work that prompted Karamzin to describe his travels in literary form. Many of Karamzin's contemporaries followed his example, but none of their work is nearly as important as his own. Some features of the *Sentimental Journey* are present in Karamzin's *Letters*. In his pretty descriptions of nature, he dreams of village idylls with rococo shepherds and shepherdesses. The short passages based on scenes that he has observed or on chance conversations and developed into miniature sentimental novellas, sometimes of several hundred lines, give him an opportunity to develop his sentimental style, which had already appeared in his poems before his trip. The outpourings of his heart, particularly his reactions to nature in Switzerland, are in the same sentimental vein.

One has only to read the first letter, which must have been written later as an introduction to the entire work, to find the same kind of vocabulary that is characteristic of Karamzin's novellas and poems. In the sixty or seventy lines of the letter, one finds the words "tears" three times, "cry" twice, "grief" (*grust'*) and its derivatives four times, "touched, affected" twice, "orphaned" twice, "distress" (from the Russian *gore*), "melancholy," and "softened" once each. In all, there are fifteen lexical items in the same vein and a number of expressions with similar meanings.

Despite occasional patriotic remarks, Karamzin views the West as a Westerner, or rather simply as a man of the West. He may well have been the first Russian European—although he did not really get to the essence of Western culture.

7. He was not interested only in Europe, however. Twelve years after his trip, Karamzin began work on his history of the Russian state, the first eight volumes of which appeared in 1818. Apart from the scholarly value of the work—which one should not overlook, despite its many shortcomings—this history was also a literary success for Karamzin. In his account of his travels, several sections on France and England had already developed into popular scholarly discussions, distinguished stylistically from the rest of his prose. One could say that in his history Karamzin gives up his attempts to cultivate the language of polite society and returns to the old tradition of language, to the "high style." Evidence of this is the use of rather numerous stately Church Slavonicisms and Karamzin's masterful technique of writing long, intricate, yet comprehensible sentences, the periods that had distinguished his early prose as well. Until the end of the nineteenth century these characteristic techniques served as a model for various genres in Russian literature, for the solemn speech, the sermon, the panegyric, and even for scholarly essays.

8. Karamzin did not take part directly in the literary controversy over language and style reform. These matters were not decided until after 1810, when the younger generation formed the "Karamzin School." Significantly, literary societies were formed, and for the first time in Russia they became involved in literary disputes.

One group, the Society (*Beseda*) of Lovers of the Russian Word, attacked Karamzin and were led by an adherent of the old and "genuinely Russian," Admiral Aleksandr Semenovič Šiškov (1754–1841). The writers in this circle were not very important, but literary historians are often unjust in judging them. Šiškov, whose literary talent is attested by his children's poems, was a thoughtful theoretician. To some extent he was right in reproaching the Karamzinians for destroying the Russian lexical system with their "new language" and for adulterating the Russian language with fragments of a foreign system that he considered

French. Šiškov was wrong in taking old Russian to be the same thing as Church Slavonic, which he knew only in the late Russian version of the eighteenth century. The position of the archaists and their "old language" was not long tenable. Many of their members—and there were some of them even among the romanticists—moved away from the views of the *Beseda*. Šiškov's archaism died a natural death.

The Karamzinians formed their own literary society, the Arzamas (1815–1818). In addition to the important poets P. A. Vjazemskij and V. A. Žukovskij, who later went over to the romantic movement, the Arzamas included V. L. Puškin, K. N. Batjuškov, the young Aleksandr S. Puškin, who belonged to the group only nominally, and a number of other adherents of Karamzin's reforms, lovers of literature, some of whom were later important diplomats and ministers. The closed meetings of this small group, the minutes of which were preserved by Vjazemskij, were actually pleasant social gatherings, at which the poetry of the Šiškovian group was cleverly ridiculed and sometimes seriously criticized. Although few pronouncements of the Arzamas were published, they had a strong effect. It is questionable, however, whether the society did more than give ideas to its members, who were, with the exception of A. S. Puškin, already mature writers. The group disintegrated when a liberal-minded member, General M. F. Orlov, tried to persuade the others to publish a journal that would include political articles.

Even without the polemics of the Arzamas, which hardly made an impression on the public, the days of archaism were numbered. Neither Karamzin himself nor any of the older Karamzinians actually belonged to the Arzamas. They were not really needed. The language of Karamzin had already won the day.

9. The most important, faithful, and attractive follower of Karamzin was his friend Ivan Ivanovič Dmitriev (1760–1837). Dmitriev was from the same region of the Volga as Karamzin. He entered the guards at fourteen and there met Karamzin and began to write verse. In the 1790s, Dmitriev contributed to Karamzin's journals and in 1795 published his own first book of poetry. In the years preceding 1814, he was a senator and a minister and ne-

glected literature almost entirely. But he remained the host of a circle frequented by younger poets and even exiled Poles, such as Adam Mickiewicz.

Although A. S. Puškin regarded Dmitriev as merely a member of the Karamzin School who had outlived his time, Dmitriev's works kept coming out in new editions; and Žukovskij was not the only one who called him "Karamzin's second hypostasis." As late as 1823, Vjazemskij said that "the new era in our language" had begun with Karamzin and Dmitriev and especially praised Dmitriev's narrative art and the "good cheer, wit, and refined mockery" of his poems. Another contemporary, A. E. Izmajlov, thought that Dmitriev meant to Russian verse what Karamzin had meant to prose. Like Karamzin, Dmitriev considered his task to be primarily to create a new literary language, as is attested by the countless lexical and stylistic changes in his poems in succeeding new editions. Above all, his corrections show that he was attempting to make his language lighter and more flexible and to use the colloquial language of "good society."

From his correspondence with Karamzin and from his reminiscences, it is clear that Dmitriev kept up with the literary work of his contemporaries. He often tried to influence young poets—even Aleksandr S. Puškin, using Karamzin as an intermediary—and to persuade them to remove vulgarisms from their language. Among the words that he considered vulgar were *podmoga, davnym-davno, tak-kak, otvet, vot, ču, prijut, teplit'sja, jurknut'*, the Gallicisms *ser'ëzno* and *naivno*, and "elegiac" words used in imitation of folk songs. His correspondence and his reminiscences are a mine of information on the history of Russian literature. The style and language of his works are not at all uniform; he suited them as best he could to the genre he was writing in. There is a marked difference between his epistolary and poetic styles, according to V. Vinogradov, a Soviet scholar.

The main groups of Dmitriev's poems are satires, of which *Čužoj tolk* [Other People's Opinion] (1794), with its brief, trenchant parodies on the poor odes written by the archaizing classicists, and *Modnaja žena* are especially noteworthy. Notable also are the numerous fables, mostly on the traditional themes of this genre, but distinguished from the deliberate stylistic clumsiness and talkativeness of most eighteenth-century fables. The fables are further distinguished, by their refined language, from those of I. Krylov (see chapter VI). Like Dmitriev's later epigrammatic fables, they are often brief and pointed "apologues," which, after 1825, may be compared with the works of I. Krasicki, the Polish master of this genre.

An example:

The Fly

An ox was going home from work to rest, pulling the plow
    as he went.
A fly was sitting on his horn,
And on the way they met another fly.
"Where have you been, sister?" the second one asked.
"Where have we been? We've been plowing!"

Or:

A Skiff Without a Rudder

Without a rudder, driven by the wind, a skiff went racing
    out to sea.
It struck a rock and was dashed to pieces.
The same misfortune awaits us in the river of life!
Without good sense—farewell, frail skiff!

Here one finds a symbol that was also popular among the romanticists.

Or:

A Soap Bubble

On the thousand colors of its rainbow
A soap bubble hovered proudly in the air.
The wind blew, and suddenly the bubble became a drop—
    the fate of the sycophant!

Poetry such as this was alien to the romanticists, and they reacted to it by writing parodies (as did Aleksandr Puškin and Nikolaj Jazykov in 1827).

Dmitriev also wrote a great many elegiac and pseudopopular songs that were intended for the drawing room and consisted of variations on Karamzin's sentimental love themes. Some of them became quite popular, such as *Stonet sizyj goluboček* [The Gray Dove is Sighing]—it "sighs day and night/its dear friend/has flown away for a long time." The vocabulary of the poem is made up of words in the same minor key: "sighing," "cooing" (the then current metaphor for "being tender"), "being melancholy," "little dove" (metaphoric for "my darling"), "dear little friend," and even "tender branch" (on which the dove sits), and "grains of wheat" (that the dove, tormented by longing, prefers not to peck).

Dmitriev's lyric poems are written in the same tone, as are his epistles to his friends, his epigrams, and his occasional poetry; one finds the tone even in some of his odes. A vein of light irony runs through Dmitriev's verse narratives (which he called *skazki* or "fairy tales" and modeled after the fairy tales of *La Fontaine*). A "realistic ballad," *Karikatura* [Caricature] (1791), is unique among Dmitriev's works: a soldier who has served his time returns to his village and discovers that his wife has fallen in with criminals and is in prison. In telling the story, Dmitriev uses a number of expressions taken from the low vernacular.

The influence of French literature on Dmitriev is even more noticeable than on Karamzin. But, all in all, one cannot help feeling that subscribing to Karamzin's principles proved detrimental to Dmitriev and prevented him from developing more fully.

10. One of the first Russians who was a poet by profession was Vasilij L'vovič Puškin (1770–1830), Aleksandr Puškin's uncle, "bodily and also (stylistically) my uncle on the mount of the muses," as the nephew humorously observed. Vasilij Puškin was a good-natured character and a frequent butt of his friends' jokes. This poet, who has been for no good reason almost entirely forgotten, was an admirer of French literature. He was so dedicated to his profession that his last remark on his deathbed was said to have been a literary appraisal: "How dull Katenin's essays are!" His nephew Aleksandr wrote that he had "died like an honest warrior on his shield, *le cri de guerre á la bouche*." We say that Vasilij Puškin has been forgotten unjustly because he was a

master of verse technique (*bout-rimée*) and because he further modernized the Russian language. He had a remarkable ability to express his thoughts in pointed aphorisms, as his verse epistles attest. In addition to two polemic poems, *Opasnyj sosed* [The Dangerous Neighbor] (1811), full of bold images of situations in a brothel, and *Captain Xrabrov* (1829–1830), a parody on romantic poems, Puškin wrote a number of epigrams in imitation of the French, good fables of the kind that Dmitriev wrote. Above all he wrote the poetic manifestoes of the Karamzin School, letters to his colleagues in the Arzamas, among them Vjazemskij, Žukovskij, and his nephew, Aleksandr Puškin. These letters show clearly the close relationship between the Karamzinians and the tradition of classicist poetics. Besides "enrichment of the language" and beauty, V. L. Puškin requires of poetry a serious content ("sense" as well as "words"). In his view, what the Russian people need most is "enlightenment" (*"prosveščenie"*).

11. Among the many poets who joined the Karamzin School were several who later became romanticists. Of these, Petr Andreevič Vjazemskij and Vasilij Andreevič Žukovskij, in particular, should be mentioned, because of the considerable amount of their work done in the Karamzin style. We shall have more to say about them later.

The last classicist writer of tragedy, Vladislav Aleksandrovič Ozerov (1769–1816), was not personally connected with the Karamzin group. He enjoyed great but short-lived success. Although Ozerov took few liberties with the precepts of Russian classicism, Karamzin was known to be a supporter of the "true" Shakespeare—we do not know whether and to what extent he favored the practical application of Shakespeare's poetics. Ozerov's tragedies *Èdip v Afinax* [Oedipus in Athens] (1804), *Fingal* (1805), *Dmitrij Donskoj* (1807), and *Poliksena* (1809) betray a strong influence of French late classicist drama, especially of Jean François Ducis (1733–1816). But he handles unity of place somewhat more freely. The content of his work is often moralizing (in *Oedipus*, even in the Christian sense); and although his heroes are still kings, princes, or renowned warriors, they are, as Šiškov remarked, no longer heroic. The Karamzinians were also disappointed by the lack of local color (*Fingal*, for example, has a pseudo-Celtic setting) and by the feelings of the heroes, which they did not find tender enough. Although Ozerov did not exactly attempt to develop the character of his heroes—that would have amounted to a violation of the principle of unity of time, which he observed rather strictly—he did succeed in showing changes in their feelings and intentions (as in *Fingal*). Ozerov's tragedies were tremendously popular with the public but were coolly received by fellow writers. His *Dmitrij Donskoj*, for example, had a Russian theme and patriotic subject matter (the battle on Kulikovo Field, 1380), but was marred by unsuitable romantic entanglements: the heroine, for instance, a Russian princess, is stopping, oddly enough, at an army camp. Ozerov went insane in 1812 and died in 1816.

Jurij Aleksandrovič Neledinskij-Meleckij (1752–1829), a rococo figure, should also be mentioned. He was a rich nobleman and, for a time, a high dignitary and the hero of many love affairs. Within the framework of Karamzin's renovation of the language, Neledinskij was best known as a composer of songs. His songs are fit for "good society" but contain, by and large, more popular elements, lines and whole stanzas, than do Dmitriev's. Neledinskij's elegies and love poems are closely connected with his songs.

Karamzin's youngest follower was Žukovskij's friend Andrej Ivanovič Turgenev, who died early (1781–1803). His poems—some of which were first published in 1961—his letters, and the brief, elegiac outpourings of his heart, reminiscent of Ossian, reveal considerable poetic talent. It is significant that, as early as 1800, Turgenev wrote a quatrain "To Goethe's Portrait" and characterized Goethe as a poet who submitted entirely to "the laws of the heart."

Mixail Vasil'evič Milonov (1792–1821) can also be called a Karamzinian. He is known primarily as the author of satires and epistles. As often happens, only one of his lyric poems is remembered today, *The Leaves Are Falling*, an adaptation of C. H. Millevoye's *La Chute des Feuilles*. Puškin quotes passages from it in Lenskij's poem in *Evgenij Onegin*.

The Ukrainian Nikolaj Ivanovič Gnedič (1784–1833) is particularly remembered for his translation of the Iliad, on which he worked tirelessly from 1807 to 1829. His true accomplishment was the "vindication of the honor of the Russian hexameter." His translation is still printed and read. Gnedič also translated the *Homeric Hymns*. In 1800, he began to compose poems in the Ossianic vein and wrote an idyll that was well known at the time, *The Fishermen* (1821). In the 1820s, he joined the romanticists Baron Anton Del'vig and Aleksandr Puškin, and translated modern Greek folk songs—an attractive contribution to Russian romantic philhellenism.

Another outsider to the Karamzin School was Aleksandr Xristoforovič Vostokov (1781–1864), one of the founders of Slavic philology. He was the illegitimate son of a Baltic German nobleman, Baron von Osten-Sacken, from the island of Oesel. A hopeless stutterer, Vostokov decided to become a librarian. In 1802, he began to write poems, at first as a classicist, in a rather old-fashioned vein. His poems appeared until 1821 and gradually approached the Karamzin style. His important *Essay on Russian Versification* (1817) no longer bears the stamp of orthodox classicism. Vostokov early gained the reputation of being a master and arbiter. He experimented in the field of prosody, wrote poems without rhyme, and attempted, especially in his translations, to imitate ancient meters. He called his first small volumes of verse *Opyty* [Experiments]. His last poetic works, influenced by A. S. Puškin, are translations of Serbian folk songs, to which Del'vig called his attention. Vostokov's main scholarly work was a *Discourse* [Rassuždenie] *on the Slavic Language* (1820), which, along with the works of Josef Dobrovsky, was the foundation of Slavic philology. His important Russian grammar appeared later (1831–1833) and was often republished.

12. Konstantin Nikolaevič Batjuškov (1787–1855) was a significant poet who went far beyond the limits of the Karamzin School, from which he had set out. After a good education that emphasized languages, Batjuškov worked first as a public official and then as a librarian. The Napoleonic Wars took him to Finland and later to Western Europe. As a young man, he published poems that reveal his maturity and mastery. Around 1810, he fell in with the Karamzin School and took part in the Arzamas. In 1822, permanent insanity put an end to his diversified life.

Batjuškov represents a classicism no longer operating within the limits of Russian classicist theory. His views are known to us from his remarks on poetic theory. Batjuškov was close to classical poetry as well as to Italian poetry, which was not otherwise especially important to Russian classicism. Like various contemporaries, including Aleksandr Puškin for a time, he sought to follow the French poets Evariste Parny and André Chénier and his fellow Russian Žukovskij. But he was essentially interested in modifying the "coarseness" of Russian; and in his efforts to attain euphony, he achieved some astonishing effects. It was often no more than isolated lines that caused Puškin to call him a magician—at the same time that he sharply criticized other passages in his poems. Batjuškov frequently wrote in iambic lines of unequal numbers of syllables but also composed in regular lines and stanzas.

The subject matter of his poems is far removed from the fantasy and romantic longing that Žukovskij introduces into poetry. Batjuškov's subjects are entirely of this world but alternate between epicurism and an elegiac mood that later turns to pessimistic desperation. His translations and imitations of Italian poetry and of classical anthologies of poems and elegies are among his best works. He appears to have reached the greatest perfection that Russian classicism was capable of. But few of his poems outlived the age of Puškin. Among the few that did are *The Dying Tasso*, *To the Ruins of a Castle in Sweden* (an elegy), and *The Shadow of a Friend*, a poem written as he was leaving England. All three of these poems are set in foreign countries, and Russia appears only as an object of longing. Some poems from his anthologies remained popular for a long time, such as these lines that one would hardly expect from a classicist:

О, память сердца, ты сильней
рассудка памяти печальной.

O, memory of the heart, you are stronger than the sad
    memory of reason.

13. Poets who wrote on "night and tombs" were also related to the Karamzin School.

Gavriil Petrovič Kamenev (1772–1803) is famous for a single poem. He was from Kazan' and visited Moscow only briefly. His verse and prose are altogether typical of preromantic literature of the night. Apart from his epic *Gromval* (1804), which has been incorrectly called the first Russian ballad and which appears to have had no influence on the development of the Russian ballad, his works are not well known.

Ivan Petrovič Pnin (1773–1805) appeared to be a promising writer, more on the strength of his preromantic poems than of his political radicalism, which he expressed, for instance, in 1804 in his *Essay on Education in Russia*; but he died at thirty-two.

Vasilij Vasil'evic Popugaev was born in 1778 or 1779. The date of his death is unknown. He was for a time a very productive writer and was influenced by the Karamzin style.

Both Pnin and Popugaev were close to the political radicalism that originated with Aleksandr Nikolaevič Radiščev (1749–1802).

Aleksej Fedorovič Merzljakov (1778–1830) is of interest as a translator of classical poetry and as the composer of imitation folk songs. He was highly influential as a professor of poetics at Moscow University. His theoretical views were not narrow but generous, as is attested by the fact that romantics studied under him and that he especially encouraged Tjutčev.

Nikolaj Fedorovič Ostolopov (1783–1833) is remembered, not so much as a notable writer, but as the publisher of a three-volume literary lexicon, *Slovar' drevnej i novoj poèzii* (1821 ff.), that proved useful to his contemporaries.

Aleksandr Fedorovič Voejkov (1779–1839) was a member of classicist and romantic literary circles and later became professor of Russian literature at the University of Dorpat (now Tartu) from 1814 to 1820. He was a contributor to various literary journals and, beginning in 1820, published several periodicals himself. He was never able to give up the classicist tradition altogether. His translations, satires, and letters were soon forgotten, with the exception of the literary satire *Dom sumasšedšix* [Insane Asylum], written before 1830, which had, however, lost all its relevance by the 1830s.

III

Early Russian Romanticism

1. This chapter deals with the general characteristics of romanticism already mentioned and discusses the lives and works of the principal romantic poets and prose writers. The originality of a work was an important aesthetic value to the romantic writer; and, as a consequence, writers of this school are likely to be quite different from one another. It is all the more remarkable, therefore, that wherever one turns in Russian romantic literature, one finds the same motifs, images, and symbols. Apart from the anticlassicist and anti-Enlightenment sentiment and the general way of looking at man and the world that developed from this feeling for originality, the common features of romanticism go back to both the influence of Western European models and the influence of prominent early Russian romanticists.

The influence from the West came from several sources. Since Russian romanticism did not begin until after 1810, it was naturally affected by the later romanticists. The strongest influence was that of George Gordon, Lord Byron, who especially affected the second generation of romantics, after 1835. The only writers influenced by German romanticism were those acquainted with German literature, and that was by no means all writers, although many Russians came to know German romanticism in French translation. E. T. A. Hoffmann was very important to the development of Russian prose. The influence of philosophical romanticism goes back to Friedrich Wilhelm Joseph von Schelling and his school and perhaps even more to "scientific" fantasy—the romantic "metapsychology" and natural philosophy (see chapter

V). Schiller and, to a lesser extent, Goethe were also associated with romanticism, perhaps because they were thought ultimately to have destroyed classicism. Russian romanticists considered their main task to be to destroy the classicist tradition. They preferred new genres, ones that had not been used by the classicists, and favored, among other forms, the ballad (as shown, for example, in the work of Schiller). The Goethe to whom the Russian romanticists turned was, by and large, the Goethe of *Sturm und Drang*.

The influence of English romanticism was surprisingly strong, even apart from Byron. Walter Scott was thought to be an unequaled master of prose, although he was read mostly in French or Russian translation. Even minor English poets were influential. An American poet, Washington Irving, was also imitated, by no less a poet than Aleksandr Puškin. With the onset of romanticism, the influence of Ossian began to give way.

The direct influence of French literature was relatively slight. Preromantic poets, such as C. H. Millevoye, N. J. L. Gilbert, Evaríste Parny, and André Chénier, who were not romanticists—though they were by no means any longer classicists—were appreciated, translated, and imitated. The influence of the French romanticists, whom Puškin did not even consider romanticists, was limited.

Russian romanticists were concerned primarily with questions of style and only secondarily with ideological problems, of which they often had only a hazy notion. Russian romanticism developed in four waves. The first wave began about 1815; and literary historians used to think, not altogether correctly, that this school centered around Aleksandr Puškin. However, one no longer calls Puškin's romanticist contemporaries the "Puškin Pleiad." Žukovskij and Vjazemskij, who had formerly belonged to the Karamzin School, were also part of this first wave. As early as 1825, the influence of romantic ideology began to make itself felt. Varied groups representing the second wave were formed, one of them around the young Prince Vladimir Odoevskij. From 1830 on, followers of various philosophical schools began to fall in with the romanticists, even Hegelians who were willing to overlook Hegel's criticism of romanticism. This second group soon divided into two camps, "Westernizers" and "Slavophiles," of whom the latter are more properly called romanticists. Around 1830, a new, third current of romanticism began, one that cultivated a reflective pessimism. Mixail Jur'evič Lermontov is a typical writer in this vein. There were diverse and complex relationships among these three schools of romanticism.

Only a few years later, works of the fourth and last school of Russian romanticism began to appear, works that pointed the way to realism. These writers made up what was called the "Natural School" and were less concerned with the positive ideas of romanticism than with criticizing reality. Their criticism amounted to portraying reality in dark, repellent colors. Some members of the Natural School never mention positive ideals or, if they do, speak of them only in passing (see chapter IV, sec. 16); some of them were not at all sure about these ideals.

The crisis in Russian romanticism set in toward the end of the 1840s. There were romanticists, of course, who remained true to their ideals—for example, Fedor Ivanovič Tjutčev (1803–1873), the most important Russian philosophical poet; or less significant figures, such as Fedor Glinka (1786–1880). Some rather important epigones went on writing for decades in the spirit of romanticism, men such as Apollon Grigor'ev (1822–1864) and Count Aleksej Konstantinovič Tolstoj (1817–1875).

The momentum of the romantic movement attracted some writers who thought the school merely fashionable. Their works often read like parodies. A typical writer of this kind is Aleksej Vasil'evic Timofeev (1812–1883).

A special group of romanticists is composed of those writers who took a stand on some important question. Among them are the "archaists," who refused to go along with stylistic innovations in the early part of the romantic period. A very few writers who lived during the romantic period remained unaffected by romanticism, and we shall deal with them individually.

2. Vasilij Andreevič Žukovskij (1783–1852) went over to the romanticists from the Karamzin School. His poetic peculiarities have caused some literary historians—chiefly A. N. Veselovskij—

to set him apart unjustly from the romanticists. Žukovskij was too gentle a personality to adopt the radical tone of the romanticists, and he was profoundly religious in a way that reminds one of the German Pietists. As a result, he was neither a Byronian nor a revolutionary.

Žukovskij was the illegitimate son of a landowner named Bunin and a captive Turkish woman. He had a good education and made literary friendships very early at the boardinghouse for noblemen at Moscow University. Among his friends were Andrej Turgenev (see chapter II, sec. 11) and his brother. In 1802, after a number of attempts to write in the classicist and Karamzin vein, Žukovskij published a translation of Thomas Gray's *Elegy Written in a Country Churchyard* and soon became well known. Even later, his best and most popular poems were often translations; foreign literature inspired him to produce work of his own. From 1815 on, Žukovskij was a particularly active member of the Arzamas (see chapter II, sec. 8). He was a master of the parody and wrote a number of humorous poems.

In 1817, Žukovskij was appointed tutor in Russian to the Prussian Princess Charlotte, who, as Aleksandra, married Crown Prince Nicholas, subsequently Nicholas I. This new position put Žukovskij in touch with all the courts of Europe. In 1826, he began to tutor Crown Prince Alexander, who was to become Alexander II. It is doubtful that it was really Žukovskij's influence that later caused Alexander to undertake his reforms; but, in any case, by virtue of his connections at court, Žukovskij was always ready to protect those who had run afoul of the government.

Žukovskij did not write much original poetry and often published his works in bibliophile editions, *For the Few* (1821 ff., later printed in Karlsruhe). He translated a great deal, especially Schiller, Uhland, Goethe, the English romanticists, and later, even Byron. His version of J. P. Hebel's *Alemannische Gedichte* is excellent. He later turned to Oriental poetry, following the the example of the German poet Friedrich Rückert. Žukovskij translated the *Odyssey* from the German interlinear translation and popularized the work in Russia. He wrote only a little prose, a few novellas and popular philosophical treatises that reveal his pietistic devotion. An unhappy love for a cousin cast a shadow over his personal life.

In 1840, after he had finished tutoring, Žukovskij moved to Germany and married the daughter of a painter named von Reutern. He lived in Dusseldorf, in Wiesbaden, in several cities of Switzerland (1848), and in Baden-Baden, where he died in 1852.

Žukovskij was on close terms with Aleksandr Puškin from 1818 on and was later friendly with Gogol', with whom he shared a similar piety. He knew a number of German writers, Goethe among them; and his acquaintance with Justinus Kerner is especially interesting. Kerner translated Žukovskij's fairy tale of *Ivan Tsarevich and the Gray Wolf*, which appeared in 1852 under the name "Joukovski." Kerner also undertook to translate *The Eternal Jew,* a poem that Žukovskij did not finish.

3. Žukovskij's translations are of particular importance to Russian literature in view of their artistic quality. They made Schiller so familiar to the Russian reading public that he seemed almost a "Russian poet", according to Dostoevskij. The slightly Russified *Alemannische Gedichte* are among the few idylls that are still read in Russia. We have already mentioned the importance of Žukovskij's translation of the Odyssey. Žukovskij put into his translations the same soft touches of color that came naturally to his own writing. The sound and effect of some of his original and translated ballads, especially Goethe's *Der Erlkönig*, are therefore considerably altered. His best adaptation is probably his poetic version of Friedrich von Fouqué's *Undine.*

Žukovskij was aware that his interpretations were not always adequate. He revised his translation of Gray's *Elegy* to bring it closer to the original but lost some of the beauty of the sound in the first version. The danger of remaining true to the original is even more clear in his translation of Gottfried August Bürger's *Lenore.* In its Russian version, *Svetlana*, the ballad opens with an attractive account of popular Russian fortune-telling on the eve of the festival of Epiphany (Russian *Kreščenie*). Svetlana laments her fiancé, who has been at war and is missing; a vision of him dead and a nocturnal ride later prove to have been a dream. The next morning, her fiancé returns home, alive. Later Žukovskij attempted to write a more "genuine" translation of *Lenore*. Although he still took some of the edge off Bürger, this second version was more accurate; on the other hand, it lost much of the beauty of the less pointed *Svetlana*. Incidentally, the translation of foreign literature became the subject of an important polemic (see sec. 26 below, on Katenin).

4. Although Žukovskij's original poems have a personality all their own, they are less popular than his translations. The language of his original poems is light and represents an extension of Karamzin's linguistic reform. Žukovskij speaks to us in a manner that does not seem alien, despite the turns that Russian cultural history has taken. His own early ballads still include the figure of the unhappy singer, who is related to some of Karamzin's characters. Later, Žukovskij wrote on more serious subjects: religion, art, love. In Žukovskij, love, which in the eighteenth century was little more than a social game, is the deepest quality of the human soul and is based on mysterious relationships between souls in spheres of being about which we know nothing. The same is true of all other genuine experiences the roots of which are hidden from us. If it is impossible to realize these genuine qualities in the here and now, we can only long for them in the beyond. An indefinite place far away and the experiences of the soul that lead to the place are therefore important aspects of Žukovskij's poetry: memory that assuages longing and hope that promises fulfillment. Since our *here* is hopeless, the poet turns to the words *beyond* or *distant place*, an unknown land that we long for. But it is not merely our yearning that informs us of this distant place. We catch glimpses, signs, voices, and visions of light from this magic, faraway land, from these unattainable heights. Žukovskij wrote frequent variations on this theme. Perhaps Schiller's little-known poem *Lied* was his model.

The symbol of the "vision of light" is Žukovskij's butterfly that descends to the flowers from on high: "He soared from the heights to the heavenly realm of splendid being and was filled with memories of pure heavenly beauty" ("*Motylek i cvety*"). Or a guardian angel "sometimes lets us see heaven through a veil so that one's heart on this dark earth should know about it, and he speaks of it, with his soul, persuasively and clearly in everything that is lovely here and that animates the world" (*Lalla Rookh*). Moreover, the unhappy man, the "poor singer," is directed from above toward his goal in this world. Although emissaries from the world of darkness, witches and devils, also appear frequently in Žukovskij's ballads, he is not, of course, so naive as to believe in the literal existence of these two worlds of light and darkness. They belong to the realm of the invisible and inexpressible. Language is capable of reproducing only visual beauty, as Žukovskij says in these lines from *Nevyrazimoe* (1827):

The inexpressible cannot be put into words. For glaring features and brilliant beauty there are, of course, words. But the quality connected with brilliant beauty, the vague thing that moves us, this voice of enchantment that sounds only in the soul . . . what language can one use for that? . . . The soul is elevated to the heights, everything immeasurable is compressed into a sigh, and only silence speaks an intelligible language.

In Žukovskij, the inexpressible is connected with the "beyond" and the "distant land" and with words such as "angels," "flying," "hovering," "being animate" (of inanimate things), "magic," "enchanted," and, of course, "hope" and "memory." All of this is related to Žukovskij's view of the world, which we find set forth in his essays.

5. The past is particularly important to Žukovskij, because "somewhere back there" is man's true home. In memories, which are the basis of recognition, we have access to this original home. Recollection is not a rational capacity. True existence is accessible only to feelings. Žukovskij even speaks of "dream-like visions when one is awake." According to the romantic psychologist G. H. von Schubert, this sphere is the "night side of the soul," on which both art and poetry are based. For Žukovskij, poetry is part of the sacred sphere. In his *Camões*, after the work of the same title by F. Halm, Žukovskij says: "Poetry is the earthly sister of celestial religion," "Poetry is God in the holy dreams of earth."

The essence of the human ego is ultimately expressed in dreams and visions. Man approaches God through the experiences of the depths of his soul and of the abyss of his heart, but not through the religion of the masses, which Žukovskij says "has replaced the religion of Christ with the fanaticism of shamans and fakirs." Religion should be cleansed of everything "that is superstitious and that has been devised out of feeble ignorance."

These theoretical ideas were not particularly influential; but the "delightful sweetness of his verse," as Puškin put it, assured Žukovskij of a lasting effect on succeeding generations of poets, on A. S. Puškin, Ivan Kozlov, Jakov Polonskij, A. A. Fet, I. S. Turgenev, down to the symbolist A. A. Blok.

6. Prince Petr Andreevič Vjazemskij (1792–1878), at first a faithful adherent of Karamzin, also turned to romanticism. He took part in the Arzamas and was on friendly terms with several members of the society, in particular Žukovskij and Batjuškov. After the Napoleonic Wars (1812–1814), Vjazemskij discovered European romanticism and called Aleksandr Puškin's attention to Byron. He carried on a long correspondence with Puškin, on the problems of poetry, among other things. He was responsible for getting Puškin's "Southern Poems" published and wrote essays in which he called the poems "romantic." By "romanticism," he meant primarily a literature that stressed a reform in poetics and that stood for political freedom.

In 1825, Vjazemskij began to take a keen interest in the journal of the romanticist N. Polevoj, *Moskovskij telegraf.* Later, he joined Puškin and his literary friends in working for Anton A. Del'vig's *Literaturnaja gazeta* and for Puškin's *Sovremennik.*

As a government official in Poland, Vjazemskij became acquainted with Polish literature, wrote excellent translations of the fables of I. Krasicki, and made an effort to be accepted in Polish society. During the reign of Alexander II (starting in 1855) he was suspected of being reactionary by Russian society, which was in a radical mood. His literary friends had all died, and from 1860 on, he led a secluded life. Toward the end of his life, he began to write again and composed political epigrams and lyric poems.

Vjazemskij kept a diary for years and saw to it that his literary remains were preserved. After his death, his works and diaries were rather carelessly published, with capricious omissions. His complete remains have still not been published.

7. When Vjazemskij went over to the romanticists, his poetry changed completely. Here and in chapter V, sec. I, P. A. Vjazemskij is discussed as an example of the romantic style, especially of the semantics of romantic poetry, since Vjazemskij was one of the first in Russia to espouse romanticism, and his romantic poems have received too little attention. His lyric poems are particularly suitable for lexical analysis. I shall call this method "microanalysis."[1] Vjazemskij's poems of the 1820s are of three kinds. He wrote a number of occasional poems. His most successful genre was the epigram. Following French models, he developed a type of song on topical subjects, in couplets, with a refrain that was usually repeated; and, finally, he wrote lyric poems in which his contemporaries, including Puškin, found too much "intellect." It would be wrong, however, to assume that Vjazemskij remained a rationalist or that he was blind to romantic subjectivism. On the contrary, he succeeded in a number of lyric poems in expressing essential romantic motifs. Against a centuries-old tradition, he defended the positive significance of passion (*strast'*) in his poem *Volnenie* (1829). In the various forms of nature, such as a waterfall, he saw symbols of the human soul (*Vodopad*, 1825; *More*, 1826; *Lesa*, about 1830). He emphasized the importance of subjective experience (*Mnimoj sčastlivice*, about 1825). One of his poems is dedicated to the memory of Byron (*Bajron*, after 1824). He wrote poems that Puškin imitated (*Metel'*, from the series *Zimnie karikatury*, 1828). Later, he was one of the first to adopt the pessimistic romanticism that we have called the third wave of romanticism (*Xandra*, about 1830; *Ja perežil*, 1837). In his later poetry, he returned again to motifs from the romantic view of the world; and on meeting Tjutčev, who was near his own age, he wrote several lyrics in Tjutčev's poetic vein.

1. See Dmitrij Čiževskij, "Einige Aufgaben der slavistischen Romantikforschung," in *Die Welt der Slaven*, I (1956), 1.

Vjazemskij's early romantic poems are also distinguished by a lexical feature. In them, he attempts to maintain the romantic mood through the use of a selected vocabulary. Later poets, including Puškin, availed themselves of this stylistic device, although perhaps not always with a clear intention in mind. Before we turn to quotations, we should remember that individual words sometimes belong to definite "semantic fields." In our quotations, we shall call attention to several of the fields that were particularly popular with romanticists. The words of interest to us in Vjazemskij's *The Narva Waterfall* (1825), below, are given in italics:

НАРВСКИЙ ВОДОПАД

Несись с *неукротимым гневом*,
Мятежной влаги властелин!
Над *тишиной* окрестной *ревом*
Господствуй, *бурный исполин*!

Жемчужною, *кипящей лавой*,
За валом *низвергая вал*,
Сердитый дикий, величавый,
Перебегай ступени скал!

Дождь брызжет от *упорной сшибки*
Волны, *сразившейся* с волной,
И влажный дым, как облак зыбкий,
Вдали их представляет *бой*.

Всё *разъяренней*, всё *угрюмей*
Летишь, как *гений непогод*;
Я мыслью погружаюсь в *шуме*
Междоусобно-бурных вод. . . .
. . . .

Твой *ясный* берег чужд *смятенью*,
На нем цветет весны *краса*,
И вместе миру и *волненью*
Светлеют те же небеса.

Но ты, созданье *тайной бури*,
Игралище глухой войны,
Ты не зерцало их *лазури*,
Вотще *блестящей* с вышины.

Противоречие природы,
Под *грозным* знаменем *тревог*,
В залоге вечной *непогоды*
Ты бытия приял залог.

Ворвавшись в сей предел *спокойный*,
Один *свирепствуешь* в глуши,
Как вдоль пустыни *вихорь знойный*
Как *страсть* в святилище души.

Как ты, *внезапно разразится*,
Как ты, растет она в *борьбе*,
Терзает лоно, где родится,
И *поглощается* в себе.

The Narva Waterfall

Flow on with unbridled anger, sovereign of restless waters! Rule over the surrounding stillness with your roar, stormy giant!

Casting wave after wave of pearly, boiling water, angry, wild, and majestic one, overflow the steps of rocks!

Rain splashes from the stubborn battle of the waves contending with one another; and like a vacillating cloud, damp steam gives notice of their war.

Evermore furious, evermore gloomy, you fly along like a genius of foul weather; in my mind I sink into the din of the internecine stormy waters...

.   .   .   .   .   .

This uproar is alien to your clear bank; on it blooms the beauty of spring; and the same heaven lights peace and disorder.

But you, creation of the secret storm, plaything of remote war, you are no mirror for the azure of heaven, which is shining in vain above.

Contradiction of nature, you acquired your existence under the threatening sign of alarm as a pledge of eternal bad weather.

Bursting into these peaceful parts, you rage in isolation like a hot storm in the desert, like a passion in the temple of the soul.

Like you, it (passion) bursts out suddenly; like you, it grows in battle, rending the womb where it is born, and devours itself.

The general composition of the poem depends on the antithesis between the violent waterfall, personified in a number of epithets and verbs, and the peaceful, lovely scene surrounding it. This opposition is symbolic of the conflict between human passion and tranquillity. One finds in the poem an accumulation of words that can be assigned to definite semantic fields. The basic forms of the words are:

Motion and agitation:	nestis', burnyj, nizvergat', perebegat', letet', nepogoda (twice), volnenie, burja, igrališče, vixor', razrazitsja.
Anxiety:	gnev, mjatežnyj, serdityj, dikij, upornyj, meždousobno-burnyj, smjatenie, groznyj, trevoga, svirepstvovat', strast'.
Strife:	sšibka, srazit'sja, boj, vojna, bor'ba.
Heat:	kipjaščij, lava, znojnyj
Sublimity:	ispolin, veličavyj, genij
Secrecy:	tajnyj, gluxoj
Noise:	rev, šum

The antonyms of these semantic fields are also present and can be assigned: "tranquillity"—"tišina," "jasnyj," "spokojnyj," "mir"; and "beauty"—"jasnyj," "vesna," "krasa," "svetlet'," "lazur'," "blestet'."

The contrast in the last two stanzas makes the waterfall a symbol for the "contradiction of nature" within itself. The first seven fields may be considered metaphors for the romanticist the poet confesses to be in the fourth stanza: "ja mysl'ju pogružajus' v šume." Significantly, one finds in the twenty-four lines of the poem no less than forty words that belong to "romantic" semantic fields. The middle stanza, which is omitted, contains only four antonyms: "bezmjatežno," "nežno," "otdyxat'," "tišina."

One should note that semantic fields can cross one another and that a word may belong to two or more fields. This is the case with "kipjaščij," for instance; it could also have been assigned to the field "motion." One should keep in mind that semantic fields are a natural part of the objective characteristics

of language and that they also serve as working hypotheses for
scholarly analysis.

Although Vjazemskij uses synonyms wherever possible in
the poem above, in other situations he merely repeats words.
Let us take, for example, the poem *Volnenie* (1829, abridged):

Волнение

Желанья! бурные желанья! . . .
Волненье! темное волненье!
К чему *мятежно будишь* ты
Остывшее воображенье
И *обличенные мечты?* . . .
Вы с новой *силой* овладели
Моей *взволнованной* душой;
Как *мчится облако без цели,*
Стремглав гонимое грозой;
Как *ветр играет* им в *полете*
По *дикой прихоти* своей,
Так, мной господствуя, влечете
Под *бурю пламенных страстей.* . . .
Как часто сын *стихии бурной,*
Искатель бедствий и чудес,
Скучает *тишиной лазурной*
Над ним раскинутых небес. . . .
Печально у скалы прибрежной
Он, сидя, молит *непогод.* . . .
В душе *палимой страстью* знойной,
Он, ужасаяся, *бежит*
Картины *ясной и спокойной,*
Где все о прошлом говорит. . . .
"Бушуйте волны *бездны* синей,—
С *восторгом* восклицает он:
"Мятежной предаю *пучине*
"Мятежной жизни бурный сон."

Agitation

Desires, stormy desires! . . . Agitation, dark agitation! Why do you wake
insurgently the imagination that has grown cold and dreams that have

been exposed? . . . With renewed strength you have possessed my agitated soul: as a cloud races aimlessly, driven headlong by a storm, as the wind plays with it in flight according to its wild whim, so you [desires] rule over me and draw me into the storm of fiery passions. . . . How often the son of the stormy elements, seeker of misfortune and miracles, is bored with the still azure of the heavens stretched above him. . . . Sitting sadly on the boulders of the shore, he prays for stormy weather. . . . Scorched in his soul by burning passion, aghast, he flees the lucid, peaceful scene where everything bespeaks the past. . . . "Rage on, waves of the blue abyss," he cries with ecstasy; "to the restless gulf of the sea I give the stormy dream of restless life."

Here, too, the words of the same semantic fields are partly repeated:

Motion and agitation:	mčat'sja, stremglav, gnat', groza, vetr, igrat', polet, nepogoda, burja, burnyj (three times), stixija, buševat'
Anxiety or excitement:	želanija (twice), volnenie (twice), mjatežno, mjatežnyj (twice), budit', voobraženie, mečty, vzvolnovannyj, dikij, prixot', vostorg, strast' (twice)
Secrecy:	temnyj
Heat:	plamennyj, paljaščij, znojnyj

New fields are added, such as "strength," "*sila*"; "abyss," "*bezdna*," "*pučina*"; but these fields are not so frequently represented as before. There are also fields of antonyms. In addition to the fields already encountered—"tranquillity," "*tišina*," "*spokojnyj*"; "beauty," "*jasnyj*," "*lazurnyj*"—other fields are introduced: (spiritual) "coldness," "*ostyvšyj*" and "understanding," "*obličennyj*." The twenty-seven lines quoted here contain thirty-seven words that can be assigned to romantic semantic fields.

The real theme of the poem is developed in the second half. The desires and longings of the romanticist are directed at agitation, storms, even passions and adventures ("*čudesa*"). When he says that he would like to avoid the "lucid, peaceful scene where everything bespeaks the past," the poet is probably aiming good-natured criticism at Žukovskij, whom we have already met.

In this connection, it is interesting to note that the variability of semantic fields in the poem dedicated to the memory of Byron (1824–27) is considerably greater. Here it is often a question of word groups, not just individual words:

> Поэзия! твое святилище природа! . . .
> Так ты свой черпай *огнь* из *тайных недр* ея. . . .
> Наука водит нас . . .
> И чадам *избранным* указывает след
> В *безвестный* для толпы и *чудотворный* свет.
> Счастлив поэт, когда он внял от колыбели
> Ее *таинственный* призыв к *заветной* цели.
> Счастлив, кто с первых дней приял, как лучший дар,
> *Волненье, смелый пыл, неутолимый жар*;
> Кто детских игр беглец, объятый *дикой* думой,
> Любил *паденью* вод внимать с скалы *угрюмой*,
> Прокладывал следы в *заглохшие* леса,
> Взор вопрошающий вперял на небеса
> И, *тайною* тоской и *тайной* негой полный,
> Любил скалы, леса, и облака, и волны. . . .
> Чем *дале* от *людей*, тем мене он один.
> Везде он слышит глас, *душе* его *знакомый*:
> О страшных *таинствах* ей возвещают *громы*,
> Ей *водопад ревет*, ласкается ручей.

O, poetry! Your temple is nature! . . . Draw your fire thus from its secret depths . . . Science leads us . . . shows the select the way into the wondrous world that the masses do not know. Happy is the poet who has heard from the cradle its mysterious call to the sacred task. Happy is the one who from his first days received, as the greatest gift, agitation, bold flame, unquenchable fire, who, seized by a wild thought, ran from children's games, who loved to hear the fall of water from a dark rock, made his way into wild forests, turned his questioning gaze to heaven, and, full of secret yearning and bliss, loved the rocks, the forests, the clouds, the waves . . . (who) was less alone the farther he was from men. Everywhere he hears a voice well known to his soul: the thunder proclaims terrible secrets to his soul, the waterfall roars for it, the stream caresses it.

Further on in this poem, we encounter the then current

characteristics of the image of the poet: "striving to infinity," "illumination of language"; the poet awakens man "*strastno-sladostno*" (passionately-sweetly) with a "lightninglike word"; with a word, he "illuminates the night of the soul and of being; in this word never before uttered" ("*nesbytočnoe*") "is all the joy of hopes, passions, desires ("*želanija*"), and fiery thoughts that were created from dreams and that were destroyed by reason." That is, one finds here the same vocabulary and the same line of thought as in the previous selections. Once more, the symbols of genuine experiences are warmth ("*ogon'*," "*žar*," "*pyl'*"); burning thoughts ("*znojnye dumy*"); spiritual agitation ("*volnenie*," "*smelyj*," "*neutolimyj*," "*dikij*," "*ugrjumyj*"); noise ("*gromy*," "*revet'*"). One is particularly aware of the secret (*tajnyj*, used three times, "*tainstvennyj*," "*zavetnyj*," "*tainstva*") that is accessible only to the select ("*izbrannyj*") and of the *new language* ("*glas*," "*jazyk*," "*narečie*," "*slovo*"). The first poem cited contained a conversation with nature, an address to the waterfall and to the waves of the stormy sea. Here the poet hears the voice of nature, which is familiar to him, and in his new language passes it on, to other men. The characterization of this language as "new," "lightninglike," "nonexistent" (that is, until now) is significant.

Vjazemskij's use of the expressions "night of the soul" and "night of being" (that is, the night side of nature) is characteristically romantic. In this connection, it would be profitable to examine the introspective poem *Unynie* [Dejection] written in 1819, probably soon after Vjazemskij had become acquainted with Byron) and the equally important example of political invective, *Negodovanie* [Indignation] (1820). But for the purposes of our literary history, it is enough to make a somewhat cursory microanalysis of the poems quoted above. We shall return frequently to the concept of semantic fields.

There is a different use of lexical elements in the poem *K mnimoj sčastlivice* [To the Imaginary Fortunate One] (about 1825), written to a woman who thinks herself fortunate but who, according to Vjazemskij, enjoys only illusory happiness in her everyday life and is a party to a loveless marriage.

твоя . . . младость
Есть дня *холодного блестящая* заря.
Нет прозаического счастья
Для *поэтической* души: . . .
Сердцам *избранным* дан язык,
Непосвященному невнятный;
Кто в *таинства* его с рожденья не проник,
Тот не постигнет их награды благодатной.
Где в двух *сердцах* нет *тайного* сродства,
Поверья общего, сочувствия, понятья,
Там *холодны* любви права,
Там *холодны* любви объятья! . . .
Ты веришь, что . . .
Долг может счастье заменить!
А ты, разбив сосуд *волшебный*
И с жизни оборвав поэзии цветы,
Чем *сердце* обольстишь, когда рукой враждебной
Сердечный мир разворожила ты?

Your . . . youth is the gleaming dawn of a cold day. There is no prosaic joy for a poetic soul: . . . Selected hearts are given a language that the uninitiated do not hear; whoever has not seen through to its secrets from birth will not receive its beneficial reward.

Where there is no secret affinity in two hearts, no common belief, no sympathy of understanding, there the rights of love are cold, there the embraces of love are cold.

You believe that . . . duty can replace love! And after you have broken the enchanted vessel and have torn the flowers of poetry from life, with what will you tempt the heart when with a hostile hand you have disenchanted the world of the heart?

But the poet goes on to say:

Любуйся тишиной под небом безмятежным,
Но *хлад рассудка, хлад* до *сердца* не проник;
В нем *пламень* не потух; так под убором *снежным*
Кипит невидимо земных *огней тайник*. . . .
Еще тоскуешь ты о *бурях*, небе *знойном*,
Под коим зреют в нас душевные плоды.

Завидуя мученьям милым
И *бурным* радостям, неведомым тебе,
Хотела б жертвовать ты счастием постылым
Страстей волненью и борьбе.

Enjoy peace under tranquil skies; but the cold of reason, the cold has not yet reached your heart; the fire has not yet gone out in it; thus the hidden fires of earth burn invisibly beneath the cover of snow. . . . You still long for storms, for the sultry sky under which the fruits of the soul ripen within us.

You envy the sweet tortures and the stormy joys unknown to you; you would like to sacrifice your odious joy for the turbulence and struggle of passions.

Here again one finds the same vocabulary. Warmth and coldness are presented as antonyms; the depth of the heart is the measure of the authenticity and sincerity of feelings. The truly sensitive life is "enchanted" ("*volšebnyj*") and must not be "disenchanted" ("*razvorožennyj*"). The desire for true happiness is the desire for tortures ("*mučenija*") that the poet calls "sweet tortures," for storms ("*burja*," "*burnye*," "*radosti*"), for a "glowing sky," for passions ("*strasti*"), for turbulence and struggle ("*bor'ba*").

The quotations above illustrate at least one aspect of the romantic body of thought and of the romanticist's vocabulary. We shall return to Vjazemskij's later poetry, though only briefly.

8. The unfortunate Kondratij Fedorovič Ryleev (1795–1826) was only loosely connected with the romantic movement. He was an officer in the Napoleonic Wars; he retired from the service in 1818, and in 1821 became a judge in St. Petersburg. He took an active interest in literature and knew the most important poets of the time. In 1820, appalled at the political stagnation, he joined a secret organization, the Decembrists—as they became known after their short-lived, unsuccessful uprising in December 1825. He played a modest part at first and in 1824

became one of their main leaders. After the unexpected death of Alexander I, in December 1825, the poorly prepared revolt broke out and was put down. Ryleev made no secret of his views, his position in the organization, and his participation in the revolt. With a number of his comrades, he was sentenced to death. He was not "pardoned" and sent to Siberia, as were most of the conspirators; he was hanged publicly, on July 25, 1826, with four other participants in the revolt.

We are not concerned with Ryleev because of his tragic fate, but because of his position as an important poet of a particular kind. After some insignificant poems on various subjects and some patriotic odes inspired by the Napoleonic Wars, Ryleev wrote a satire, *To a Favorite Courtier of the Tsar* [Kvremenščiku] (1820). The courtier was clearly intended to be Arakčeev, then a favorite of Alexander I. Ryleev wrote other, somewhat old-fashioned poems and political odes, including a call to great deeds addressed to Tsar Alexander in 1821, and an ode, to the same effect, addressed to the Grand Duke Alexander, then a child who would later become Tsar Alexander II. Ryleev's poems in the civic vein and a shorter, equally political poem are also archaic. Two poems are on literary themes: an epistle to Gnedič (1821), in which Ryleev particularly acknowledges Ozerov (see chapter II, sec. 11), and a poem on the death of Byron (1824), whom he praises as a soldier and a poet of freedom. Byron had "unraveled everything under the sun; oblivious to the persecution of fate, he obeyed only his genius"—words that hardly amount to recognition for a romantic poet. Ryleev's principal works are quite different. Although his comrades seldom expressed their political views except at political meetings, Ryleev was able to put his opinions into poetry. Inspired by the *Śpiewy historyczne* [Historical Songs] of the Polish late-classicist poet J. U. Niemcewicz (1757–1841) and by Ukrainian historical songs, Ryleev wrote his *Dumy* (1821–1823). The designation *Dumy* is taken from Ukrainian epic songs. Ryleev's *Dumy* are, in effect, historical ballads. They are made up of twenty-five poems and deal with episodes from Russian history, from Oleg, a Kievan prince mentioned in the Primary Chronicle, to the poet Gavriil R. Deržavin, who is, of course, not a political hero. Often

Ryleev borrows directly from Karamzin's history, the first eight volumes of which had come out in 1816 and 1817. But instead of concentrating on the Russian state as Karamzin had done, Ryleev focused his work on individual Russians, whom he portrayed as freedom-loving. In some of his *Dumy*, he seems mainly concerned with artistic matters, as in *The Death of Ermak*, a story set against a stormy Ossianic night landscape. Here Ryleev approaches the romanticists. Although the language of some of his poems is solemn and archaistic, one feels, nevertheless, that the poet has learned, not only from Karamzin, but also from Puškin—who, incidentally, liked only a few scenes in Ryleev, scenes taken from the life of the peasants.

Ryleev's two poems on Ukrainian history are more important and more polished. The first of them, *Vojnarovskij* (1822–1824), tells of the sad fate of a Ukrainian patriot who fought in the Northern War on the side of Charles XII, was later seized by Russian agents in Hamburg, and was exiled to Siberia, where he met the German historian G. F. Müller. This encounter and Vojnarovskij's death are the main incidents in the poem. Ryleev got rather far along in his work on another poem, *Nalivajko*, taken from the history of the Ukrainian Cossack rebellions of the seventeenth century. The third poem, *Mazeppa*, was barely begun; and there are only fragments or sketches of other poems. In these epic tales, Ryleev rid himself of any trace of classicism. Although the political speeches of his heroes express little besides a general love of freedom, they are still effective today.

9. Another poet who was close to the Decembrists, although he was not prosecuted in this connection, was Aleksandr Sergeevič Griboedov (1794 or 1795–1829). He is one of the most important writers in nineteenth-century Russian literature and owes his fame to a single work, *Gore ot uma* [Woe from Wit].

Griboedov was an officer in the Napoleonic Wars. His work as a diplomat in Persia saved him from being condemned as a member of the Decembrist organization but later proved to be fateful. In early 1829, while Griboedov was on a diplomatic mission to Persia, the Russian embassy there was attacked by a mob and Griboedov was murdered.

Griboedov's early plays, some of which were written in collaboration with other poets, among them Katenin (see sec. 25 below), and his few poems are not remarkable; we know little of his literary plans at the time of his death and have only a few unimportant fragments to go on. Consequently, Griboedov is known to posterity as the author of *Woe from Wit*, which was the product of long and arduous labor. But this single work is a masterpiece of fine chiseling. It is a comedy, written in iambic lines of varying lengths, like Batjuškov's poems, and it contains on almost every page at least one sentence now familiar as a proverbial expression to everyone who speaks Russian.

The plot of the play has caused later generations to wonder if the hero, Aleksandr Čackij, is an adequate representative of wit and intellect. After three years of traveling abroad, Čackij returns home to the house in which he was reared and can find nothing better to do than to share his ideas at every opportunity with Moscow bureaucrats and noblemen, who, he realizes perfectly well, are incorrigible adherents of the good old days. This is hardly a sign of intelligence on Čackij's part. But the author is intelligent and allows his hero to make satirical attacks on old Moscow and on modern Gallomania, the exclusive use of the French language and of French customs. Čackij's disenchantment is even greater when the object of his love, Sof'ja, with whom he has grown up, is alternately indifferent and hostile to him and prefers a miserable little official. The setting for all four acts of the play is the home of Sof'ja's father, Famusov, a prominent official. All the acts take place on the same day, beginning in the early morning and ending with a small dance in the evening. The play concludes with a scene in the entrance hall as everyone is leaving the house.

Although the love story is not important, it is skillfully developed against a background of satirical comedy and does not obtrude. In all four acts, one finds a splendid, colorful gallery of Moscow types, who exemplify the faults of society. The liberal— or pseudo-liberal—circles also come in for their share of criticism. The burden of the classicist comedy, whose second-rate Russian practitioners have almost all been forgotten (see chapter VI, sec. 2, on A. A. Šaxovskoj), is evident in the inadequate individualization of most of the characters, who merely represent certain types, and in the somewhat too persistent and obvious satire of their speeches, which consist largely of series of pointed maxims. As has been mentioned, many of these maxims have become proverbs. Examples are Famusov's saying of his official activities, "I am rid of a piece of business as soon as I have signed it," or Sof'ja's friend Molčalin's remarking that he attempts in life "To curry everyone's favor, not to be on bad terms with anyone, even with the porter, so that he won't show me the door, and with the house boy's dog, so that he won't bite me."

Below are some quite neutral or sharply satirical maxims from the work of Griboedov:

Happy people don't look at the clock.	Sčastlivye časov ne nabljudajut.
Happy is the man who believes; he feels at home in the world.	Blažen, kto veruet, teplo emu na svete.
Whole regiments of teachers, as many as possible for as little as possible.	Učitelej polki, / čislom pobolee, cenoju podeševle.
But he'll go far in the world; they're fond of unscrupulous people now.	A vpročem on dojdet do stepenej izvestnyx, / ved' nynče ljubjat bessovestnyx.
Mind and heart don't get along with one another.	Um s serdcem ne v ladu.
The news is fresh, but one hardly believes it.	Svežo predanie, a veritsja s trudom.
What will Princess Mar'ja Aleksevna say about it?	Čto stanet govorit' knjaginja Mar'ja Aleksevna?

Although Griboedov belonged to the younger generation, he was an "archaist"[2] in the romantic school. He was thus described

2. [In the terminology of Ju. N. Tynjanov, in his *Arxaisty i Novatory* (Leningrad, 1929).—EDITOR]

by Wilhelm Küchelbecker, a Russian writer of German descent who was in somewhat the same position. As a consequence, one finds in Griboedov's play many of the features of classicist comedy: the carefully pointed language, characters with names suggestive of their personalities—the heroine's maid, Liza, who seems to have been taken from a French comedy and reminds one, for instance, of Dorine in *Tartuffe*—the unity of time: the action takes place in a single day. *Woe from Wit* is particularly indebted to Molière's *Le Misanthrope*.

Griboedov's few poems are closer, however, to romantic poetics; and the tragedy that he had planned was to have been a romantic tragedy. Unfortunately, only small fragments of it have been preserved.

Gore ot uma was widely circulated in manuscript. At first the censorship did not allow it to be printed, and then several scenes were permitted. The play was not staged until 1831, after Griboedov's death, and it was not passed by the censor to be printed until 1833, with many deletions.[3]

10. At the center of this entire era is Aleksandr Sergeevič Puškin (1799–1837). As is usual among the greatest poets, Puškin did not confine himself to a single school of writing. But there are in his work and in his literary development so many elements of pure romanticism that it is easier to understand him as a part of the romantic era than to understand Dostoevskij as a part of his realistic period or the Polish postromanticist Cyprian Norwid as a part of the romantic or "positivistic" school, the Polish counterpart of Russian realism.

Puškin was born in Moscow, but his parents later made their home in St. Petersburg. His old, aristocratic family was not really rich and could not afford to give Puškin an expensive education, but they were at least able to surround him with an atmosphere of culture, which suited his own inclinations. His father was interested in literature and was a dilettante poet; his uncle Vasilij L'vovič Puškin, (chapter II, sec. 10), felt that Aleksandr was meant to be a poet. His mother was the granddaughter of a general of the

3. [Some parts of this play were published in Bulgarin's *Russian Talia* in 1825.—EDITOR]

Petrine era, Abram Gannibal, who was originally from Ethiopia. She was the niece of an even more famous Admiral Gannibal. She preserved many traits of her foreign grandfather. In keeping with the custom of the time, she was given a French education, and her private letters reveal some training in literature.

While still a child, Puškin began to share the literary interests of his father and uncle and saw poets, such as Karamzin, come and go at his parents' home. Apparently, he first wrote poetry in French; and his father's library, which he used eagerly, consisted mainly of books in French.

At school, he was nicknamed "the Frenchman." He attended the lyceum at Carskoe Selo, reserved for children of the nobility and intended to prepare young men for important positions in government service. Puškin was accepted at thirteen, through family connections. This exclusive school, where pupils wore uniforms, came to mean much more to Puškin than merely a place to study.

Among his fellow students were young men as interested in literature as he was, none of them, incidentally, from the highest nobility. Some of these young poets later belonged to Puškin's circle, in particular Baron Anton A. Del'vig and the Baltic German writer Wilhelm Küchelbecker. Their work appeared in hand-written student publications, some of which have been preserved. The innocuous classicist N. F. Košanskij gave theoretical and practical instruction in poetics, which was taught as a separate subject at the school, in keeping with tradition.

The poems that Puškin wrote at the lyceum make up almost a fourth of his poetic literary remains; he wrote first in a late-classicist vein and then approached more and more the style of the French elegists. A comedy, a novel, and a novella that Puškin wrote at school, partly in collaboration with other poets, have not been preserved. Significantly, Puškin and his friends wrote in Russian.

Although Gavriil Deržavin was considered at the lyceum to be the greatest Russian poet, the influence of the Karamzin School, particularly of Vasilij Žukovskij, was gradually beginning to be felt. At examinations in January 1815, Deržavin was among the guests; and in his presence Puškin read a poem that was among his few attempts at an ode. It was written in a slightly archaistic style, and it mentioned Deržavin by name. Deržavin took an interest in the work and was delighted with it. Soon Puškin met Žukovskij, who was to have an important influence on him. In 1816, Puškin was taken into the Arzamas society. He was unable to attend meetings but began to correspond with Petr Vjazemskij. In the same year, he met Karamzin and P. Ja. Čaadaev (chapter VII, sec. 3), the latter of whom was still a guards officer. Public opinion was still dominated by the effects of the Napoleonic Wars, but we know little of the reaction to these wars at the lyceum.

Upon graduating, Puškin took a position with the Foreign Office but was in no way overburdened. He was free to devote himself to his writing and to the wild life with friends that panegyrical biographies have sought in vain to justify. In these same years, Puškin drew closer to literary circles. It was also at this time that the activities of the Arzamas came to an end.

Puškin's style had gradually been breaking away from the classicist tradition. His major work of this period was his fairy-tale poem *Ruslan and Ljudmila,* which he claimed to have begun at the lyceum and which he finished in 1820. The poem reminds one only roughly of the heroic-comic poems of the eighteenth century. It is actually closer to the light French poems of La Fontaine, Voltaire, and Jean-Baptiste-Louis Gresset and to C. M. Wieland's *Oberon,* and was perhaps also influenced by Lodovico Ariosto. It has nothing of the coarseness of the Russian heroic-comic poems of Vasilij Majkov and other writers of this genre. It is closer to the elegant *Dušenka* [Psyche] by I. Bogdanovič, published in 1778, and to the more serious *Baxariana* (1803) by M. M. Xeraskov, a counterpart to the equally Masonic *Zauberflöte.* Some scenes reveal the influence of the first volume of Karamzin's history, which had recently appeared. Many motifs are from Russian fairy tales, and some were probably taken from Žukovskij's verses written in 1814, in which he discusses the possibility of writing his own heroic, phantasmic poem under the title *Vladimir.*

In Puškin's *Ruslan and Ljudmila*, the hero, Ruslan, goes out in search of his wife, Ljudmila, daughter of the Kievan Prince Vladimir. She has been taken from Ruslan on their wedding night by a magician. Ruslan's adventures would have appeared innocent enough if Puškin had not broken up the narration into impressive scenes, at times described pretty landscapes, and used the effective epithets that are also characteristic of his later work and that often serve to personify things: *"padut revnivye odeždy"* ["the jealous garments fall"]; *"zamki bezžalostnyx dverej"* ["the locks of merciless doors"]. Well-executed comparisons lighten the poem (for instance, a frightened hero is said to resemble an awkward actor), as does the subtle irony, which turns serious situations into humorous ones, as when the heroine plans to commit suicide but does not. The prologue, added to the second edition published in 1828, creates the false impression that the work is closely connected with Russian fairy tales. This connection consists of nothing more than turns of speech and the occasional use of popular language, which was inadmissible according to the precepts of classicism and for which Puškin was reproached by well-meaning critics. Examples of words objected to are *udavlju, ščekotit, čixnul,* and *rukavica.* But the poem did not represent a final break with classicism.

Nor did Puškin take leave entirely of the classicist tradition in his lyric poetry. Although Batjuškov was surprised by one of Puškin's short poems, *Ljubimec vetrenyx Lais* [To Jur'ev] (1820), he sensed its poetic greatness and did not feel that there was any essential difference between it and his own late-classicist work. The notable poem *Derevnja* [The Village] (1819), with its pointed remarks on serfdom, offers little that is stylistically new; and the poem *Vol'nost'* [Freedom] (1817), which was to change Puškin's career, is a classicist ode, as the poet emphasizes by referring to French models. It was not just the antimonarchistic tone of this ode, in which Napoleon and Paul I are likened, that was fateful to Puškin: his many political epigrams, some of which have undoubtedly been lost, and the great show he made of his love of freedom attracted unfavourable attention. Only the intervention of influential patrons, among them Žukovskij, prevented Puškin from being punished quite seriously. As it was, he was sent to the South of Russia, as an official with rather vague duties. His superior in the Foreign Office, the Deputy Secretary of State I. Kapodistria, a Greek, wrote a character reference for Puškin that his superior in the South, General Inzov, must have taken to be a recommendation.

11. This enforced journey broadened Puškin's horizons considerably. On his way, he met the intellectual family of General Raevskij and traveled with them to the Northern Caucasus and the Crimea. Bessarabia, where Puškin was to perform the few duties expected of him, seemed to him an exotic region. The Rumanian (Moldavian) nobility with their semi-Oriental way of life, the Greek refugees, preparing for a new war with the Turks, the Jewish and Armenian merchants, and the wandering Gypsies offered rich material for Puškin's poetry. A visit to Odessa, a semi-European city with an Italian opera and a population one third Italian, added to his impressions. In the spring of 1823, Puškin was transferred to Odessa. In this exotic region, he met two poets who were to be of importance to his development, the romanticist A. F. Vel'tman and V. I. Tumanskij, who was well versed in Western European literature.

Tumanskij was on friendly terms, not only with Puškin's St. Petersburg friends, but also with Wilhelm Küchelbecker, whom he had come to know well in Paris. Puškin had access to Polish society in Odessa; and he met the most important members of the Decembrists, as he had done in Bessarabia.

Just before and during his journey, Puškin read Byron (probably in French translation), Shakespeare, and André Chénier. One of his first poems in his new style is *Pogaslo dnevnoe svetilo* (1820). The content reminds one of Childe Harold's departure from home. In his apostrophe to the sea and to the sails of his ship, Puškin sets the stage to take leave of his earlier life and touches on the theme of disappointment, which is typical of early Russian romanticism (although the word "disappointment," *razočarovanie*, does not occur in the poem.) One finds here a greater concision and strength of expression than in Puškin's early poems.

In 1824, toward the end of his stay in Odessa, he wrote the poem *K morju*, in which he says farewell to the sea. Napoleon and Byron, who had died in 1821 and 1824, respectively, seemed to Puškin to have embodied the free spirit of the sea; but perhaps a turning away from Byron's strong influence is also concealed in the poem. These brief twelve lines are hardly a satisfactory response to Vjazemskij's request to dedicate a poem to Byron. Puškin uses the words of the "romantic" semantic fields less than does Vjazemskij in the poems we have quoted. Nevertheless, he gives his vocabulary a particular coloring. He addresses the sea, which calls out in reply ("*ty ždal, ty zval*"); the sea is referred to as an element ("*stixija*"), as an abyss ("*bezdna*"), and is personified and given spiritual qualities; it is free ("*svobodnaja stixija*"), proud ("*bleščeš' gordoju krasoj*"), capricious ("*prixot'*"); and it is compared to the spirit of Byron: mighty, deep, and dark ("*mogušč, glubok i mračen*"), untamed ("*ničem neukrotim*"). Another poem written at the same time reflects more clearly Puškin's romantic mood: *The Book Dealer's Conversation with the Poet*, the latter in this case being a romantic poet. Here Puškin introduces a theme that he is to pursue later, the loneliness of the poet and his indifference to his popularity with the mob (*čern'*).

12. Puškin's most important work during these years was his "Southern Poems," some of which were completed or continued after he had returned to the North. Their themes are typical: *The Captive of the Caucasus* (exotic), *The Fountain of Baxčisaraj* (equally exotic), *The Robber Brothers* (brigand romanticism), *The Gypsies* (the free natural man). In addition, he began work on a novel in verse, *Evgenij Onegin* (see sec. 14 below). In the summer of 1824, Puškin was exiled from the South because of a dispute with the governor, R. Voroncov, who was usually considered a liberal. Puškin was ordered to live in the solitude of his parents' estate in the province of Pskov, where he was forced to stay until 1826.

The first three of the Southern Poems can be called unreservedly Byronic, mainly on account of their form. They served for decades as models for Russian epic poetry, according to the critic V. Žirmunskij. Their salient features are free form, use of a narrator, an implied tone of intimate conversation with the reader, and an assumed vagueness. The narration concentrates on particular episodes between which there are gaps that must be filled in by the reader's imagination. There is much lyrical effusion by the narrator, and there are other insertions: descriptions of nature and people play an important part. The poem takes on the character of an intimate conversation with the reader, who is often addressed directly, or of a conversation in the presence of the reader with the hero of the poem, whom the author questions and reproaches and to whom he expresses his sympathy. There are allusions to intimate episodes, moods, and experiences of the author or his friends, about which the reader does not know. The author cultivates a certain vagueness in the story and in the various episodes. The free form is often emphasized by the fragmentary character of the work or by referrences to parts of the poem that have supposedly been omitted. All these features are conspicuous in Puškin's early narrative poems.

The first of these poems, *The Captive of the Caucasus* (1820–1821), is made up of a series of lively scenes. A Circassian warrior arrives at his aul[4] with a Russian prisoner characterized as a refugee from the civilized world (*otstupnik sveta*) and a friend of nature (*drug prirody*) who has been enticed to the unfamiliar region by "the joyful vision of freedom." At night, a Circassian girl brings the prisoner a pitcher of mare's milk. Without any explanation or transition, the girl is presented as a friend of the prisoner. In the first part of the poem, much attention is paid to pretty pictures of the mountains and of the lives and conflicts of this "wonderful people." The second part is made up of conversations between the prisoner and the girl; he confesses to her that he is a victim of passion and unhappy love, that for him "happiness is dead." The Circassian girl is moved and helps him escape. But when the prisoner has reached the opposite bank of the river and looks back, he no longer sees the girl; and "in the moonlight, rings of waves disappear in the murmuring water," a suggestion that the girl has committed suicide. It is obvious that the story is rather thin and that the individual scenes are loosely connected. Puškin's genius is most evident in pretty passages juxtaposed with lesser ones and in his descriptions, as of a Circassian song or as in the conclusion of the poem:

> The liberated prisoner went on a distant way;
> and already Russian bayonets glittered in the mist
> and cossacks called from the hill
> where they were keeping watch.

4. [*Aul*: a village in the mountains populated by Moslem Caucasians.— EDITOR]

In a brief epilogue, Puškin extols the Russian war of conquest in the Caucasus—to the displeasure of Vjazemskij, who otherwise praised the work extravagantly.

It was not until 1825 that a shorter poem, or rather a fragment of a poem that Puškin had apparently burned, *The Robber Brothers*, was published. The poem is a gloomy description of the flight of two brothers from prison and of the death of one of them.

The third poem tells of *The Fountain of Baxčisaraj* (1821–1823) and the former palace of the Crimean Tatar Khan (actually, this "fountain" was no more than a slowly dripping "fountain of tears") and recalls a tragedy provoked by jealousy in the harem of the khan. The khan's former favorite wife, a Georgian, stabs a Christian woman who has been taken prisoner and who has become the object of the khan's passionate love; the victorious Georgian woman is drowned. The poem concludes with recollections of the Crimea. The action of the poem is only hinted at, and the main subject matter consists of the encounter between the two women and of the monologue of the Georgian woman.

The last of the Southern Poems, *The Gypsies*, written in 1824, did not appear until 1827. Ideologically, it is more important than the others, as it contains the essential motif of Dostoevskij's speech on Puškin. Once more, the hero, Aleko, is a refugee from the "world"; but he is fleeing not simply for personal reasons: he is being pursued by the law. He is repelled by the "way of the world" and by urban culture. In his search for freedom, which he longs for but is not quite certain of, Aleko enters into a love affair with the Gypsy woman Zemfira. The values that he attributes to their love are essentially those of the world that he has left behind. For a time, he appears to fit into the life of the Gypsies; but when Zemfira is untrue to him, he kills both her and his rival and, as a consequence, is forced to leave the Gypsies. In addition to the two main characters, Zemfira's father plays an important part and tells the story of his life. The description of the life of the Gypsies is an organic part of the work and introduces the action; the poem ends with the old Gypsy's parting words. The "wild" (*dikij*, in the sense of primitive) freedom amounts to a kind of "golden age," perhaps an idealization of Rousseau's view of the original condition of man. It is Aleko's tragic flaw to "wish freedom primarily for himself." Like a wounded crane left behind by his comrades, he remains alone in the wilderness, rejected for his crime by the primitive community.

In the poem, Puškin displays new colors and devices, among them the description of the motley life of the Gypsies by means of an accumulation of words, of an "unorganized" enumeration (or a "catalogue," to use E. R. Curtius's familiar term for it) and dialogues that are as effective as speeches on the stage. The old Gypsy's account of Ovid, who was allegedly banished to Bessarabia, does not seem really to fit into the rest of the poem; but perhaps the legend serves to foreshadow Aleko's own experiences: he is so bound to his home by memories that, even if he had not committed a crime, he could not have torn himself away forever from his habitual environment, his "world." The epilogue contradicts the belief in unalloyed happiness among the "poor children of nature"—a theme to which Puškin returned—and includes an allusion to Puškin's own exile.

The Southern Poems provoked a lively response from supporters and opponents of romanticism. Vjazemskij wrote an introduction to *The Fountain of Baxčisaraj*, in which he developed a rather vague concept of romanticism, based on German models that he knew only superficially.

While in the South, Puškin also wrote a blasphemous poem, *Gavriliada*. Although there is some beauty of expression in the poem, it is now included among Puškin's works, sometimes even in popular editions, only for its usefulness as antireligious propaganda. In form, it is a heroic-comic poem, but in ease and elegance of language it is superior even to *Ruslan and Ljudmila*.

13. Though banished to the North, Puškin was at least able to live fairly close to St. Petersburg. He was subjected to an irritating surveillance by the police and was at first very lonely, although he soon began getting in touch with his neighbors. Occasionally he was visited by old schoolmates, among them Anton A. Del'vig and Ivan I. Puščin, who was later to become a Decembrist. He also met a younger poet, a student at the University of Dorpat, N. Jazykov (see sec. 22 below). More than a hundred of Puškin's letters on literary topics have been pre-

served from this period, many of them written to Žukovskij and Vjazemskij. It was important for Puškin's later work that he became acquainted with folk literature, much of which he learned from his old nurse.

Like all the Russian reading public of the time, Puškin was familiar with Karamzin's *The History of the Russian State*. In it, he found a subject that seemed to lend itself to a historical drama: the beginning of the interregnum in the late sixteenth and early seventeenth centuries. We have only recently discovered that the same subject had attracted the attention of an early eighteenth-century Hamburg composer, Johann Mattheson, who wrote an opera called *Boris Godunov*.[5] In the early nineteenth century, Schiller had begun to treat the same material in his *Demetrius*. Puškin made use of the fall of the last legitimate tsar, Boris Godunov, to write a play in the Shakespearian manner.

This subject has proved popular in literature. Several writers have attempted to complete Schiller's unfinished drama. Later, in Russia, various treatments were given to the same material, in particular the last part of A. K. Tolstoj's trilogy; and Puškin's *Boris Godunov* was ably translated into German by Henry von Heiseler, who also wrote a play of his own, *Die Kinder Godunovs*. Finally, one should not forget Musorgskij's musical version, one of the most important Russian operas.[6]

Following an old and probably erroneous tradition, Karamzin thought that Boris had assured himself of the throne by murdering the last son of Ivan the Terrible, the child Prince Dimitrij. An avenger appeared, however, in the person of the mysterious "False Dimitrij," a pretender who came on the scene in Poland, took up arms against Tsar Boris, and defeated him. Soon afterward, the False Dimitrij was murdered in Moscow and the tumultuous "Time of Troubles" (1604–1613) continued. But Puškin does not go into the particulars of these events.

Puškin's drama consists of twenty-three scenes, some of them very brief. The form was unusual for the Russian stage and has

5. [The earliest Western European work on this subject was *El gran duque de Moscovia* (1617) by Lope de Vega.—EDITOR]

6. [*Boris Godunov*, first performed at St. Petersburg in 1874 and considered to be the composer's great masterpiece.—EDITOR]

seldom been imitated. There were difficulties with censorship, but its form was responsible for the fact that the play was not produced until 1870. As a closet drama, however, *Boris Godunov* soon became extraordinarily popular.

The play does not actually have a protagonist. Apart from the attention given Boris, the play devotes several scenes to the fate and character of the False Dimitrij. In several other scenes, the people are the hero. In all, Boris appears in six out of twenty-three scenes; the False Dimitrij, in eight; other characters who, in the absence of Boris or Dimitrij, play a part in the prologue or serve to connect the individual scenes, appear in five scenes; and finally, the people are involved in four scenes and are present on stage in two others. The Moscow courtiers, including a not entirely historical Puškin, an ancestor of the poet, form a group of their own. Over and above all this, the poet mixes the serious and the comic in a "Shakespearian" fashion that had not previously been permitted in Russian drama; two scenes are comic. Furthermore, Puškin allows some of the characters in his verse drama to speak in prose. There are a large number of pointed lines, some of which have become proverbial. The language is simple. Puškin avoids words associated with the "high style" and only occasionally uses archaic-sounding words and phrases. Often he is content merely to use the antiquated conjunction "*da.*" The language of the various characters is suited to their personalities.

Although Puškin thinks that Tsar Boris was troubled by a bad conscience, he sees the False Dimitrij as nothing more than a bold adventurer. The only motive that he ascribes to his efforts to obtain the throne is the desire for power. The secondary characters, the cunning, self-centered boyars, the Polish grandees, the ambitious Marina Mniszech, who later marries the False Dimitrij, and the clergymen are subtly characterized in succinct dialogue. Behind all the events of the play are the people, whose change in mood Boris Godunov perceives. Their mysterious role is clarified in the concluding scene of the play, when they fall uneasily silent at the news of the death of Tsar Boris's young son, Tsar Fedor—murdered by the boyars. Two characters who play no active part in the events of the drama are perhaps intended to symbolize a superior earthly and heavenly justice.

They are Pimen, the chronicler, who will tell future generations about the crime, and the "fool in Christ" (*jurodivyj*), who dares say whatever he wants and who likens Tsar Boris to King Herod in the Gospels, since the entire tragedy is based on the supposition that Boris obtained the throne by murdering Ivan's young son, Prince Dimitrij.

Puškin's drama represented such a decisive break with Russian theatrical tradition that at first his play provoked opposition, even from his friends.

14. The epic "novel in verse" *Evgenij Onegin* was no less unusual. Puškin began it in May 1823 in Bessarabia, published it chapter by chapter, and concluded it with the eighth chapter in the fall of 1830. Naturally, one notices Puškin's intellectual development over a span of seven years, but by and large he was able to maintain a unity of style.

The subject of the novel is unusual: not one, but two, unhappy protagonists. Young Evgenij Onegin leaves St. Petersburg, where he has spent his dissolute early years enjoying society life, and goes to live on an estate that he has inherited from his uncle. The daughter of a neighboring family, Tatjana, falls in love with him. Onegin rejects her love, for he is disenchanted (*razočarovannyj*), a typical representative of the generation of 1820. He soon leaves the village; he has killed his friend Lenskij, the fiancé of Tatjana's sister Ol'ga, in a duel provoked by a trivial incident. Several years later, he meets Tatjana in St. Petersburg. She has married a general and has changed from a provincial girl into a fashionable socialite. Now it is Onegin's turn to fall in love with her, but she rejects him.

The novel is still under the influence of Byron. One encounters the "free form" (*dal' svobodnogo romana*) that allows the author to call the reader's attention to various episodes and to ignore for a time the two leading characters. This is an aspect of the work that has not escaped kindly disposed critics. But the descriptions of St. Petersburg, of Onegin's life in the country, and of Tatjana's family, and especially the sketches of the many secondary characters attest to the great artistry of the author. One should also mention the lyric passages, which sometimes run for several stanzas. Of particular interest are Puškin's remarks on literature, some of which are pointedly polemic (as, for instance, those directed at Wilhelm Küchelbecker), and his observations on general questions. Some stanzas deal incidentally with the intellectual interests of different circles and generations of early nineteenth-century Russian society and assume something of the nature of a cultural history. We find out what Onegin and Tatjana read, what Onegin and Lenskij talk about (Lenskij studied in Germany at the University of Göttingen), and what sort of poetry Lenskij writes—it is rather like the elegiac poetry that Puškin wrote after 1817. Of the earlier Russian writers, Mixail V. Lomonosov, Denis I. Fonvizin, Ja. B. Knjažnin, and V. A. Ozerov are mentioned or quoted; of Puškin's senior contemporaries, A. S. Šiškov and A. A. Šaxovskoj are quoted; of the more recent poets, Žukovskij, Katenin, Vjazemskij, Del'vig, Küchelbecker, Jazykov, and Baratynskij are quoted. The older generation reads Richardson and Rousseau; Tatjana's generation reads Madame Cottin, Madame de Krüdener, Madame de Staël, and probably Goethe's *Werther*. Onegin's contemporaries like wildly romantic literature: Charles R. Maturin, M. G. Lewis, C. Nodier, and, of course, Scott and Byron. Lenskij reads Schiller and probably the Poetic Edda (*otryvki severnyx poèm*); besides Jean François Marmontel, Onegin reads Bernard Fontenelle, J. G. Herder, Alessandro Manzoni, Adam Smith, P. Bayle, and Gibbon. In addition, Puškin mentions or quotes the classical poets Ovid, Homer, Juvenal, and Tibullus and the Italians Tasso and Petrarch. In short, the heroes and their times are characterized by a literary encyclopedia. Onegin's education, his uncle's life in the country, and the childhood of Tatjana's mother are also described. Occasionally Puškin includes scenes from the life of the serfs, such as Tatjana's *njanja* (nurse) and Onegin's peasants. There are also a number of personal references and autobiographical digressions.

It was no problem for Puškin to accommodate all these many colorful elements in a "Byronic poem." He emphasizes the freedom of the form by omitting stanzas or lines. In later editions, he discards stanzas that he has already published but leaves their number or a space for them in the text. Some attractive stanzas from an omitted chapter dealing with Onegin's journey after his unfortunate duel were published separately by Puškin. They represent an interesting autobiographical source, on the poet's stay in Odessa, for instance. There is evidently much of Puškin's own life in the novel—Onegin is even introduced to the reader as a good friend of Puškin.

As in Puškin's other Byronic poems, he addresses the reader, the characters, and even the work (*"idi že k nevskim beregam, novoroždennoe tvorenie"*) and includes monologues of his own. Closely connected with these features are the light humor and elements of parody (as in Lenskij's poem) and the parodic use of the traditional epic form; for instance, the epic theme is announced in the next-to-last chapter, instead of at the beginning of the work, as one would expect:

> Я классицизму отдал честь —
> хоть поздно, а вступление есть.

I have paid my respects to classicism; here is an introduction, late though it may be.

Puškin created for his novel a special fourteen-line stanza, which is not a variation of the sonnet. The rhyme alternates according to the following scheme, in which the numeral represents the number of syllables in the line; a small letter represents feminine rhyme; and a capital, masculine rhyme: *9a, 8B, 9a, 8B; 9c, 9c, 8D, 8D; 9e, 8F, 8F, 9e; 8G, 8G.* This scheme corresponds, by and large, to Puškin's pattern of thought. In the first quatrain, the theme of the stanza is announced; in the next two quatrains, it is developed; and in the last two lines, the theme is concluded, often with a joke or a maxim.

The language of the poem is perfectly polished; it is the quintessence of the idiom that Puškin had coined in his early narrative and lyric poems. He deliberately employs foreign words used by the Russian upper class in everyday speech (*breget, frak, žilet,* and the like), prosaisms, and occasional neologisms. Humorous rhymes on foreign words such as

> И бесподобный Грандисон,
> который нам наводит сон.

> And the incomparable Grandison,
> Who puts us all to sleep.

are particularly numerous in the last (eighth) chapter, as are words to which Puškin attaches a new meaning. Neologisms, on the other hand, are found only occasionally in his poetry. The word *mjatežnyj* means "agitated" (originally, "rebellious") and is used by Puškin to describe the soul. The sensation of being agitated is characterized as "deep and sincere." The word *trepetnyj* (trembling) describes the tender impulses of the soul and has a similar meaning. The word *obman* (deception) takes on an aesthetic meaning in Puškin; of enthusiasm for poetry, he says:

> с каким живым очарованием
> пьет обольстительный обман

> With what lively enchantment she drinks the bewitching deception.

Words belonging to the semantic field of emotion (such as *trepetnyj, burnyj, volnenie*, and so on, and *živoj*, perhaps based on a French model) are connected with genuine, sincere, profound experiences, as are words belonging to the semantic field of warmth (*ogon', teplo, žar, plamja,*) and their adjectives, as well as words that otherwise designate signs of disease, such as *gorjačka* (fever) and *bred* (delirium). But this usage is not new; in classical Greek and Latin, one finds *vir ardens* and *anima inflammata* and in Old Russian literature, *teplye slezy*, the fervent tears of a contrite sinner. The antonyms of these words are also used in a metaphorical sense. The word *son* (sleep, dream), is important and is used as a synonym for all the experiences of the "night side of the soul." For example:

> сны поэзии святой . . .
> средь поэтического сна . . .
> и сердца трепетные сны . . .
> кто странным снам не предавался . . .

и в сладостный, безгрезный сон
душою погрузился он . . .
исполнены страстей и лени
и снов задумчивой души.

dreams of sacred poetry . . .
in the midst of a poetic dream . . .
and the troubled dreams of the heart . . .
who did not give himself up to strange dreams . . .
with his soul he sank into a sweet and innocent dream
filled with passions and idleness and the dreams of
   a pensive soul.

In this connection one reads of the "depths of the soul," of the "depths of the heart," and so on. Words such as *strast'* (passion) and *bezumie* (insanity) take on a positive connotation. Unlike Vjazemskij and other romanticists, Puškin is not inclined to accumulate words from these semantic fields, but one often encounters lines such as these:

(Татяна) . . . одарена
воображением мятежным;
умом и волею живой
и своенравной головой
и сердцем пламенным и нежным

(Tatjana) was endowed with an active imagination,
a lively mind and will, and a fiery, tender heart.

Or Puškin says of himself:

Любви безумную тревогу
я безотрадно испытал.
Блажен кто с нею сочетал
горячку рифм: он тем удвоил
поэзии священный бред.

I have drearily experienced the mad anxiety of love. Blessed is he who has joined with it the fever of rhymes. In doing so he has increased the sacred delirium of poetry.

Puškin's epithets are notable for making their objects animate or for personifying them. A child's doll is "obedient" *(poslušnaja)*; the dice of a cheat are "obliging" *(uslužlivye)*; a lorgnette is "searching," "jealous," "disappointed," "inattentive," and "importunate" *(razyskatel'nyj lornet, revnivyj, razočarovannyj, nevnimatel'nyj, neotvjazčivyj)*—all of which would have been thought catachresis by strict archaists.

Evgenij Onegin is undoubtedly one of the finest works in Russian literature. Merely to have portrayed Russian society over two important decades (1810–1830) would have been enough for a poet to do. In addition, Puškin wrote into his novel various elements of his view of life and the world. It would be a mistake, however, to turn to the novel for "instruction," to seek a moral in it. Puškin also set down in other works his ideas on life and art.

Later attempts by Puškin to continue *Evgenij Onegin* did not get very far. He was perhaps most successful at portraying the Decembrist circles and their times (presumably Onegin was to have come in contact with these circles). Unfortunately, only fragments have been preserved from this "tenth chapter" of the novel.

15. Later on, Puškin wrote and planned epic works. Besides the two short humorous epics *Graf Nulin* and *Domik v Kolomne* (1825 and 1830) and an epic reworking of Shakespeare's *Measure for Measure* *(Andželo*, 1833), two historical poems are of particular importance.

Poltava (1828) was written in a few days and deals with the tragic love of the young Maria Kočubej for the Ukrainian hetman Mazepa, who is pictured in the poem as ambitious and self-centered. Mazepa has joined forces with Charles XII of Sweden and, in 1709, at Poltava, he is decisively defeated, along with Charles, by Peter the Great, who also appears in the poem. Maria goes mad when Mazepa orders her father executed, and not until she is mad does she recognize Mazepa for the bloody monster he is. Madness is also a part of the night side of the soul and enables the madman to recognize that which the normal person cannot comprehend. The combination of a romantic tragedy with a historical episode is not advantageous to either motif, although the poem, which is constructed Byronically, contains excellent passages and develops several of Puškin's important thoughts, among them his high opinion of the role of Peter the Great in Russian history. Nevertheless, the poem ends with a pessimistic epilogue on the transience of the great figures of history.

Tsar Peter is also one of the central figures in the poem *Mednyj vsadnik* [The Bronze Horseman] (1833). The theme deals with the great flood in St. Petersburg in 1824, to which S. P. Ševyrev also devoted a poem, *More sporilo s Petrom* [The Sea Quarreled with Peter] (1829). As in *Poltava*, Puškin combines observations on the historical greatness of Peter's deeds with a portrayal of the personal tragedy of a little man. During the flood, the clerk Evgenij loses his fiancée, with whom he has hoped to lead a quiet and conventional life. Evgenij goes mad and *"projasnilis' v nem strašno mysli"* ("suddenly his thoughts became dreadfully clear"). He protests against Tsar Peter, whom the famous monument portrays as a "bronze horseman" on a rearing horse. Like Maria Kočubej, Evgenij sees more clearly in his madness than he has ever seen in his right mind. He asks about the future of Russia, which the "miraculous architect" has built on an abyss and which is racing somewhere and will stop somewhere—no one knows where. The conflict between the fate of an individual and historical necessity is the problem that Evgenij faces, and he believes that he has heard the "ponderous gallop" of the bronze horseman behind him ever since his moment of indignation in front of Peter's statue. In the introduction to the poem, devoted to the beautiful and majestic capital, and in various passages of the poem Puškin appears definitely to be defending Peter's work. He is engaging in polemics, not only with Ševyrev, who, as a Slavophile, was somewhat skeptical of Peter, but also with the great Polish poet Adam Mickiewicz, in whose work St. Petersburg comes off rather poorly. Later, Puškin considered writing a history of Peter the Great; and from his notes that have been preserved, it is obvious that he would have had to change much of his eulogistic attitude toward Peter.

The Bronze Horseman is also an important work of art in its form, especially in the often-praised "dynamic character" of its presentation. The stirring account of the building of St. Petersburg on a miserable and desolate site and a description of a day and a year in the life of the city take up two pages of the poem. The sea, which struggles with the Tsar for control of the city, is portrayed as an animate being. It attacks St. Petersburg like a beast of prey and draws back, carelessly dropping its plunder as it goes.

One should discuss Puškin's fairy tales together with his epics. One finds that his attitude toward folklore is not yet marked by the great respect and partial exaggeration later characteristic of the Russian romanticists. Like Žukovskij, Puškin treats not only purely Russian fairy-tale motifs, but makes use of foreign folk and art tales as well. For his *Parson and His Man Balda*, he turns to the Russian motif of the devil who has been deceived. Here Puškin uses an original poetic technique, one that is close to Russian folklore meter and that he also employs in a fragment about a she-bear, *Medvedica*. *King Saltan* and *The Dead Princess* treat Russian motifs in a verse that is lovely, but by no means folk verse; and *The Fisherman and His Wife* goes back to the Grimms' fairy tale, which Puškin knew in French translation. The theme of *The Golden Cockerel* is taken from Washington Irving's *Alhambra* (1832). On occasion, Puškin tried to make use of Russian folk meters in his fairy tales. One wonders if there can be anything genuinely "folk" about an art fairy tale.

Tsar Nicholas found parts of *The Bronze Horseman* suspect and did not permit the poem to be published. After the suppression of the Decembrist Revolt in 1825, the Tsar had granted Puškin a kind of amnesty, receiving him personally and proposing that, from then on, he be Puškin's censor. In time, this "kindness" proved to be a menace, as when *Boris Godunov* was not approved for publication. Puškin became even more closely connected with the court of the Tsar when, in 1831, he married the beautiful Natalja Gončarova. It was because of his wife, Puškin believed, that he was "honored" and made a "gentleman of the chamber," a rank normally conferred on young noblemen but one that would enable him to escort his wife to court. This new position changed his life considerably and made him more enemies than friends. In 1837, Puškin's jealousy of Georges d'Anthès, an adventurer who had been adopted by the Dutch ambassador, led to a duel in which Puškin was fatally wounded. The whole affair was due to a misunderstanding. Puškin had mistakenly taken d'Anthès to be the author of an anonymous insulting letter.

16. As he had in *The Bronze Horseman*, Puškin succeeded in his Little Tragedies in putting intellectual subject matter into an attractive form. The plays include *The Covetous Knight, Mozart and Salieri, The Stone Guest*, and *The Feast During the Plague*.

The Stone Guest (1830) is an attempt to give a new treatment in four scenes to the old theme of the fall of Don Juan. Puškin was familiar with Molière's moralistic interpretation and presumably with the text of Mozart's opera. But Puškin's Don Juan is an intelligent man, a poet, whose tragic fall is not a punishment for his sins but a consequence of his genuine love for Donna Anna.

The Feast During the Plague (1830) is a translation of most of act I, scene 4 of the dramatic poem *The City of the Plague* by the Scottish poet John Wilson (1785–1854). Puškin makes the plague a symbol of the dangers that confront everyone but that give an "inexplicable pleasure" to the "mortal heart."

> Есть упоение в бою,
> и бездны мрачной на краю,
> и в разъяренном океане,
> средь грозных волн и бурной тьмы,
> и в аравийском урагане,
> и в дуновении Чумы.
> Все, все, что гибелью грозит,
> для сердца смертного таит
> неизъяснимы наслажденья.

There is ecstasy in battle, at the edge of a dark abyss, in the raging ocean in the midst of threatening waves and stormy darkness, in an Arabian hurricane, and in the breath of the plague. Everything, everything that threatens us with destruction conceals within itself inexplicable pleasures for the mortal heart.

Nevertheless, a priest succeeds in moving one of the participants in the feast to "deep reflection."

In his last years, Puškin eagerly studied English literature in the original; but his *The Covetous Knight* is not really, as he says, a translation from the English poet W. Shenstone (1714–1763). Shenstone never wrote a poem of this title or content. This Little Tragedy seeks to give an intellectual interpretation of avarice.

> Что не подвластно мне? Как некий демон
> отселе править миром я могу.

What is not subject to me? From here I can rule the world like a demon.

These are the words of the "covetous knight" as he views his riches, which serve no purpose. But he does not need actually to make use of his power. He acknowledges:

> Я знаю мощь мою: с меня довольно
> сего сознания.

I know my power; and this knowledge is enough for me.

Nevertheless, avarice can destroy the most basic human relationships, in this case those between father and son. The problem suggested by Puškin was later treated by Dostoevskij, who was concerned with psychological rather than social poverty.

The last of the Little Tragedies, *Mozart and Salieri* (1830), deals with an aesthetic problem. Puškin based his play on the legend that Mozart was poisoned by his envious Viennese colleague Antonio Salieri. But in Puškin, Salieri's envy is due not to Mozart's success, but to his original, spontaneous manner of composition, which, in Salieri's view, is a dangerous precedent for art. Salieri considers art to be almost a craft, based on strict theory. Mozart's music awakens in others a sense of helpless longing but cannot really advance their work.

Two larger dramatic works were not completed. *Rusalka*(1829–1832) is the story of a girl who has been deserted by a prince, drowns herself in a river, and becomes a water nymph. *Scenes from the Age of Chivalry* (1835) was evidently to have been Puškin's Faust drama. Its heroes are Bertold Schwarz, the inventor of gunpowder, and Johannes Gutenberg—that is, the men who, in

Puškin's view, created the forces that gave rise to the modern world. Only Schwarz appears in the completed part of the play, and the main hero is the singer Franz. In these two fragments and in a number of short plays (among them one on Pope Joan, who was perhaps supposed to appear in *Scenes from the Age of Chivalry*), there are many excellent passages; but we know little about Puškin's further plans for the plays.

17. Puškin left a number of prose works. Although various critical and personal notes have been preserved from his younger years, his literary development seems to have been from poetry to prose. One should not rely on this fact, however, to try to demonstrate that literature always develops from verse to prose.

As early as 1827, Puškin was working on a novel, *The Nigger of Peter the Great*, which was dedicated to Gannibal (see sec. 10 above), an ancestor of his mother. Not quite seven chapters of the work were completed. In the novel, the blackamoor, Gannibal, who has studied in Paris, is summoned back to St. Petersburg by the Tsar. His return gives Puškin an opportunity to describe life in the new capital. Peter the Great finds the blackamoor a wife from a good boyar family. Whether the story was to have taken a turn for the better or for the worse, we do not know. It is possible that Puškin intended to tell of the unhappy marriage as it really was; but it is also possible that in the novel the bride was to have come to love her blackamoor—whom Puškin portrays as one of the best men around Peter the Great—just as Shakespeare's Desdemona learns to love Othello. The fragment is distinguished by its fine, lucid language and succinct narration, which is dynamically relieved by dialogue. Puškin published only two chapters of the novel (1829 ff.).

In 1830, Puškin brought out *The Tales of Ivan Petrovič Belkin*. Although he provided the fictitious author with a biographical introduction, Puškin wrote all five stories himself. Belkin is supposed to have heard the tales from different people, whose style he sometimes uses in narrating. *The Shot* is told by an officer. The hero of the story, a Byronic type, chooses not to fire when his opponent in a duel shows no fear. He saves his shot until his opponent is happily married. The confusion and anxiety of the

opponent and his young wife satisfy the demonic hero, and he fires
his pistol at the wall.

Two other stories, *The Snow Storm* and *The Stationmaster*, have
romantic themes. The first of them is an improbable story of
fateful love. When a snowstorm prevents a bridegroom from ar-
riving on time for his wedding, his place at the altar is taken by
another man who is thought to be the groom. Immediately
after the wedding the stranger leaves. Years later he chances
to meet the woman he has married by accident and falls in love
with her before discovering that she is his wife. The story of *The
Stationmaster* is often misunderstood. A traveling officer abducts
the daughter of a stationmaster, who supposes that she has had a
fate like that of the prodigal son. In his despair he drinks himself
to death. But his daughter apparently marries her abductor, and
later, a rich lady, visits her father's grave. In both stories there are
lacunae and obscure points appropriate to romantic prose and
verse tales.

The Coffinmaker is a parody on the romantic horror tale: a
coffinmaker is visited one night by his former customers, some of
whom he has cheated. But as it turns out, he has merely had a bad
dream after a merry evening.

In tone, *Mistress into Maid* is reminiscent of Karamzin.[7] A
young noblewoman is supposed to have told Belkin this sentimental idyll about the young son of a landowner and the heroine who
disguises herself as a peasant girl.

All of the *Tales of Belkin* are distinguished by succinct, pithy
language, brief subordinate clauses, and modest use of epithet
and metaphor. The tales almost fit the ideal that the classicists
were unable to realize. They are typical short stories. *The Coffinmaker* is only eight pages; *Mistress into Maid*, about twenty; and
each of the other three, about twelve pages. They mark the beginning of the tradition of the modern Russian short story.

Puškin also wrote several long novellas that one could call
novels, although he did not use the term. He himself published
the romantic novella *The Queen of Spades* (1834), which in theme
is a direct forerunner of the works of Dostoevskij. A poor officer

7. [It also has some features in common with Oliver Goldsmith's comedy *She
Stoops to Conquer* (1773).—EDITOR]

of the army engineers, named "German" (in Russian; presumably "Hermann," since he is German), wishes to find out from an old countess the secret of three cards that will always win. When he intrudes into her room and threatens her with a pistol, she dies of fright. Later she appears to German as a ghost and tells him the three cards, but the secret does not help him. After winning at the table for two evenings, he loses on the third; instead of an ace, the queen of spades turns up. German goes mad. Although this story is interwoven with a love story, Puškin compresses the involved action into twenty-five pages.

The Captain's Daughter (1836) is a genuine novel, although it is only a hundred and thirty pages. In writing it, Puškin made use of his research on the history of the Pugačev rebellion (1773–1774; see below). The central character is a young officer who is in love with the daughter of the commandant of a small fortress near Orenburg. The commandant is killed by the rebels. On behalf of the girl, the hero travels to the province occupied by Pugačev and is suspected of having gone over to his side. Pugačev himself is the only historical character who figures in the main action of the novel, although Empress Catherine II appears in the concluding chapter. Perhaps because he introduced only two historical personages, Puškin was able to write a striking and concentrated novel of historical events from a limited point of view.

Two other long works remained incomplete and were published posthumously. One of them is the brigand novella *Dubrovskij*. A young nobleman turns outlaw, as did Michael Kohlhaas,[8] in an effort to avenge an unjust verdict against his father. Romance is introduced when the hero falls in love with the daughter of his enemy. Puškin completed only one volume of this novel. In the second volume, the hero was probably supposed to have gone abroad, but we know nothing more about Puškin's plans.

8. [Michael Kohlhaas is the chief character in a short novel by the same name published in 1808 by the German writer Heinrich von Kleist. Kohlhaas, a sixteenth-century horse-trader, is victimized by a nobleman's dishonest practices and subsequently becomes a "bandit of honor," organizes his own rebel-robber band, and storms the surrounding castles and cities in a quest for justice. —EDITOR]

The second work, of which only a small part was completed, is *Egyptian Nights*. Queen Cleopatra is said to have sold her favors in exhange for the death of the lover with whom she had spent the night. In Puškin's work, an improvisator reads a poem on this theme; but in the St. Petersburg audience there is a woman who can match Cleopatra, and there the novel leaves off.

A number of literary plans and beginnings of novels by Puškin have been preserved. Much of the material is very interesting, for instance, *The History of the Village Gorjuxino*, which is ascribed to Belkin and which was presumably inspired by Washington Irving's parodic history of New York, and, like its model, contained social motifs.

The themes and individual motifs in Puškin's prose are entirely within the romantic tradition; outlaws (Dubrovskij, Pugačev), artists (the Italian improvisator and his opposite number, the Russian poet, in *Egyptian Nights*), visions and clairvoyant dreams (*The Queen of Spades* and *The Captain's Daughter*), and, especially, paradoxical subjects (*The Snowstorm, The Stationmaster*, and *Egyptian Nights*) are concisely presented. Particularly in some of *The Tales of Belkin* and in the novels, Puškin writes in short sentences and with an economy of poetic ornamentation that is almost unique in Russian literature.

18. Early in his life, Puškin probably felt himself destined to be a "writer by profession." In the eighteenth century, journalism was not thought to be fashionable. Karamzin dared for a time to practice journalism professionally; and by the nineteenth century, there were already journalists from the nobility. The *Poljarnaja Zvezda* of Kondratij Ryleev and Aleksandr Bestužev and the *Mnemozina* of Prince V. F. Odoevskij were indications of the new attitude toward the profession of journalism. Prince Petr Vjazemskij was a permanent contributor to Nikolaj Polevoj's magazine. A number of drafts of critical essays from Puškin's early years have survived; and in 1830, he took an active interest in Anton A. Del'vig's *Literaturnaja Gazeta*. He did not, however, contribute to this journal of the Moscow romanticists. His efforts to found a journal of his own did not meet with success until 1836, when he began publishing the quarterly *Sovremennik* [Contempo-

rary]. Journalistic as well as creative prose played an increasingly important part in Puškin's life.

In addition to writing a great many literary reviews and essays, Puškin also revised foreign works. Among them are the memoirs of the American John Tanner, who, as a child, was abducted by Indians and later returned to the civilized world; the memoirs of a French officer who had taken part in the campaign of Peter the Great against the Turks in 1711; and a fragment of an epistolary prose work on Maria Schoning, an impoverished young Nürnberg woman. With the fragment is a note by Puškin, saying that Maria was supposed to confess to a crime that she had not committed, in order to be executed and thus escape poverty. *The History of the Pugačev Rebellion* (1834, in two volumes) is a historical work. Among Puškin's quasi-journalistic writings is his description of his trip to the Caucasus in 1829 (*Putešestvie v Arzrum*); here he combines a serious report, literature, and a parody on Chateaubriand. Although the critical and polemical essays are stylistically rather different, the longer nonfictional prose works have much in common with Puškin's novellas.

Of *The History of Peter the Great* that Puškin planned to write, only the research material that he gathered has survived.

19. One should, of course, value Puškin primarily as a lyric poet and take particular note of his place in the history of the Russian lyric. One first encounters genuine features of Puškin's poetry in his youthful elegies, to which many of his later poems hark back. Turning away from laments for lost youth (at eighteen) and vague longings (of the kind that he later put into Lenskij's poems— *temno i vjalo*, [dark and dull]), he proceeded to create clear, though often unusual, images and to express himself surely and concisely.

Later generations have been especially impressed by the clarity and transparency of Puškin's lyrics. For this reason only, such poets as A. N. Majkov and even A. Apuxtin were taken to be legitimate successors of Puškin: their verse was sonorous and smooth and their manner of presentation fairly concrete. Fifty years after Puškin's time, his particular poetic qualities were called realism. We shall return to this point later.

Unlike Puškin's epic works, his lyrics can hardly be characterized briefly. There are several important features that run through
all his poetry written after his exile in the South. The dawn of a
new era was marked by his final break with classicist poetics.
First of all, he gave up the traditional genres. Classicist forms
were broken up and their place taken by the free form of the "Byronic poem." Even Puškin's fragments are complete works of art,
such as *Kakaja noč', moroz treskučij, Al'fons saditsja na konja* (a
reworking of the Polish writer A. Potocki's phantasmic novella
A Manuscript Found in Saragossa [1804]), the five-stanza poem
Strannik (a reworking of the first chapter of John Bunyan's
Pilgrim's Progress), and *Dva čvstva divno blizki nam*, an eight-
line poem, of which only the first four lines were finished.
Enigmatically, even the completed lyric poems open infinite
perspectives. In some cases, Puškin called his published poems
"fragments" (*otryvki*); in other cases the subject matter requires a
"continuation"—Puškin goes beyond what has actually been
said (as in *Poèt—"Poka ne trebuet poèta"*). The last lines of some
poems suggest a continuation, for instance, by means of a missing
rhyme.

The verse forms in Puškin's poetry are not especially numerous.
Iambic tetrameter is the predominant line and is varied only when
a stress is dropped. In at least twenty-five percent of Puškin's
lines, the accent is missing from the third foot, so that the line
looks something like this:

$$\text{X X́ X X̋ X X X X́ (X)}$$

One also finds missing stresses in other feet:

egó primér drugím naúka	X X́ X X́ X X́ X X́ X
poká ne trébuet poéta	X X́ X X́ X X X X́ X
ón malodúšno pogružén	X́ X X X́ X X X X̋
neotxodjá ni šágu próč'	X X X X́ X X́ X X̋

Trochees and ternary meters are less usual in Puškin's work,
and anapests are very unusual. With few exceptions, Puškin's
rhymes are exact, so that he had occasion to complain half-

jokingly about the poverty of Russian rhymes. He does not always develop his stanzas regularly.

It was obviously Puškin's intention to be concise. He often shortened his original drafts and omitted lines that he considered good enough to use in other works. This concision is an essential characteristic of the poetry of Puškin's time.

The themes of Puškin's poems are difficult to summarize, since he particularly valued variety and thought of the poet as an echo of the world (*Èxo*, 1831). Romantic themes are common in his work (see also chapter V, sec. 12). The following are among them.

In the night, or "night side of the soul," man's soul finds its answer or at least searches for it (see *Stixi sočinennye noč'ju vo vremja bessonicy* [1830], the fragment *Skaži mne noč'* . . . [1825], and even the appeal to the winter night *Vesna, vesna, pora ljubvi* . . . [1827]). The night is, of course, only the background for the deeper emotions of the soul (*Noc'* [1823], *Nenastnyj den' potux* [1824]); more importantly, in Puškin's longer works, it is often the background for events. Man is often pictured as a wanderer in this world; the life of the poet serves as an example. One thinks of *Telega žizni* (1823), *Zimnjaja doroga* (1826), *Besy* (1830). Incidentally, *Besy* was not written in winter, and some of the lines remind one very much of Vjazemskij's *Metel'* from the series *Zimnie karikatury* (1828). Dreams are also a romantic theme. As we have mentioned, they are for the mature poet a symbol of the deeper, more significant emotions of the soul (see *Razgovor knigoprodovca s poètom* [1824], *Fontanu Baxčisarajskogo dvorca* [1824]; the new interpretation of *son* has already been discussed). Dreams reveal man's inner being, as in *The Queen of Spades* and the scene omitted from *Boris Godunov*; or they have clairvoyant properties, as in Tatjana's dream in *Evgenij Onegin* or Grinev's dream in *The Captain's Daughter*. Even madness, which also reveals the depths of the soul, and the word *bezumnyj* take on positive connotations, for instance, as early as 1820 in *Pogaslo dnevnoe svetilo*, in *Puskaj uvenčannyj ljubov'ju* (1824), in *Pod nebom golubym* (1826), and especially in *Ne daj mne Bog sojti s uma* (1833). The last of these poems is an idealization of madness. The madmen in Puškin's longer works are, of course, also important, especially Evgenij in *The Bronze Horseman*. One

category of Puškin's works is made up of the many poems that deal
with the profession, mission, and life of the poet and that create a
typically romantic image of the poet from various points of view.
The poem *Prorok* [The Prophet] (1826) is characteristic in several
respects; here Puškin portrays the poet's calling in biblical
terms and makes skillful use of Church Slavonicisms. He does not
hesitate to include unusual Church Slavonic words (such as
vlačit'sja, persty, zenicy, otverstyj, and *glagol* in the sense of
"word" [*slovo*]) and morphologically archaic forms (*gad morskix*,
genitive plural, or *vižd'*, imperative). One finds a similar poetic
playing with lexical word groups, foreign to the romantic literary
language, in other places in Puškin, as in the folkloric lexical
elements in the fairy tales, the "Spanish vocabulary" in various
poems, and Church Slavonic elements still to be found in *Otcy-
pustynniki* (1836), and in various scenes in *Boris Godunov*.

Breaking with the classicist theory of genres, Puškin wrote
ballads, a characteristic genre of Russian romanticism. Often he
turned to the fantastic or numinous ballad. The formal aspect
of Puškin's poetry was a part of the stylistics of Russian romanticism, just then developing, and includes his attention to the
ballad and to stylization, his interest in the Orient, the Middle
Ages, the narrator of folk tales, and Dante and Byron. But as
we have already said, Puškin does not fit entirely into the framework of romanticism.

Other formal features of Puškin's poetry are his efforts to
achieve concision and to write fragmented forms. His works are
not weighed down with metaphors and epithets. In time he
turned from the exuberant, periphrastic style of his youth and
attempted to designate things precisely. But despite the concision
of his poetry it remains original and substantial. For example:

> в тревоге пестрой и бесплодной
> большого света и двора . . . .
> ратник, вольностью венчанный,
> исчезнувший, как тень зари (Наполеон) . . . .
> мучим казнию покоя (Наполеон).

> in the gay and barren anxiety
> of society and the court . . . .

the warrior crowned by freedom,
who vanished like the shadow of dawn (Napoleon) . . .
tortured by the torments of peace (Napoleon).

беззаконная комета
в кругу расчисленных светил . . . .
на немые стогны града
полупрозрачная наляжет ночи тень . . . .
воспоминание безмолвно предо мной
свой длинный развивает свиток.

The lawless comet
circling the calculable star. [said of an unpredictable woman]

On the broad and noiseless city streets
night's translucent shadow falls . . .
[a reference to "white nights"]
Silently in front of me memory
unfolds its long scroll.

See also other examples above.

Puškin put it well when he referred to "*moj svoenravnyj genij*,"
"my capricious genius."

20. In the nineteenth century, it was the custom to include
several of Puškin's contemporaries in a "Puškin Pleiad," without
taking into account the style or subject of their work. A closer
examination of their work shows, however, that many of these
writers, among them those who were close to Puškin, went quite
different ways and that one cannot properly speak of a Pleiad of
poets who collaborated, consciously or unconsciously. Among the
literary and personal qualities valued by romanticism were
originality and individualism, and one can hardly imagine a
group of romantic poets marching along in step.

Baron Anton Antonovič Del'vig (presumably von Delwig
[1798–1831]) came from a family of impoverished Baltic-Germans.
He spent most of his youth in Russian-speaking regions. Like

Puškin, he attended school at Carskoe Selo and took part eagerly in literary projects. He had the reputation of knowing foreign literatures well, especially German, although he could only read German and could not speak it. He was a close friend of Puškin. After graduation from the lyceum, Del'vig moved in literary circles and was a frequent guest in literary salons. Until 1825, he held various minor, poorly paid positions and was equally unsuccessful at all of them. In 1824, the almanac *Severnye Cvety*, on which Del'vig had collaborated, appeared. In 1825, he married and became the host of a salon, which, though modest, attracted Puškin, V. F. Odoevskij, Evgenij Baratynskij, and other poets. In 1830, he became editor of the *Literaturnaja Gazeta*, which had been founded by Puškin and his friends;[9] and for a time Puškin was an eager contributor to the magazine. After various difficulties with censorship, Del'vig was forced to vacate his position in favor of Orest Somov (see chapter IV, sec. 8). The *Gazeta* closed soon after Del'vig's sudden death in 1831.

Despite their personal friendship and their collaboration on the magazine they were putting out and despite the common literary battles they fought, Del'vig and Puškin were not at all close as poets. Del'vig was early attracted to two sets of themes that never particularly appealed to Puškin: antiquity and the folk song. Del'vig attempted to imitate the classical meters without seeking an equivalent in Russian for the lengths of the classical syllables, as Aleksandr Vostokov had successfully done. And as early as the Napoleonic Wars—that is, when he was about fourteen—Del'vig wrote a patriotic "folk song." He became more and more adept in these two genres. In 1814, he wrote an idyll, the characters of which are Greeks. As he experimented with classical meters, so he experimented with the verse form of the Russian folk song; and for all the artificiality of his folk songs, they are closer to real folk songs than are the attempts made in the eighteenth century. In 1821, Del'vig began his formal imitation of folk songs and the "stylization" of his poems in the

9. [There were published, altogether, seventy-one issues of the *Literaturnaja Gazeta* in the 1830s. Issues three to twelve were edited by Puškin himself and by O. M. Somov. In 1831, Somov became its sole editor.—EDITOR]

"Russian style," such as *Ax, ty, noč' li, nočen'ka, Golova-l' moja, golovuška* (1823), *Solovej* (1825). He also translated Ukrainian folk songs. His favorite genre was the idyll, such as *Konec zolotogo veka*, and a "Russian idyll," *The Discharged Soldier* (1829). In Del'vig's poetry, one finds many lines with dactyllic endings and even rhymes with the stress on the third syllable from the end. For example:

Ne osennij, častyj doždiček	X X X́ X X́ X X́ X X
bryzžet, bryzžet skvoz' tuman,	X́ X X́ X X X X́
slezy gor'kie l'et molodec	X́ X X́ X X X́ X́ X X
na svoj barxatnyj kaftan.	X X́ X́ X X X X́

It is not the fine autumn rain drizzling through the fog; a young man's bitter tears are flowing onto his velvet coat.

Del'vig's views on poetry, which he told his friends in verse letters in his early years, are quite interesting. Particularly important is *Poetic Enthusiasm* (1822), on the isolation from everyday life of the despised and persecuted poet, who directs his words at future generations.

21. Another of Puškin's schoolmates, Wilhelm Küchelbecker (1797–1846), has long been unjustly neglected by critics and literary historians. He came from a Russified Saxon family and did not learn German until he was six. Two years older than Puškin, Küchelbecker also attended the lyceum at Carskoe Selo. Like Puškin and Del'vig, Küchelbecker was already an enthusiastic poet while in school and was certainly the best-read of the three friends. Because of his extreme seriousness, Küchelbecker was somewhat lonely and appeared at times ridiculous among his schoolmates, whose ideal was "golden youth." Puškin's many epigrams to him do not reflect the love and esteem that he felt for his odd friend.

After graduating from the lyceum, Küchelbecker became a minor official in the Foreign Office, as did Puškin and Del'vig. At the same time, he taught and was an active participant in various literary circles. In 1820, he went abroad as a private secretary. The well-educated young man made a number of literary acquaintances in France and in Germany, among them Goethe. In Paris, Küchelbecker began giving lectures on Russian literature; but the content of his lectures provoked the Russian ambassador to stop them and to send him back to Russia. Küchelbecker was then apparently forced to go to the Caucasus, but he returned to Russia in 1822 and became a member of the philosophical society that had formed around the much younger Prince V. F. Odoevskij (see chapter IV, sec. 1). In 1824–1825, Küchelbecker and Odoevskij published the influential literary quarterly *Mnemozina*, and in it Küchelbecker defended his views on literary theory. In his opinions he was evidently close to Aleksandr Griboedov; he opposed the Russian early romantic elegiac poetry and favored the old doctrine of genres, which the romanticists were against. He was also the first Russian enthusiast of Goethe. In 1825, he joined the Decembrists and took part in the Decembrist Revolt with a pistol in his hand. Characteristically for Küchelbecker, who was pursued by bad luck, the pistol failed to go off. He was the only one of the Decembrists who attempted to flee abroad; but he was arrested in Warsaw and paid for his part in the revolt by being kept for a time under strict confinement in fortresses. In 1828, as he was being transferred from one fortress to another, he ran into Puškin at a posting station. Although placed in solitary confinement, Küchelbecker was allowed to read and write. Unfortunately, only an abridged edition of his interesting diary has been published. He was not sent to Siberia until 1835; he died there ten years later, blind and sick.

Even after 1826, Küchelbecker was able to publish some of his works under assumed names in Russia; but most of his writings, such as his abridged diary, were not discovered until later. Thanks to the critic Jurij Tynjanov, a two-volume edition of Küchelbecker's verse was published in 1939; but even this edition is unfortunately not complete.

Ideologically, Küchelbecker is one of the most interesting of the Russian romanticists. He began by writing elegies that he later attacked, elegies in which he presented himself to the reader as disenchanted. Žukovskij was still his master, and Küchelbecker retained great respect for him. Next he turned to Greek writers and translated Callimachus, Bacchylides, and the Homeric hymns. Later he wrote on aesthetic questions. The fundamental concept of his poetics is *mečta*, which actually means "daydream" but which, in Küchelbecker, suggests "longing." *Mečta* is the enchantress, the true friend of the poet, the divine flame, the holy vision that comes from the depths of the heart and discloses the wonderful world to the poet. It is the "restless dream" (*son mjatežnyj*), the mystery that the poet must solve. The image of the "wonderful guest," the "wonderful messenger" who comes to the poet from the land of wonders, goes back to Žukovskij and recurs often in Küchelbecker's poems. In his view, poetic enthusiasm is opposed to dead knowledge, to the "barren rock." Books are but "corpses of faded days." The "messenger" is the "angel of poetic enthusiasm," for whom Küchelbecker later devised a name, ostensibly from an Oriental source: Isfrail, the "angel of song," the "clairvoyant of the night of the heart" (*serdečnoj noči jasnyj zritel'*).

Oddly enough, by 1820 and 1821, Küchelbecker was already writing poems on the tragic fate of poets, who are the elect (*izbranniki*) and the prophets of the heart and soul but who are persecuted and banished. It is natural for the poet to wear the "martyr's crown" for it is "dreadful to be . . . the prophet of the happy gods." On the one hand, Küchelbecker considers the poet to be omniscient, especially in the realm of "secret forces," of the "depths of the heart," of the "abyss of the heart" (he calls the depths of the soul "sea of dreams"); he even considers the poet to be a doctor of the heart. On the other hand, *mečta* is the source of the "incomprehensible tortures" that lead the poet onto the "path of thorns." There, in addition to his inner suffering, he must bear the "abuse of the crowd" and the buffets of fate. Events seemed to confirm Küchelbecker in his view; he wrote poetic obituaries to his friends Ryleev, Griboedov, Puškin, and Baratynskij. His themes are also concerned with the fate of man in general, not merely that of the poet. He celebrates nature in his pretty landscape poems, in which the waterfall, the wind, and the night are symbolic, and he writes from experience on the fate of the prisoner (*uznik*). Strangely enough, Küchelbecker is almost the only Russian poet to praise the "joys of wandering"; even in Vjazemskij and Puškin, the traditional Russian theme is the melancholy song of the troika. There are, of course, also themes dealing with freedom in Küchelbecker's poetry—the Greek war of liberation, for example.

Küchelbecker's writing was not confined to lyric poetry. He wrote several ballads, which remind one of Katenin (see sec. 26 below); he wrote plays, including a typically romantic mystery play, *Ižorskij*, the ironic portrayal of a disenchanted dreamer; and he wrote several epics, *Jurij i Ksenija, David* (in which various literary problems are discussed), *The Eternal Jew*, and others that are only partly preserved. In addition to critical prose and an interesting diary, Küchelbecker produced a romantic novella, *Poslednij Kolonna* [The Last Colonna], a work written in prison.

It was once said the Küchelbecker's writing suffered from "technical weaknesses," but this view has now been refuted. The unusual quality in his poetry that offended some critics was a certain lexical "unevenness," that is, the use of words not permitted by poetic standards then or later. His neologisms are not numerous, consist mostly of compound forms, and are in part descriptive, such as *žiznedatnyj, roskošno-svežij, pesne-ljubivyj*; sometimes, however, they are more unusual, such as *razoblekalas', rezvoskačuščij*—a word that Puškin ridiculed—and others. One often finds striking images in his work. "Man—brother of the seraphim and brother of the worms" goes back to Schiller; Küchelbecker mentions Schiller often and anticipates Dostoevskij. His poems are generally written in iambic tetrameter, a meter considered modern at the time. Some poems are in elegiac pentameters. Although he defends archaisms in his essays, there is hardly a trace of them in his work after 1825.

Occasionally, one finds in Küchelbecker an accumulation of words from the romantic "semantic fields," such as:

> беседует со мною гений
> . . . Он неожиданный слетает,
> не приманит его мольба,
> он так таинствен, как судьба;
> из бездны сердца он вещает.

Крыло прострет он надо мною —
огонь горит и моих очах.

A genius talks with me . . . He descends unexpectedly; no supplication can lure him down; he is as mysterious as fate; he prophesies from the depths of his heart. When he stretches out his wing over me, fire burns in my eyes.

Or he makes free use of the antonyms of the semantic field "warmth":

Замолк и меркнет вещий дух,
не брызжут искры вдохновения,
исчезли дивные видения,
в груди певца восторг потух.
Так постепенно тише рдеет
без жизнедатного огня
и остывает, и чернеет
под мертвым пеплом головня.

The prophetic spirit has fallen silent and grown dark. The sparks of enthusiasm no longer fly. The wonderful visions have disappeared. The ecstasy is extinguished in the breast of the singer. So gradually, without life-giving fire, the charred log glows dimmer, grows cold, and turns black beneath dead ashes.

22. Puškin was much closer in spirit to Evgenij Abramovič Baratynskij (or Boratynskij [1800–1844]) than he was to his schoolmates Anton Del'vig and Wilhelm Küchelbecker. Baratynskij came from a family of provincial nobility and, when he was thirteen, was sent to an exclusive school in St. Petersburg. He fell in with an unfortunate crowd at the school and got into trouble with them—it is doubtful that they were merely following the example of Schiller's *Räuber*—and as a result, he was not only expelled from school, in 1816, but later was forced to serve as a private in the army. When he was eighteen, Baratynskij was sent as a soldier to St. Petersburg, where he met poets and became close friends with Del'vig and Küchelbecker. As he was

allowed to live off post, he moved in with Del'vig and came into contact with the literary circles of the capital. In 1820, he was sent as a noncommissioned officer to a regiment in Finland. The wild Northern landscape and the loneliness had somewhat the same effect on him as the South had had on Puškin. By 1823, Baratynskij's literary friends the Decembrists Kondratij Ryleev and Aleksandr Bestužev were planning to publish a volume of his poetry. Thanks to the patronage of Vasilij Žukovskij and Petr Vjazemskij, Baratynskij's situation improved; and, besides, the new tsar, Nicholas I, was entirely absorbed with the prosecution of Decembrists. In 1826, Baratynskij was made an officer. He was able to leave Finland and soon retired from the army. He married and lived afterward in Moscow and on his estate. In 1827, the first collection of his poems was published. Baratynskij's new acquaintances influenced him, especially the brothers I. V. and Petr Kireevskij (in particular I. V.), Nikolaj Jazykov, V. F. Odoevskij, Aleksej Xomjakov, and others.[10] I. V. Kireevskij explained Schelling's philosophy to Baratynskij but was evidently unable to convert him to Slavophilism (see chapter VII, sec. 3). Baratynskij took part in literary activities in Moscow but withdrew from literary life after the appearance of a two-volume edition of his poems in 1835. In 1842, he published another volume of poetry, *Sumerki* [Twilight]. Like all his work, these last poems were severely attacked by the critic V. G. Belinskij, who was influential at the time and later even became famous but who had no understanding of poetry. In 1843, Baratynskij went abroad and became acquainted with literary circles in Paris (A. de Vigny, C. Nodier, P. Mérimée, George Sand). Traveling farther, he died after a brief illness in Naples.

The symbolists rediscovered Baratynskij. He was thought, unjustly, to be a philosophical poet. Undoubtedly, he is a thinker and is successful in the aphoristic form. He expresses his ideas as Puškin does, concisely, clearly, and on occasion in a surprisingly original way. But his ideas have not become household sayings, as have a great many lines by Aleksandr Griboedov. Baratynskij's

10. [Ivan V. Kireevskij (1806–1856) and Alexej S. Xomjakov, together with brothers Ivan S. (1823–1886) and Konstantin J. Aksakov (1817–1860), were founders of the Slavophile movement.—EDITOR]

literary formulas are seldom theoretical. He was a notable lyric poet who was less concerned with expressing his thoughts than his personal experiences. Even after Ivan Kireevskij had acquainted him with the philosophy of Schelling, Baratynskij's extraordinarily concise formulations were seldom philosophical in the strict sense. They are aphorisms for the few; but this is certainly not a defect. For example:

> Две области, сияние и тьмы
> исследовать равно стремимся мы.

We are equally concerned with exploring two spheres, light and darkness.

On examining a skull, the poet calls himself

> мыслящий наследник разрушения

the thinking heir of destruction.

> дарует между нас и славу и позор
> торговой логики смышленный приговор

The clever judgment of tradesman's logic distributes both praise and shame among us.

Pointed but not readily understandable formulas such as these had no hope of becoming popular, and many educated Russians have forgotten them.

Generally speaking, Baratynskij's lyrics are elegiac in nature. In his later years, his melancholy mood darkened to a profound, all-embracing pessimism, although his personal life was happy, at least as far as it is revealed in his poetry.

According to the poet, there are two possible attitudes for man: hope, which is associated with restless agitation; and hopelessness, which is associated with tranquillity (*Dve doli* [1823]). As a young man, Baratynskij wrote the pretty, traditional elegies that so upset his friend Küchelbecker (*Razuverenie* [1821]; *Čerep* [1824]; *Istina* [1824]; *Ljubov'* [1824]); but he soon tried to make his experiences more universal (*Stansy* [1827]). He sees the image of *Poslednjaja smert'* [Final Death] that will visit all the earth. But he does not look upon death as hostile; rather, it is a force that reconciles, resolves mysteries, and releases one from one's bonds (*Smert'* [1828]). Man is merely a "creature who has been born too early," "a sigh with wings" (*Nedonosok* [1835]), condemned to hover forever between heaven and earth and not to find peace in either place. The "splendor of senseless eternity" is therefore burdensome.

Baratynskij also wrote *The Last Poet* (1835), a poem with a disturbing vision of the near future when there will be no place for poetry in the world and when the world will be indifferent to art. Like Küchelbecker, Baratynskij had once thought that heaven was the true home of the poet (*Del'vigu* [1821]); in *The Last Poet*, he appears to have lost even this sense of being connected with the world above.

A great many of Baratynskij's poems have to do with the profession of the poet, among them his early epistles (those to Anton Del'vig, Nikolaj Gnedič [1823], Nikolaj Jazykov [1831], Prince Petr Vjazemskij [1834—especially the beautiful letter on the death of Goethe in 1832], and to Adam Mickiewicz—*K**** [1827], *Ne podražaj* [1827]), and a group of other poems, including *Podražateljam* (1829), *Byvalo otrok* (1831), reminiscent of Puškin's *Èxo, Boljaščij dux vračuet pesnopenie* (1832), *Rifma* (about 1840). Baratynskij thought of the poet as a teacher or tutor (*nastavnik*), a prophet, and even a god. He felt that poetry is directly connected with the world beyond; and even the sound of it (rhyme) is, in effect, a voice from the beyond. But the meaning of poetry is twofold. On the one hand, the work of a true poet, whom Baratynskij considered a martyr, is disturbing and tormenting (the poet is a *dušemutitel'nyj poèt*); on the other hand, the harmony of poetry has the mysterious power to calm passions. The poet's soul is cleansed of suffering (catharsis) and finds peace.

Baratynskij touches on a number of romantic themes, such as the philosophy of art (*Skulptor* [1841]). His defense of popular beliefs and superstitions is characteristic; proud reason can do no more than state the "sense of a popular proverb" (*Staratel'no my nabljudaem svet* [1828]). Prejudice is but a fragment of a previous truth, is the unrecognized father of present-day truths, and is rejected by our "proud century" because the deeper sense of "prejudice" eludes us. Primitive man had an inner bond with nature, and nature responded to him with "mutual love." Nature gave man premonitions in a language we no longer understand. Since present-day man scorns "feelings (presentiment), puts his trust in reason, and has given himself to vain research," the "heart of nature" is no longer open to him; and he receives no prophecies (*Primety* [1839]). The other world is hidden only by imaginary ghosts. The "home of spirits" will open to man when he has unhesitatingly set aside this false world of ghosts, the "cloud" (*Tolpe trevožnyj den' priveten* [1839]). Here one hears overtones of the philosophy of the night that was already being developed by Fedor Tjutčev (chapter V, sec. 10 f.). Baratynskij does not necessarily reject reason. Thought unfolds like a flower and bears the seed of new plants (*O, mysl'*! [1832]). The poet thinks of himself as a creator who goes beyond everyday, physical reality to the thought before which earthly life pales as before a sharp sword (*Vse mysl', da mysl'* [1840]).

Baratynskij also wrote nature lyrics. His images of nature, such as autumn (*Padenie list'ev* [1823], *Osen'* [1836–1837]), a waterfall (*Vodopad* [1821–1824]), and a storm (1824), portray not a dead but a living nature, the wordless language of which man "can understand only with his heart." Its turbulent elements, storms and hurricanes, are close to the soul of the poet. Noise and thunder (*šum, rev, gram*) are the voices with which nature speaks to the poet.

Baratynskij wrote a number of epigrams, which, like his poetic maxims, are more profound than witty.

In his efforts to make fresh use of language, Baratynskij accepted the positive changes in meaning that Puškin had made in words such as *mjatežnyj* and *bezumnyj*. At times, he plays with the separate elements of romantic semantic fields (see the beginnings of *Vodopad, Poslednjaja smert'*, and other poems). Neologisms are characteristic of Baratynskij; generally, he uses them in his poetry to avoid a customary expression. As neologisms, they are weak; that is, they are easily understood, since many of them are negations, or antonyms, of words used in normal speech:

bezzabotlivyj, beznagradnyj, bezvesel'e, nedružnyj, neobščij (in the sense of "unusual"), *nečuždaja žizn'*. Neologistic adjectives formed with suffixes are less usual: *pustynničij, prygučij, ulybči-vyj*, and the like. Neologisms in Baratynskij's nouns are perhaps somewhat bolder: *navestitel', lelejatel', upoj* (instead of *upoenie*), *naxod, vyčur, pokorstvo*; and the compound words: *žiznexulenie, sedobradatyj, dušemutitel'nyj, tjaželo-kamennyj, burno-pogodnyj, sladostno-tumannyj, proxladovejnyj*. Some of the neologisms in this last group sound archaic.

Baratynskij's narrative poems *Piry* [Feasts] (1821), *Èda* (1825), and *Bal* [The Ball] (1825–1828) are related to Puškin's Byronic poems in composition and have simple plots. *Èda* is a Finnish girl who is seduced by a foreigner; the heroine of *The Ball* violates social convention, becomes a man's mistress, and pays for her passion with her death; the epic *Feasts* contains a number of observations but no real action. In many respects, these poems are markedly different from the style of other poetry of the time and perhaps for this reason have been unjustly neglected.

23. In a formal sense, Nikolaj Mixajlovič Jazykov (1803–1846) wrote the most brilliant poetry of the age of Puškin. One should not overlook the part he played in destroying classicist poetics.

We have two different images of Jazykov. First, he was a dissolute student at the University of Dorpat and an active member of his fraternity; then, while still in Dorpat, he became a lyric poet. Jazykov was the son of a rich noble family in Simbirsk. When he was eleven, he went to St. Petersburg to study at a technical institute; but his enthusiasm for poetry and other things interfered with his studies, which did not interest him at all. In 1822, he went to Dorpat and remained there for seven years as a student in the philosophy department. From his poetry, one gets an idea of what Jazykov was like at the time, especially in his early phase; but one does not really get to know him completely. Many of his poems are partly or wholly unsuitable for publication. From his correspondence, one knows that he took a serious interest in world literature and the theories of art of the German romantics. He had begun to publish his poetry while still in St. Petersburg. Among others, Anton Del'vig and Puškin took note of him; and during Puškin's "Northern exile" in Mixajlovskoe, Jazykov became acquainted with him. Puškin considered Jazykov more of a poetic ally than were any of his schoolmates or even Baratynskij. But Jazykov was not an uncritical admirer of Puškin. In his letters, he points out weaknesses in *Ruslan and Ljudmila*, in the first chapters of *Evgenij Onegin*, and, later, in Puškin's fairy tales.

In 1829, Jazykov went to Moscow, where he was especially close to the Kireevskij brothers, Petr and Ivan. With Petr, he shared a serious interest in folklore and, with Ivan, an interest in the Russian tradition and past, of which they both took a favorable view. In 1833, Jazykov published his selected poems. Afterward, he lived on his estate; but in 1838, he went abroad to seek relief for a spinal disorder and from the crippling effect that it had had. Until 1843, he lived in Germany, France, and Italy; and during this time, he made friends with Gogol'. After attempts at a cure had proved unsuccessful, Jazykov returned to Moscow and, in the heated atmosphere of the 1840s, joined the Slavophiles.[11] Like Gogol', Jazykov did not completely agree with their theories; but he took part in their literary battles with political radicalism and Westernism. Jazykov was a close literary friend of the poetess Karolina Pavlova. He died in 1846.

As we have said, there are two aspects of Jazykov the poet. But as for his art, one can safely say that he was the most accomplished versifier among Puškin's contemporaries. From 1819 on, this technical mastery is in evidence in his early poems, which are written in part in iambic lines of different lengths. When one considers Jazykov's accomplishment, Puškin's part in the development of modern Russian poetry does not seem quite so great. While in Dorpat, Jazykov turned away from the poetic epistles of his youth and began to concern himself with modern poetry; soon he gave up stanzaic construction in favor of extreme "free form." A large number of his poems are called elegies, but the term suggests neither a specific form nor a specific subject matter. Jazykov's epistles are splendid. Some of them are written to unknown and, at times, dubious ladies; others are to various

11. [On Slavophiles, see Chapter VI.—EDITOR]

casual friends and acquaintances, two of them even to the graphomaniac poet, Count D. Xvostov. There are also epistles to Puškin, and later to the Kireevskij brothers, to Konstantin and Ivan Aksakov, to the poets D. V. Davydov, Baratynskij, and Vjazemskij, to the young Ja. P. Polonskij, to K. K. Pavlova, to Count V. A. Sollogub (see chapter IV, sec. 15) and to Gogol'. These epistles are outpourings of Jazykov's feelings at the moment. All of them contain brilliant lines, pretty images, and well-turned phrases.

Various small groups of Jazykov's poems are devoted to single themes. One thinks first of his student songs with the perpetual, monotonous motifs of this genre, generally written to be sung to the melodies of traditional student drinking songs. Although some of these songs represent astonishing accomplishments in verse technique, by and large they are not an important part of Jazykov's sizable literary legacy. In the 1820s, Jazykov wrote several poems on homesickness and some ballads and balladic poems on themes from Russian history. Here one reads of the singer Bajan, battles with the Tatars, the legendary Evpatij Kolovrat, and the battle on Kulikovo pole [Snipe Field]. Several of these poems are also concerned with Scandinavia and the Baltic region. There are lovely descriptions of nature in the part of the country where Jazykov met Puškin. Later, Jazykov wrote poems in Bad Gastein, Johannisberg, and Nice. Although one of his poems is in praise of the Rhine, he grew more and more homesick while he was abroad. Two recurrent motifs reflect Jazykov's view of the world: the poet as genius, as the "elect of heaven," as "priest," and the lonely sailor at sea who may reach the distant land of his desires if he is strong enough in mind and will (*Plovec* [1829]). In his later years, Jazykov made sporadic attempts to write poems based on the Psalms and political poems against the Westernizers. Jazykov's long fairy tales, among them *Žar-ptica* [Firebird] (1836), are far removed from real folklore.

In Jazykov, one often finds attractive images of a kind unusual in Russian literature. He compares forgetting momentary, whimsical moods and feelings with the "vapor of breath" that disappears from clean glass (*tak par dyxanija/sletaet s čistogo stekla*); or, contrary to the Russian romantic tradition, he notices that the wave is a catachrestic metaphor for the agitated human soul: "the wave sparkles and foams in the rays of golden light, but remains cold." One also finds pretty images of night. The iambic tetrameter line that is prevalent in Puškin is typical of Jazykov as well.

A peculiarity of Jazykov is his predilection for unusual words and bold neologisms, which he creates masterfully for the context at hand. Jazykov's neologisms are more numerous and more daring than Baratynskij's; they are "strong" neologisms. Among his "weak" coinages are compound words, such as *krovopijstvo, carevenčanie, vodobeg, čertopljas, vetrokrylyj, vetroletnyj, nepro-xodimo-bespokojno, svobodno-šumnyj,* and *dostopamjatno-živoj.* Other examples are *razglašenie, podaren'ice, podružnik,* the verbs *putevodit', protoržestvovat', peretoskovat',* the adjectives and participles *potemnelyj, brodjažnyj, rassvetnyj, razobmanutyj, povsjudnyj,* and so on. Here the changes that Jazykov makes are sometimes minor, for instance, *gololed'* for *gololedica.* But one also finds in Jazykov a great many strong neologisms, such as the nouns *kričal'ščik, tainstvennik* (for *sekretar'*), *lošadinnik, čužemy-slitel', stolbnica,* the adjectives *zvonkokopytnyj, pennokipučij, burnonogij, nepoščadnyj, otryvnyj, zabral'nyj,* the verbs *duša prjamit'sja, sostukivat'sja* (with cups), *perekočkat'* (*put'*), and so on. The meanings of some words are changed: *pravoslavno* means *istinno; prostuda* means *oxlaždenie* (normally, these words mean "of the Orthodox faith" and "a cold"). The meanings of word combinations are altered especially often: *pustynnaja sinica, dorožnyj poèt, vozmutitel'nye oči, otkrovennoe* (that is, causing one to be open) *vino, zakonnik Feba, kamennosečnyj kumir, besprijutnyj sad, tabačnyj brat,* and the like.

Jazykov used the plural of nouns that existed only in the singular and the singular of *pluralia tantum,* a practice that one also finds later in Russian verse. It is, of course, sometimes diffi-cult to tell whether one is dealing with a neologism or simply a seldom-used word.

24. The age of Puškin saw a great many men turn to literature. It is as though the atmosphere of the times required everyone to engage in some literary, linguistic, or creative activity. There

have been a number of such periods in the history of the Slavic literatures, for instance, Czech literature in the late Middle Ages or Croatian literature in Dubrovnik in the sixteenth and seventeenth centuries. In any case, it is important to bear in mind that it was not just due to the influence of Puškin that literature flourished in Russia at this time.

When we speak of "lesser writers," we are thinking of writers outside the mainstream of literary development. Some of them wrote a great deal.

The first of these "lesser writers" one should mention is Dmitrij Vladimirovič Venevitinov (1805–1827), whose early death prevented him from writing very much. He came from an old aristocratic family, went to the boarding school for young noblemen at Moscow University, and was a member of V. F. Odoevskij's circle (see chapter IV, sec. 1). In 1824, Venevitinov began working in the Moscow archives of the Foreign Office; in 1826, he moved to St. Petersburg, and there he died, early the next year.

His poems deal mainly with questions requiring philosophical treatment, in particular with the question of the vocation of the poet. He writes somewhat more glowingly on this subject than do other Russian romanticists. In Venevitinov's view, the poet is the pupil of the muses, the son of the gods, or, in more general terms, the supreme being among men; the poet is able to express his experiences adequately and poetry is superior to the power of reason. Venevitinov played a particularly important part in the development of philosophical Russian. All of Odoevskij's circle were engaged with the philosophy of Schelling. In several essays, some of them published posthumously, Venevitinov gave the best account of Schelling's ideas on aesthetics.

Venevitinov's elegiac poems are in the style that had become traditional by 1825. He left fragments of plays, epics, and a novel.

Prince Aleksandr Ivanovič Odoevskij (1802–1839) was from an old aristocratic family. He was educated at home and entered the guards at an early age, in 1821. In 1825, he joined the Decembrists and was arrested along with the others and exiled to Siberia, although he had been a member of the secret society for only a short time and, when questioned, denied having had close ties with the ideology and activities of the group. After years at forced labor, he was allowed to settle in Siberia, and in 1837 he was permitted to go and fight as a private with the Russian army in the Caucasus. That same year, he met Lermontov. In 1839, Aleksandr Odoevskij died of malaria. Whether or not he really wrote a great number of poems that have been lost, as his friends in Siberia maintained, is a matter of conjecture.

Aleksandr Odoevskij's poems are historical ballads, concerned with the love of freedom; but above all, they are elegiac reflections on personal experiences, such as the tragic death of Aleksandr Griboedov. Among Odoevskij's early poems is *Bal*, in which the poet sees a brilliant ball as a party of dancing skeletons. Like Baratynskij, Aleksandr Odoevskij is given to expressing his thoughts pointedly. Especially characteristic is a twelve-line poem on the poet. The enthusiasm of the poet who has not yet begun to write and seek his "too early crown" is his "sacred dream" (*son svjaščennyj*), for this poet reveals to the world the "unknown song," one that has been hidden like a sound in the "still lyre." Every line of the poem is pointed, sometimes rather obscurely, as is the case with many of A. I. Odoevskij's elegies. One also finds in Odoevskij's work early Slavophile ideals, as in *Slavic Girls* (1828 or 1829).

Fedor Nikolaevič Glinka (1786–1880) was also associated with the Decembrists, but he was imprisoned for only a short time and then exiled to Karelia. Glinka began writing poetry at an early age and subsequently wrote a classicist tragedy on liberty (*Vel'zen or Holland Liberated*, an unhistorical work [1808–1810]). He wrote patriotic poems during the Napoleonic Wars, religious hymns, lyric poems, and in later years, together with his wife, he wrote a long religious epic, *Mysterious Drop* (the milk of the Mother of God, a legend apparently of his own invention but analagous in some respects to the legend of the Holy Grail). Apart from its pretty passages, Glinka's poetry is distinguished by its use of words from various lexical levels, a feature that prompted Puškin to comment ironically on the "dashing" ("*uxarskij*") vocabulary of the religious poems. Glinka also uses dialectal forms and foreign words (Finnish and Ukrainian). At an early age, he began translating Czech songs. His themes are those that later became typical of Russian romanticism. Amid living nature, which speaks a secret language, the sea, waterfalls, and night landscapes particularly attract the poet. Within the human soul, he turns his attention to dreams and madness, that is, to the "night side of the soul." Man is a pilgrim in a boat. Later this comparison was typical of Aleksandr Poležaev and Lermontov. The "Plantonic" image of flying and hovering recurs often in Glinka. Like other Russian romanticists, he devotes several poems to the poet, who has two different egos, and to poetry, the task of which is to tell the inexpressible, *neizrečennoe*. One finds these motifs repeatedly in Glinka's later poetry. Later, too, under the influence of the movements of the 1840s, his naive patriotism of the Napoleonic Wars was transformed into Slavophilism.

Petr Aleksandrovič Pletnev (1792–1865) was a professor of literature at the University of St. Petersburg. He is remembered mainly as a friend of Puškin, who dedicated *Evgenij Onegin* to him. He was also a friend of Gogol' and of other writers. In the 1820s, Pletnev published some poems of his own that dealt with typical romantic themes: night, the sea, poetic enthusiasm, and so forth. They are noteworthy for the interest that Pletnev took in shorter forms (cf. later Tjutčev).

Denis Vasil'evič Davydov (1784–1839) was the most original of the lesser romantic poets. As an officer in a hussar regiment, Davydov waged guerrilla warfare against Napoleon's troops in Russia. In his poems, he displays two different personalities. Apart from his famed hussar poems—on wildly martial themes, wine, and tobacco—he wrote important love elegies, which reveal a quite different side of him. His love culminates in a romantic mood of prayer. Davydov is also a witty epigrammatist and is the author of a well-known satirical song directed at liberals or pseudoliberals. He is by no means a dilettante in prose; as one reads him, one realizes that he is familiar with Russian and Western European literature and that he does not regard writing as a mere hobby.

25. Ivan Ivanovič Kozlov (1779–1840) enjoyed a special kind of fame. He was an officer in the guards and later an official. In 1816, he became paralyzed; and in 1821, he went blind. During his illness, Kozlov developed into an accomplished linguist, translating poetry by Byron and the English romanticists, French and Italian works, and the "Crimean Sonnets" by the Polish poet Adam Mickiewicz. It was not just his personal misfortune that made Kozlov popular, but his melodic, sentimental poetry as well, which was much like that of his friend Žukovskij. Especially famous were Kozlov's own poem *Černec* [The Monk] (1825), in which the hero loses his family tragically; and his translation of Thomas Moore's *Those Evening Bells, Večernij zvon*, in which one finds various striking romantic images. In other poems of Kozlov one finds thoughts on the "secret" language of nature that "whispers of miraculous things." The subject matter of the lyric poem *Bezumnaja* [The Mad Woman] (1830), which has almost no story, is typical. Since Kozlov did not begin writing until 1821, there are in his poetry scarcely any of the classicist overtones so audible in the writing of many Russian romanticists.

26. Pavel Aleksandrovič Katenin (1792–1853) occupies a rather unusual place in the history of romanticism. As a translator, he was a belated popularizer of French classicist tragedy; but he was also one of the first Russian romanticists and, in some respects, he was a forerunner of the subsequent romantic nationalism. In his late work *Invalid Gorev* (1836), Katenin strikes notes that one does not hear again until the time of the Russian realist poets, some fifteen years later.

Early in his career, Katenin was a public official and an army officer. In 1820, he was discharged from the service; and in 1822, he was banished from both capitals over a minor affair. From 1833 to 1838, he served in the army again, primarily in the Caucasus; then he was discharged for good and spent the rest of his life on his estate.

Some of Katenin's contemporaries thought of him as a romanticist in his writing; others viewed him as a belated classicist. His most important, if not his most extensive work, his ballads, are certainly a part of Russian romanticism. The first of them was a

Russified translation of Goethe's *Der Sänger* (1814). This was followed by *Nataša* (1815), *Ubijca* [The Murderer] (1815), *Lešij* [The Wood Spirit] (1815), and *Ol'ga* (1816). These ballads, particularly *The Murderer* and *Ol'ga*, are counterparts of Žukovskij's gentle ballads. Katenin's images are purely Russian, and the *Sänger* is even moved to the court of the Kievan Prince Vladimir. In *Ol'ga*, Gottfried Bürger's *Lenore* is set in a Russian village, and the language is not that of polite society, but of the common people. Even romanticists accustomed to using the "modern" language of the time felt that many of Katenin's expressions were intolerably vulgar—in *The Murderer:* "*na mesjac pjališ' oči*"; "*ne bab'e delo*"; "*ja s ruk sbyl duraka*"; "*mesjac . . . prokljatyj*"; "*ne sterpevši kazni . . . izdox*"; and the famous apostrophe to the moon: "*Smotri, plešivyj!*" ["Look here, bald-headed one!"]. There are a great many similar passages in Katenin's other ballads. In contrast to *Ljudmila*, Žukovskij's milder version of *Lenore*, Katenin uses coarse, biting language in his *Ol'ga* and comes closer to the spirit of Bürger's ballad. In Žukovskij, the mood around the gallows is described; "*šorox tixix tenej*," in Katenin: "*adskoj svoloči skakan'e, smex i pljaski v vyšine.*" In Žukovskij, ghosts are described: "*Legkim, svetlym xorovodom v cep' vozdušnuju svilis', vot za nimi poneslis'*"; in Katenin: "*Svoloč' s pesnej zaunyvnoj poneslas' za sedokom.*" Žukovskij writes: "*Veetsja legkij veterok; budto pleščet ručeek*"; in *Ol'ga*, Katenin writes: "*Slovno vixor' by poryvnyj zašumel v boru syrom.*"[12] Nikolaj Gnedič disapproved of *Ol'ga*, and he was not alone; he was joined by Konstantin Batjuškov, Ivan Dmitriev, V. L. Puškin, and Petr Vjazemskij. Aleksandr Griboedov supported Katenin, however; and A. S. Puškin remained full of praise for Katenin's ballads. Puškin's ballads *Ženix* [The Bridegroom] (1825) and *Utoplennik* [The Drowned Man] (1828) are similar to Katenin's in

12. Following are parallel translations of the quotations above; Žukovskij is Z; Katenin, K: "Rustle of the gentle shadows (ghosts)" (Z); "the leaping of the hellish riffraff, laughing and dancing on high" (K). The spirits "formed a light and luminary ring in an airy chain and chased after them" (Z); "with a mournful song the riffraff chased the rider" (K). "The light breeze is blowing as though a brook were splashing" (Z); "as though the stormy wind were roaring in a damp pine forest" (K).

style and language. In his late idyll *Invalid Gorev*, Katenin adds realistic detail to his vernacular language. In his view of the national character (*narodnost'*), Katenin is a true romanticist. Wilhelm Küchelbecker thought of Katenin this way, as a genuine romanticist, although Katenin wavered between considering himself a "true romantic" (according to his friend N. Baxtin in 1828) and denying that there could be such a thing as Russian romanticism, since romanticism seemed too closely related to the Western Middle Ages (1830). On the other hand, the language in many of Katenin's works is such that he was unjustly included among the classicists. The reasons for this were his translations of French classicist tragedies and comedies and his use of Church Slavonicisms, which are certainly no more numerous or difficult in Katenin than in the writers of the Karamzin School. Katenin's translations (Dante, *Poema del Cid*), his attempts at drama (in particular the tragedy *Andromaxa*, 1827), and his original works on classical themes (Sophocles, Homer, Sappho) and Old Russian themes are interesting in form and content but did not secure their author a significant place among his contemporaries.

Katenin was more influential as a teacher (*maître*), and both Aleksandr Puškin and Griboedov acknowledged their debt to him. Katenin's critical articles, which appeared in the *Literaturnaja Gazeta* (1830–1831, published by Del'vig with Puškin's active collaboration) were highly regarded, and deservedly so.

IV

Romantic Prose

1. Prose was not at first an important part of Russian romanticism. But, as we have seen, in the course of his development Aleksandr Puškin turned more and more to prose. Other prose writers were also read and appreciated. We shall examine in some detail the most important of them, Nikolaj Vasil'evič Gogol', and consider his contemporaries as merely a background for the works of Gogol'.

The first writer to be discussed left no verse, but he has been mentioned several times already. He is Prince Vladimir Fedorovič Odoevskij (1804–1869), cousin of Aleksandr Ivanovič Odoevskij. We still do not know V. F. Odoevskij well enough, although attempts have been made in the last few years to make his work more widely available. V. F. Odoevskij was a restless personality, and during his years at the noblemen's boarding school of Moscow University he gathered around him a group of friends who were interested in philosophy. After graduation, they remained in touch and adopted the name *Ljubomudry*, the literal Russian equivalent of "philosophers." Among the writers and thinkers in Vladimir Odoevskij's circle were Dmitrij Venevitinov, Mixail Pogodin, Ivan and Petr Kireevskij, Fedor Tjutčev, and Stepan Ševyrev. Later, V. F. Odoevskij and Wilhelm Küchelbecker became friends, and together they published the quarterly *Mnemozina*. Vladimir Odoevskij seems to have been instrumental in calling attention to German philosophy, in particular to the study of Schelling and his followers. After the Decembrist Revolt, the philosophical circle dissolved. From 1827 to 1830, the same circle published the magazine *Moskovskij vestnik*. In 1825, V. F. Odoevskij went to St. Petersburg and met the Schellingian professor D. M. Vellanskij, who appears to have broadened Odoevskij's knowledge of German philosophy. Odoevskij turned to German mysticism, which was one of Schelling's sources. We find reflections of this interest in Vladimir Odoevskij's extensive writings on philosophy and aesthetics, which to a large extent were made known posthumously, and in his novellas, some of which were not published or not completed. Although V. F. Odoevskij calls Schelling the discoverer (the Columbus) of the soul, one wonders why he does so when one considers that Odoevskij learned of Schelling's works from Schelling scholars whom one thinks of as psychologists: H. G. von Schubert, J. J. Wagner, Lorenz Oken (actually, Ockenfuss), and others. Perhaps he meant to imply that Schelling rejected the sovereignty of reason. V.F. Odoevskij was influenced by Schelling and by mysticism, primarily that of Böhme and his followers; he was also indebted to Schiller's aesthetic, and he made use of the writings of the Eastern Church Fathers. His extensive sources have not been entirely accounted for. Many thoughts that Vladimir Odoevskij merely touches on turn up in other Russian romanticists, of whom a number were in contact with Odoevskij.

Later, in 1844, V.F. Odoevskij put together a number of his novellas to make the lovely and almost forgotten *Russkie noči* [Russian Nights]. The stories are framed by a conversation among friends discussing the fundamentals of the romantic view of the world. The author takes part in the discussion, assuming the role of the "Russian Faust." By this time, after 1840, V. F. Odoevskij had modified his more pronounced views; and, as a result, his ideas are more clearly defined in his early writings and in the earlier editions of his novellas.

In scope and style, his novellas are quite different. Vladimir Odoevskij cannot really be compared with E. T. A. Hoffmann, since there are few obvious parallels in their work. In his novellas on artists, Odoevskij dealt with some of the same themes that one finds in Hoffmann; but this can be explained by the fact that they were both writing in the spirit of the times. Odoevskij's rather

severe criticism of social conditions, in particular of social conventions, is a reflection on the reality of life in Russia. Odoevskij's
criticism of the Enlightenment goes deeper than does Hoffmann's.
On the other hand, Odoevskij does not have Hoffmann's careless
but lively narrative art. By and large, Odoevskij's novellas are
simply-related happenings that charm the reader with their
content and their almost inevitable "moral"; the style is seasoned
only by the gentle humor of the author and by his occasional
biting satire. Odoevskij worked on his novellas long and pains-
takingly and attempted always to individualize the speech of his
characters. He made interesting use of jargon and appears to have
been the first writer in Russian literature to employ rogue's slang
(in *Živoj mertvec*, which appeared in 1838, that is, after Gogol's
work had begun to come out.)

For the most part, the themes of Vladimir Odoevskij's novellas
are purely romantic. The defense of madness, which he associates
with creative genius, is a prevalent theme in his novellas on artists
(*Sebastian Bach, Beethoven's Last Quartet, The Improvisator, G.
Piranesi*—all of them in *Russian Nights*), in which he portrays
great musicians and artists as men possessed and strangers in this
world. V. F. Odoevskij was himself a musician and made a considerable contribution to Russian music; among other things, he
introduced Richard Wagner to Russia. Several novellas have to
do with the intervention of supernatural forces, for example, the
nature spirits. There are satirical novellas aimed at the nobility
(*Princess Zizi, Princess Mimi, Nasmeška mertveca*), which Odoevskij knew well and which Lev Tolstoj later portrayed. But the
height of V. F. Odoevskij's satire is his "negative Utopias," which
recall Baratynskij's pessimistic poems (the decline of social life
and of the life of the individual in a world based on the ideas of the
Enlightenment: *Poslednee samoubijstvo* in *Russian Nights* and
Gorod bez imeni). The fantastic technological Utopian story, *The
Year 4338*, first published in 1926, consists of letters sent from
Moscow to a friend by a Chinese student and is unfinished; V. F.
Odoevskij published only a few fragments of the work. The level
of technology that he portrays in the forty-fourth century comes
as no surprise to us today. Like Puškin and Gogol', V. F. Odoevskij
also wrote "realistic stories," that is, scenes from the prosaic

everyday lives of the common people. He may have been the first to popularize the theme of the unfortunate "petty official," a motif later in Gogol' and Dostoevskij (see sec. 16 below). Vladimir Odoevskij also wrote excellent children's stories.

We cannot deal with Odoevskij's theoretical views in detail. They go back to the sources already mentioned. Odoevskij defends the ideal of total culture, in which reason does not predominate and religion and art also play important parts. Reason and empiricism give a one-sided picture of reality; the totality of things can be realized only through art (as Schiller says). This totality of being that is achieved through art is similar to man's original condition. All things in nature are connected, and every element of reality is reflected in many other things. (In addition to the influence of mystics, I find here an influence from Oken's works on natural philosophy.) In cultural history, Vladimir Odoevskij thought that there had been a diminution of man's spiritual powers. Previously, instincts (*instinktual'nye sily*) had kept man closer to nature; and nature spoke to the "primitive" prehistoric man in a language that civilized men have now forgotten (cf. Baratynskij). True art can perhaps restore these or similar powers to man; but, at least in his novellas, V. F. Odoevskij takes a dim view of the future of an enlightened mankind.

Typically, Odoevskij believes (see *Russian Nights*) that the harmful effects of the Enlightenment have already gone too far in Western Europe. What is needed is a fresh, new people to rescue and restore culture, and the Russians are particularly qualified to revive the spiritual life of Europe. So one finds in V. F. Odoevskij many of the ideas that were later to appear in Slavophilism (see chapter VII, sec. 3). After 1850, he turned to new tasks. He was an enthusiastic supporter of the emancipation of the serfs and devoted much time and energy to improving education. Whether or not he really went over to "positivism" one cannot be sure until the manuscripts of his later years are carefully examined and published.

2. Another prose writer of the time was Aleksandr Aleksandrovič Bestužev (1797–1837), who later took the pen name "Marlinskij." Bestužev was from St. Petersburg. He attended various

schools there, entered the guards in 1816, and the next year became an officer. He soon met the Decembrist poets, took part in
their literary activities (*Poljarnaja zvezda*), and joined their
secret organization. Along with his four brothers, Bestužev par-
ticipated in the Decembrist Revolt and was exiled to Siberia, but
in 1829 he received permission to go to the Caucasus as a private
in the army. There he was killed in 1837. There is a legend that he
took refuge among the Caucasian mountaineers; but, in any case,
his body was never found.

Even before his exile, Bestužev was thought to be one of the
most promising writers of the day. He had published excellent
surveys of Russian literature up to 1825 and a number of poems, in
which he had begun gradually to break away from classicist
poetics. These studies are useful in evaluating his own trend
toward romanticism. He published several novellas, some based
on Russian history, some on the history of the Baltic region. The
novella *Roman and Olga* (1823) deals with the struggle for the
liberation of Novgorod in the fourteenth century. Roman goes as
an ambassador to Moscow and is taken prisoner. His fiancée,
Olga, waits for him in vain until he is freed by brigands from Novgorod; he fights for Novgorod against Moscow and then returns
home safely to Olga. As in several of his shorter novellas, Bestužev
attempts here to render the language of the past, but confines
himself by and large to using isolated archaisms. As a result, men
of the fourteenth century appear to act and react as do Bestužev's
contemporaries. His Baltic novellas stress even more his ideal of
liberty: *Wenden Castle* (1823); *Neuhausen Castle* (1824); *Eisen
Castle* and *The Revel Tournament* (both 1825). The stories have the
same theme. Using historical sources, Bestužev portrays strong
men getting revenge (*Wenden Castle, Neuhausen Castle, Eisen
Castle*) and the incredible success of a Revel merchant's son at a
tournament, where he also wins the hand of a young noblewoman.
Bestužev sets these events between the thirteenth and sixteenth
centuries. More important than the historical color of the stories
is Bestužev's criticism of social inequality and oppression. Many
passages sound as though they were taken from the plays of
Schiller. The criticism of conventions in a chivalric society is not
particularly relevant to the story; and the action is concentrated

on a small group of characters who speak an individual but too literary language, full of witticisms, metaphors, and similes. There is even more literary decoration in the brief tales told by officers in the two short sketches *Evenings on Bivouac* and *Night Guard* (1823).

After Bestužev's exile, his literary career took an unusual turn. He assumed the pen name Marlinskij and became even more famous than he had been before. He published his new novellas in various magazines, first under the initials "A. M." and later under "Marlinskij." Although Bestužev did not hesitate to refer to the Caucasus and his stay there, few people seem to have known who the mysterious new writer was. In 1830, he began publishing novellas, the first of them on society life: *Ispytanie* [The Test], *Večer na kavkazskix vodax* [Evening in a Caucasian Spa], both 1830; and *Strašnoe gadanie* [A Terrible Fortunetelling] (1831). All the stories are exciting. The first of them is about a complicated love affair. The second novella begins on an evening in the Caucasus, and a narrator tells three stories involving ghosts, thieves, and all sorts of horrors. Bestužev next published novellas about the period of the Napoleonic Wars. *Lieutenant Belozor* (1831) is the story of a lieutenant of the fleet who finds himself in Holland during the French occupation. He is taken in and hidden by a Dutch manufacturer. The manufacturer's daughter falls in love with the lieutenant, and the love story and the hero's exciting escape are cleverly woven together. Another novella tells the story of a guerrilla officer (*Latnik* [A Cuirassier], 1832); and *More-xod Nikitin* [The Sailor Nikitin] (1834) is supposedly based on a true incident that took place in 1810: Nikitin captures an English ship in the White Sea after the Treaty of Tilsit. In 1833, a society love novella appeared, *Fregat Nadežda* [The Frigate Hope], along with several sketches of the Caucasus written partly in the form of letters. The two longest of Bestužev's novellas, *Ammalat-Bek* (1832) and *Mulla-Nur* (1836), may actually be thought of as novels. These are the first of the more important Russian novellas on life in the Caucasus and are the predecessors of Mixail Lermontov's poems and novellas and of Lev Tolstoj's *Xadži Murat*. In both works, Bestužev portrays life in the Caucasus and at the same time tells an exciting narrative. In *Ammalat-Bek*, he characterizes the primitive people of the region, through the contact of his hero with the civilized world; in *Mulla-Nur*, through the portrayal of the people's milieu. Poetical ornamentation is used sparingly in the first novella, perhaps because of the considerable action. The second novella is written in a stylized florid language in the Oriental tradition, is adorned with a great many foreign words, and thus gave rise to a tradition that has been parodied in our time by the Soviet writers Il'f and Petrov.

The plot of *Ammalat-Bek* is based on a true incident. While fighting against the Russians, Ammalat-Bek is taken prisoner. A high Russian officer intercedes for him and arranges for his release, but Ammalat-Bek murders his Russian protector. Marlinskij makes use of this incident to contrast the moral attitudes of the Russians and the Caucasian mountaineers. One finds the same method used later in Dostoevskij's *Memoirs from the House of the Dead* and Lev Tolstoj's *Xadži Murat*. In Bestužev, this contrast has little to do with Rousseau's idealization of primitive man and is more closely related to Byron. It is an attitude based on the observations of a perceptive author who views the whole Caucasian war as a tragic mistake. Ammalat-Bek is almost a Byronic hero in his quest of liberty.

Mulla-Nur is set in the milieu of a Caucasian people. Mulla-Nur himself appears only briefly, and the story is mainly about the lovesickness and adventures of young Iskander. An epilogue tells of the narrator's encounter with Mulla-Nur, a heroic brigand who has helped the unfortunate Iskander. The novella is full of quotations in Oriental languages, and the life of the Caucasian people and their surroundings are portrayed in a style heavy with Oriental decoration.

The principal feature of Marlinskij's novella style is the wealth of metaphors used by the narrator and his characters, regardless of their social rank or nationality. Here is a characteristic sample from a description of officers celebrating.

No matter how happy the guests were or how frank their conversations, the talk began to languish and the laughter faded like Cleopatra's pearls in their cups . . . even the various toasts, in the invention of which a hussar's imagination can compete with a kaleidoscope—

gradually everything grew dull. The wits were annoyed because no one listened to them; those who liked jokes were annoyed because no one made them laugh. The tongue on which, I know not why, gravity worked the quickest grew tired of raising itself to the palate. The exclamations, sighs, and the clouds of tobacco smoke climbing from the mouths grew less and less frequent; and a great yawn flew from mouth to mouth like an electric spark.

Descriptions of landscapes are similarly ornamental (cf. Gogol'). So, for instance, when asked about the weather, a modest mountaineer answers:

The mountains are covered with a gilding made by God. The sea shines like a mirror. The flag on the fortress Naryn-Kale embraces the flagpole as a garment embraces the waist of a beautiful girl. Along the coast no waves are breaking into sprays of pearls. Curls of dust on the road are not ruffled by the least trace of wind. Everything is calm at sea, peaceful on land, clear in the sky.

Marlinskij's principal characters use just as many metaphors and similes. "One must feed oneself on the spark of glances and the smoke of hope." "The explosion of her fantasy cast me too high into the air." "The floor in the salon seemed to me to sway, and I went around every china vase as though it were a stone in the sea." "The devil himself cooks snow and rocks in the mountains to catch drowned men in the murky water." Bestužev's maxims are similar. "In the book of love, the pages of mistakes are the most beautiful." "There is nothing sweeter than dreams in the morning. The debt of weariness is already paid, and the soul gradually overcomes the influences of the body."

One should add that, in the text of Bestužev's narratives, there are a great many quotations and maxims from various literatures, names, and bits of information.

3. There were, of course, historical novels in Russia; but, although some writers imitated Walter Scott very ably, their work lagged far behind the shorter novellas of Puškin, Marlinskij, and Gogol'. Among these writers of historical novels were Mixail Nikolaevič Zagoskin (1789–1852) and Ivan Ivanovič Lažečnikov

(1792–1869). They deserve to be treated more fully in a history of Russian culture than in a literary history, since they considerably influenced the way in which many Russians interpreted their country's past. Both writers were sufficiently patriotic to appeal to the hearts of their readers, and both knew how to tell an exciting story with facility and clarity. Nevertheless, their language is colorless, and they are too close to the Karamzin tradition. Perhaps it was difficult for writers of the time to avoid Karamzin's influence.

Mixail Zagoskin was the son of a provincial landowner and was an officer during Napoleon's invasion of Russia. After the war, he lived in St. Petersburg and Moscow and in 1831 became director of the Moscow Theater (at the time, all theaters were "Imperial"). He wrote several plays that were soon forgotten but was successful as a novelist. Despite his rather superficial education, Zagoskin wrote two famous novels, *Jurij Miloslavskij ili russkie v 1612 godu* [Jurij Miloslavskij or the Russians in the Year 1612] (1829) and *Roslavlev ili russkie v 1812 godu* [Roslavlev or the Russians in the Year 1812] (1831). They idealize Russian history and portray the patriotism of the Russians, during the interregnum of the seventeenth century in the first novel and the Napoleonic campaign of 1812 in the second. The personalities of the principal characters are not clearly defined, and their fate depends almost entirely on external events. In *Roslavlev*, however, Zogoskin attempts to treat a deeper theme. The heroine of the novel, Polina, gives her love and hand to a Frenchman—that is, to an "enemy of the fatherland"—and is brought to ruin by this rash action. She also suffers various reverses, such as the death of her child. The primitiveness of the story annoyed Puškin, who began a reply in the form of a novel, in which he pretended to be personally acquainted with the characters of Zagoskin's novel.[1] Unfortunately this literary reply was not finished, and Puškin did not get around to dealing with the main question of the polemic. Nevertheless, the conversations of Zagoskin's characters, who all speak very much alike, are quite lively. The ideological views

1. [Puškin's fragment of this story, likewise entitled *Roslavlev*, is written in the form of the memoirs of a lady who witnessed the events of Russia's invasion by Napoleon in 1812.—EDITOR]

sometimes expressed by the characters are primitive. Zagoskin's novel *Askol'dova mogila* [Askold's Grave] (1833) is known thanks only to Verstovskij's opera based on the novel.

Perhaps more important as a stylist was Ivan Lažečnikov, whose father, a merchant, saw to it that he had a good education. Lažečnikov studied various writers and attempted to imitate their language; but his most important novels appeared too late, that is, after Gogol' had come on the scene. These works were *Poslednij novik* [The Last Novik][2] (1831–1833); *Ledjanoj dom*, [The House of Ice] (1835), and *Basurman* [The Infidel] (1838). Lažečnikov was able to awaken the reader's interest in the past without glorifying it unduly; at times, he portrays rather vividly the darker chapters of history. His novels are less "historical" than are Zagoskin's, although their historical trappings are much richer and their historical facts are dealt with more faithfully. But for the most part, historical events are merely a backdrop for fictitious adventures. "Novik" is an imaginary nephew of Peter the Great and is supposed to have got mixed up in the events of the Northern War. The hero of the *House of Ice*, which is built on the Neva at the behest of the Russian Empress Anna, is the minister A. P. Volynskij, who is executed because of his opposition to the ruling party. Lažečnikov devises a love story for Volynskij. *The Infidel* is a fifteenth-century German doctor who fights against injustice, is put down by a court intrigue, and is executed. Historical facts in this and in Lažečnikov's other novels are limited to occasional, sometimes very colorful scenes. Lažečnikov's characters are more individualized than are Zagoskin's; and his language is embellished with "archaisms," most of them still understandable. Often Lažečnikov takes vernacular expressions of his own time to be archaic, and in this he is usually mistaken.

It is almost inconceivable that Vissarion G. Belinskij, who is often said to be a major critic, could have hailed the works of these two novelists and could at the same time have "deposed" Mar-

2. [The sixteenth- and seventeenth-century term *novik* was applied either to young noblemen beginning at the age of fifteen who were already registered for military service but had not yet served, or to such noblemen who had already served in the army but had not yet received the usual remuneration in the form of lands or estates.—EDITOR]

linskij and Baratynskij. Despite certain appealing features, the
works of Zagoskin and Lažečnikov by no means represent a step
forward to the "realistic" historical novel, but rather a step backward to the adventure novels of the pre-Karamzin period.

4. Ivan Lažečnikov was not the first writer to come from a
family of Russian merchants, a milieu already disparaged and
later called the "kingdom of darkness." The somewhat younger
Nikolaj Alekseevič Polevoj (1796–1846) had already appeared in
print. The son of a merchant, Polevoj was born in Irkutsk, Siberia,
but as a boy he had moved with his parents to their native Kursk in
European Russia. Later he began to write and publish in Moscow.
From 1825 to 1834, he published a good, modern magazine,
Moskovskij telegraf (the telegraph referred to was, of course, the
optical kind, which played an important part in communications
as early as the eighteenth century). Petr A. Vjazemskij was a
frequent contributor to the magazine, and Polevoj saw in him
an ally in promoting his own romantic ideas. In 1829, Vjazemskij
broke off with Polevoj, and in 1834 the *Moskovskij telegraf* was
closed by the authorities. Afterward, Polevoj wrote very little
of consequence, although he had published several interesting
novellas and novels of his own in his magazine. In addition to
his creative work, Polevoj wrote a *History of the Russian People*
in six volumes (1829–1833), which, as its title suggests, was
intended to be a counterpart of Karamzin's *History of the Russian
State* but which, in contrast to Karamzin's work, was no more
than a compilation.

Polevoj's creative works are in the typical genres of romantic
prose. The novel one should mention first is *Živopisec* [The
Painter] (1833), which deals with a specifically Russian theme—
the lot of a middle-class artist in the cultural life of Russia. At
the time, cultural life was controlled primarily by the "educated"
classes, the nobility and the clergy (who seldom kept pace with
each other). Polevoj does not think of the problem of his hero,
Arkadij, the son of a petty official, as a social, political, or legal
one; instead, Polevoj is concerned with the psychological conflict
between the modest, creative hero (who reminds one of some of
Dostoevskij's characters) and the society world that is interested

only in material and fashionable things. Dying of consumption, Arkadij defends various romantic interpretations of art, which range from the rebellious Byronic concept, expressed in his picture *Prometheus*, to Christian piety (that of the Nazarenes?), to which his last picture, *Christ Blessing the Children*, is supposed to be devoted. Polevoj's *Abbaddonna* (*sic*) (1834, epilogue 1838) is another novel about an artist. The main character is the German poet Reichenbach, who is torn between an idyllic love for the mayor's daughter, Henriette, and the passion to which the "Abbaddonna," Leonora, the society lady, had diverted him. The triumph of idyllic love is brought about by the realization that the true poet is alone when confronted with vanity and the "deceptive splendor of worldy relations." The short novel *Blaženstvo bezumija* [The Bliss of Madness] (1833), is also interesting. In it, imaginary love for a woman who appears as a phantom is portrayed as a great joy and is contrasted with the desolation of everyday life. The long novel *Kljatva pri grobe Gospodnem* [An Oath at the Lord's Sepulchre] (1832) deals with the political conflicts in fifteenth-century Russia. Although the novel seems unhistorical to us now, one recognizes Polevoj's gift for presenting scenes and moods of the masses. In contrast to most Russian historical novels of his time, Polevoj's work does not focus attention on great persons, or supposedly great persons, and does not go in for the usual rhetoric in the dialogue of noted people. Even before the rather weak *History of the Russian People*, this novel reveals Polevoj's unrealized intention of giving the people a place in history.

Among Polevoj's novellas, *Rasskazy russkogo soldata* [The Tales of a Russian Soldier] (1829) should be mentioned. Here he pictures the life of the common people, peasants and soldiers, plainly, without pathos, and almost in the same style of "portraying reality" (or, as it was later called, from the French, "physiological sketches") that was to become popular during the time of the Natural School (see sec. 16, below). Polevoj's style is less colorful here than in his other novellas and novels, where he uses a bright palette and different styles. His ornamentation is often too heavy, and at times he is almost on a par with Marlinskij. (Some of Marlinskij's work was published in the *Moskovskij telegraf*). Polevoj also wrote clever parodies of other writers, even of Puškin and Gogol', and humorous poems, most of which he collected in *Novyj Živopisec* [The New Painter] (six volumes, 1832).

5. Mixail Petrovič Pogodin (1800–1875) was the son of a serf, a servant of Count I. P. Saltykov. A historian and dedicated collector of old manuscripts, Pogodin was not a very productive scholar. He attended Moscow University, became a teacher in 1821, and in 1825 began to lecture at Moscow University.[3] As a young man, he was a member of Prince V. F. Odoevskij's circle and became acquainted there with Schelling's philosophy (see his *Historical Aphorisms*, 1836). Pogodin's sizable fortune enabled him to publish almanacs and the magazines *Moskovskij vestnik* [The Moscow Messenger] (1827–1830) and *Moskvitjanin* [The Muscovite] (1841–1856). He was on friendly terms with Puškin and Gogol' and later became a Slavophile and took an active interest in various Slavic countries. He began writing very early, translating, among other things, Goethe's *Götz von Berlichingen* (1828); and he wrote a drama based on the history of Novgorod, *Marfa-posadnica*, [Marfa the Mayor's Wife] (1830), for which the free, anticlassicist composition of Puškin's *Boris Godunov* served as a model. In 1832, Pogodin also published *Povesti* [Novellas] in three volumes, some tales of which are noteworthy for their unrestrained use of the vernacular. Among them is the novella *Petrus'*, in which Ukrainian is used to good effect, although Pogodin was a Great Russian. The novella *Černaja nemoč'* [The Falling Sickness] (1829) is the tragic story of a merchant's son who is extremely interested in intellectual concerns. The central character does not actually suffer from epilepsy, but he is confronted with conflicts brought on by his profound spiritual involvements. Although a priest encourages him in his efforts, his parents try to force him to lead a normal life and to get married, and in the end the young man commits suicide. The passions of the talented, spiritually tormented young man are told in a romantic, pathetic style that is in sharp contrast to the language

3. [In 1835, Pogodin was promoted to the status of full professor (ordinarius); and in 1841, he was elected to the Imperial Academy of Science.—EDITOR]

of the parents and of the priest, who is well-intentioned but alarmed at the rebelliousness of the young man. Several other novellas by Pogodin are direct predecessors of the realistic style.

For decades, Pogodin kept an amazingly frank diary, which served as the basis for N. P. Barsukov's twenty-two-volume biography of Pogodin, *Žizn i trudy M. P. Pogodina* (1888–1910). This biography is one of the most valuable sources for Russian literary and cultural history in the first half of the nineteenth century.

6. Russian-born, but of Danish origin, Vladimir Ivanovič Dal', a physician whose pseudonym was Kazak Luganskij (1801–1872), played a special part in the history of Russian literature. He was a collector of Russian folklore and, on the basis of his own findings, compiled a dictionary of the Russian language in four volumes (1863–1868). Dal's writings began to appear in 1827, and in 1832 he published the first of his novellas, *Russian Fairy Tales*. These and his later novellas draw freely on Russian fairy-tale motifs. In the 1840s Dal' began publishing his "physiological" sketches (see sec. 4 above and sec. 16 below). His novellas are of particular interest in that he made the most consistent use of anyone of his time of the style that was later to become known as *skaz*. *Skaz* is a narrative style employing devices from the spoken language that do not correspond to the normal usage of the written language. This style is generally associated with the use of a fictitious narrator whose peculiarities of language (dialect, slang, individual mannerisms) are faithfully rendered. Dal' was by no means the first to employ this style (cf. Puškin, chapter III, sec. 16); and by the time he had carried the *skaz* technique still further, in his later novellas, other masters of the style had appeared, in particular Nikolaj Gogol'. But Dal' is an important link in the development of *skaz*.[4]

7. The prose writers discussed above are towered over by the talent and the continuing influence on Russian literature of Nikolaj Vasil'evič Gogol' (1809–1852). The man's Ukrainian name

4. [In the nineteenth century, the master of the *skaz* was Nikolaj S. Leskov (1831–1895).—EDITOR]

was actually *Hohol'* (with a voiced *h*), and officially his name was Gogol'-Janovskij. Gogol's biography and genealogy are full of legends and mystery. We shall set straight some of the legends in passing, but there is little we can do about the mysteries.

Gogol' was born in the Ukraine in Poltava province, from which so many well-known Ukrainians and Russians have come. He was the son of a rather wealthy landowner, who wrote two of the first comedies in Ukrainian, and his wife, who was only sixteen. Nearby lived a relative, the former senator and minister D. P. Troščinskij, whose cultural interests are now subject to doubt but who had a large library with many European works, including those of the German romanticists, in Russian translation. In contrast to some genealogical legends, Gogol's father came from a family made up largely of clergymen. Gogol's grandfather was the first to achieve the rank of nobleman (*dvorjanin*, or, as it was called in the Ukraine in the eighteenth century, *šljaxtyč*). He deceived the authorities and others into believing that his ancestors, the Janovskijs, were connected with Ostap Hohol', an important Ukrainian military leader of the seventeenth century in the service of Poland, to whom they were probably not related. Young Gogol' was the only son in the family who survived, and at twelve he entered an exclusive lyceum[5] for noble children in Nežin. Unlike Puškin, Gogol' was able to visit his parents during vacations; and, on these visits, he became acquainted with life in the country. The teachers at the lyceum had very unequal educational backgrounds. Gogol' was not a good student; but he was, as has been recently discovered, the favorite student of one of the best teachers, G. Belousov, who taught jurisprudence and had been indirectly influenced by German idealistic philosophy. Gogol's notes on Belousov's lectures were used by all the students at the lyceum. At Gogol's lyceum, as at Puškin's, there were a number of young poets who put out handwritten magazines, which have unfortunately been lost. Gogol' probably wrote a great deal but was by no means the leading writer at the school. He was, however, the best actor. As we know from his letters, he had a dream of a special service he

5. [A lyceum was a boarding high school with a quite elaborate curriculum. —EDITOR]

was to perform for mankind. He was rather lonely among his schoolmates, and they called him "The Mysterious Dwarf" because of his small stature.

When he had graduated from the lyceum, he went to St. Petersburg. There, to his disappointment, he could find only modest positions as a petty official. At the same time, Gogol' made his literary debut, publishing a poem, *Ganc Kjuxel'garten* (by *Ganc*, he presumably meant *Hans* or *Heinz*), under the name "Alov" and at his own expense. The critics barely took notice of the book or did not know what to make of it; and the young, discouraged Gogol' bought up the remaining copies of the book—that is, almost all of them—and burned them.

The work is a kind of Byronic poem. It consists of several "scenes" with long pauses in the action between them. The main character lives in an idyllic village somewhere in Northern Germany and has a fiancée—an obvious influence from the Russian translation of Voss's *Luise*. Ganc, a romantic dreamer, leaves home and goes to the promised lands of artists, Italy and Greece, but returns disappointed and continues to live in his own idyllic setting. This wavering between bold Utopian dreams and the equally Utopian patriarchal idyll is the subject matter of Gogol's later life. The poem is weak, to be sure. The verse limps along; the vocabulary is uneven and contains a considerable number of words that can only be explained by Gogol's insufficient command of literary Russian. But the poem remained almost unknown and did not damage Gogol's later reputation.

8. It is possible that Gogol' was told that among the faults of his first work was the gaudiness of the vocabulary. He soon discovered, however, that he had a trump that he could easily play: his knowledge of Ukrainian and his limited familiarity with Ukrainian popular life and folklore. Russian writers—Ryleev, Puškin, the Ukrainian Vasilij Trofimovič Narežnyj (1780–1825), who wrote in Russian, and others—had recently written on a number of Ukrainian themes; but in 1829, Nikolaj Markevič (*Ukrainskie melodii* [1831]) and Orest Somov (1793–1833), who wrote under the pseudonym of P. Bajskij, began bringing out novellas and poems on Ukrainian subjects. Gogol' met Orest

Somov. Both Markevič and Somov provided their works with ethnographic and historical notes. Since Gogol' had probably already turned his attention to Ukrainian material, it was easy for him to make use of it. After publishing several fragments of novellas, he decided to try his luck with a collection of stories. In 1831 and 1832, the two volumes of *Večera na xutore bliz Dikan'ki* [Evenings on a Farm near Dikan'ka] appeared under the pseudonym of "Rudyj Pan'ko," a beekeeper who has supposedly published these eight stories told him by his guests.

The collection enjoyed an unexpected success. Although some reviews were severely critical, Puškin's few enthusiastic lines and the opinions of the select literary circles into which Gogol', unlike most provincial writers, was at once received, impressed Gogol' deeply. In his letters to his mother, however, he may have overestimated or exaggerated his friendship with Puškin.

The eight novellas in these two volumes portray the life of the peasants in the Slavic Ausonia, the Ukraine, with the magic of a naive belief in miracles and the forces of the "other world." The subtle irony of the works is also purely romantic. Even the tragic fall of a man is obliquely illuminated, and the reader is reminded that all the things of this world are mere fleeting shadows in the face of eternity. The interplay of the humorous and the melancholy in almost all these novellas, the splendid scenes of nature (for which Marlinskij's style served as the model), and the colorful characters in quaint costumes—all this so struck the reader that he did not even notice that much of this was not new but merely a clever adaptation of other works, many of them well known.

Some critics did take note of this but did not understand the aim of the young writer: judging from some passages, Nikolaj Polevoj doubted that the author was Ukrainian or had lived in a village. It was Gogol's intention to use various narrators for his novellas, among them an "educated" young nobleman who is mentioned in the prefaces. In comparison with Puškin in the *Tales of Belkin*, Gogol' is a great master of stylization. Other critics noticed that prefaces to the two volumes were imitations of similar forewords to the early novels of Sir Walter Scott. But it was not until much later that one began to realize that Gogol' had only a rather superficial knowledge of the life of the Ukrainian peasants. In his letters to his mother, he asked for information about popular beliefs and customs and even asked her to send him native costumes. While at the lyceum, he had begun a collection of literary odds and ends; later he was to collect a thousand Ukrainian folk songs. Despite all the errors in his descriptions in *Evenings*, he succeeded in creating the illusion of great fidelity to fact. Few seemed to notice that motifs, scenes, characters, and various incidental features of the works came from three sources and had been cleverly put together. Gogol' had drawn on the Ukrainian puppet theater (*vertep*, which Gogol's father also drew on for his comedies), romantic literature in translation (Ludwig Tieck, E. T. A. Hoffmann, Washington Irving, and others), and well-known Russian sources (Žukovskij's ballads, Somov's tales, Pogorel'skij's novellas [see sec. 15 below] and even Puškin's works).

The forewords to the *Evenings*, like those of Walter Scott's sexton, are filled with idle chatter. The beekeeper speaks respectfully of his provincial guests, talks about their clothing and about Ukrainian dishes, and finally invites the reader to visit him. Of the eight novellas, three are told by the *d'jačok* (sexton) of the village church (*St. John's Eve, The Lost Charter*, and *The Charmed Spot*). All three of them are full of Ukrainian turns of phrase and tell of tricks the devil has played. Only *St. John's Eve* ends tragically. With the help of the devil, the central character attains wealth by murdering a child and is able to marry the girl he loves; but he is brought to ruin through spiritual suffering. He does not regret what he has done, but he has forgotten the key episode on the road to wealth and is tortured at having forgotten. Some of the scenes are imitations of German romantic novellas. *Christmas Night* and *May Night* are both written in a similar "higher" style; they combine motifs from fairy tales and legends with Gogol's own inventions and borrowings to make a colorful series of scenes in which, with the help of supernatural forces (the devil and a water spirit), the hero and heroine overcome the obstacles standing in the way of their love. The fantastic element in all these novellas is genuine, whereas in the first of them, *Soročinskij Fair*, the apparition of the devil is only a clever ruse to bring the lovers happily together. In the treatment of nature and in individual scenes in these last three novellas, the author's style tends to make one think of the educated nobleman's son rather than of the author. The other novellas are quite different. The first of them, *Ivan Fedorovič Špon'ka and His Aunt*, is a fragment; the wife of the beekeeper is supposed to have used the second half of it to put under the excellent cakes she was baking. The fragment is the story of a small landowner who is on active duty as an officer and whose estate is being run by an aunt. After leaving the service, he quarrels with a rich neighbor about a part of his estate. The aunt tries to settle matters peacefully, by marrying a nephew to the daughter of the rich neighbor—and here the novella breaks off. It is pointless to speculate on how Gogol' intended to continue the story because, as manuscripts show, it was intended to be a fragment, a romantic joke. The treatment of the great spiritual emptiness of the small landowner reflects Gogol's own attitude, that of an educated, intelligent Ukrainian nobleman, toward his lesser neighbors. At the same time, this sketch is the first of Gogol's treatments of spiritual poverty (*pošlost'*) and is a forerunner of the Natural School, which grew out of Gogol's later work (see sec. 16 below).

Far more important is the novella *The Terrible Vengeance*, the story of a family under a curse (as in E. T. A. Hoffmann's *Die Elixiere des Teufels* and in Brentano's *Romanzen vom Rosenkranz*). The hero is presented in an unfavorable light and is the last of his family, a criminal magician. The positive characters are his daughter and her husband, a brave cossack *esaul*, or captain, both of whom perish in a war that the magician has brought on out of jealousy of his own daughter. But the magician is also overcome by the "terrible vengeance" exacted for fratricide, the crime for which the whole family has been damned. Stylistically this is the most peculiar work of Gogol's early period. Everything is told in flowing, musical, rhythmical language, the secret of which has not yet been unraveled, that is, has not been adequately formulated. The words form rhythmical and euphonic chains and figures; there is a succession of pretty, commonplace, and charmingly uncanny images; and the same rhythm is constantly repeated.

For all their beauty, the novellas in *Evenings* are not mere literary games. Two themes run through the stories, themes that are prominent in Gogol's later work: first, the belief in two (perhaps more) worlds, one of them that of diabolic powers that seek to tempt men and lead them to ruin. Then there is the first suggestion of the many ways in which one can fall victim to the powers of darkness *or* save oneself from them. These ways to ruin or salvation are the human passions (Gogol' later called them *zadory*), which can at times be important (in *Evenings*, love, wealth, perhaps power) but which can also be trivial and vain.

9. Quickly acquired fame may have turned Gogol's head. He left his position as a minor official and became, it is said, a very good teacher at an exclusive girls' school and then a docent[6] in world history at St. Petersburg University (he was not able to get a similar position in Kiev). Gogol's teaching at a university has often been thought the result of his exaggerated need to assert himself, but this is not so. Gogol' did hundreds of pages of research in preparation for his lectures. One speaks ironically of his plan to write a history of the Ukraine "in several volumes"; but one forgets that Gogol' was familiar with at least one of the extensive Ukrainian chronicles of the seventeenth and eighteenth centuries and knew the *Istorija rusov* [History of the Russians], a tendentious work of the early nineteenth century that had not yet been revealed to be a forgery. If Gogol' had written on the basis of these works, even uncritically, he could easily have written a work several volumes long (like N. Bantyš-Kamenśkyj's *Istorija Maloj Rusi* [History of the Ukraine], which appeared in four volumes in 1822). But Gogol' wrote only a few short sketches, including an excellent romantic essay on Ukrainian folk songs. Gogol' was industrious, however, and brought out four new volumes of fiction in 1835: two volumes entitled *Arabeski*, containing several essays and three novellas, and two volumes entitled *Mirgorod*, containing four novellas with Ukrainian themes that go back to *Evenings*.

Of the Ukrainian novellas in *Mirgorod*, only one, *Vij*,

6. [The rank of docent corresponds to that of an associate professor today. —EDITOR]

is a fantastic, "demonological" story. It concerns a pretty young witch who turns to the demonic world and the spirit Vij to help her bring her murderer to ruin—he is supposed to have read Psalms over her coffin for three nights. Although Gogol' says in a note that the novella is based on a Ukrainian legend, actually the story goes back, by way of a ballad by Vasilij Žukovskij, to an English ballad, "The Witch of Berkeley". The earth spirit Vij is unknown in Ukrainian folklore. Eerie scenes, in which Gogol' artfully joins dreams and reality, alternate with comic scenes of the simple folk. Two other novellas continue the line of stories begun with *Ivan Fedorovič Špoň'ka and His Aunt* and likewise portray small Ukrainian landowners and townspeople. The story of a quarrel between two men named Ivan (*Povest' o tom kak possorilsja Ivan Ivanovič s Ivanom Nikiforovičem*, the originality of which delighted Puškin) is perhaps the novella of Gogol' that carries grotesquery furthest. The illogical comparison of the two heroes sets the tone at the beginning: "Ivan Ivanovič is rather timid, but Ivan Nikiforovič has such wide pleats in his pants that . . . " There is incredible hyperbole, improbable happenings: for six years, the captain of the town militia has been asking every day if someone has found a button he has lost in the market place; in the courtroom, Ivan Ivanovič's brown pig steals the complaint directed at his owner; and the complete break with any logic (the incomprehensible language of both heroes' petitions and the language of the fictitious narrator) are evidently intended to show the utter triviality and emptiness of the little world of the heroes. By contrast, the idyll *Old World Landowners* is Gogol's tribute to his aesthetically and morally Utopian view of the patriarchal life (see also *Rome*, sec. 12 below). This life has much to recommend it; and although Gogol' presents his old-world landowners in an ironic light, he does emphasize that their life has certain human values, ranging from their somewhat careless willingness to forgive to their true love even beyond death. It is inconceivable that V. G. Belinskij could have interpreted this story as a merciless satire.

One of Gogol's novellas, *Taras Bul'ba*, is historical and was considerably expanded and revised in 1842. Gogol's interest in history suggested new subjects for his creative work. He wrote one or several fragments of historical adventure novels, began a drama, *Alfred*, which is based on English history and has remarkable crowd scenes, and wrote *Taras Bul'ba*, which contains a rapid succession of scenes of the fighting between the Cossacks and Poles in the sixteenth or seventeenth century. The large crowd scenes combine elements of Ukrainian historical songs and of the *Iliad* of Homer. In attempting to present historical reality, Gogol' portrays the Cossacks as a totally unified people, without taking into account their subdivisions, classes, and private interests. The middle-class and rural population are completely overlooked. It is a poetical picture that deliberately ignores facts that Gogol' must have known. Later, the Ukrainian and Russian writer P. A. Kuliš (see sec. 16 below) presented a historically faithful picture of the Cossacks in his novel *Čorna rada* [The National Assembly]. In Kuliš's novel, the Cossacks are divided by class interests, and the work is an effective literary reply to Gogol's *Taras Bul'ba*. Even the later revision of *Taras Bul'ba* did not make the work more historically credible. What is new in *Taras Bul'ba*, in comparison with the primitive psychology of previous historical novels, is the more complex treatment of psychology. When Andrij, the son of the main hero, goes over to the Poles, he is not simply a traitor. In his love for a beautiful Polish girl, he has found the "home of his soul"; and he is brought to ruin, as a romantic hero, by his father. One should emphasize that Gogol's attempt at a historical novel is something new in Russian literature.

Apart from the negative picture of the Poles in his novel, Gogol' was one of the few writers among his contemporaries who did not condemn the Poles after their unsuccessful uprising of 1831. (Incidentally, Vjazemskij was also opposed to the anti-Polish attitude of Puškin and Žukovskij).

Arabesques contains three more novellas, based on life in St. Petersburg. These are no idylls; they are stories of the tragic fall of men through passion, the forerunners of Dostoevskij's later novels. Two of the heroes are brought to ruin by love; a third, by striving for wealth and recognition. *Zapiski sumasšedšego* [The Memoirs of a Madman] is the story of a petty official who falls in love with the daughter of the head of his department. Since he has no chance of actually winning her, he fulfills his desires through megalomania and is finally taken to an insane asylum, where he imagines that he is King Ferdinand of Spain. The peculiarity of the story is in the gruesome mixture of tragedy with the grotesque, confused thoughts of the madman recorded in his dairy. *The Portrait* is the story of a painter who finds money in a fantastic manner, becomes a society painter, and squanders his true artistic ability. The second part of the novella, which was considerably revised, tells of a mysterious portrait that corrupts the artist who obtains possession of it. The man pictured in the portrait is demonic—in the original version, a forerunner of the Antichrist—and is capable of living on in the portrait. The history of the portrait serves to illustrate Gogol's aesthetic view that art is closely related to religion. This novella is a variation of Gogol's romantic philosophy of art, which he sets forth in the three theoretical discussions in *Arabesques*. A third novella on artists, *Nevskij Prospekt*, was considered by Puškin to be Gogol's most significant novella. It tells of a young painter who commits suicide when he discovers that the girl with whom he has fallen in love is a prostitute. The cause of despair goes deeper than the fate of the hero of this story; it is the same doubt that recurs in Dostoevskij, and it has to do with whether beauty necessarily leads to good. The poor artist, Piskarev, is contrasted with the officer Pigorov, who is spiritually impoverished. Pigorov's romantic adventure begins at the same time as the painter's; but even after he has been disappointed, insulted, and beaten by the honest husband of the woman, who proves to be just as honest, Pigorov is bothered for only a few hours. Both of these quite different love stories are set in St. Petersburg, on the Nevskij Prospekt. The city, which is described in detail at the beginning of the story, is illusory and controlled by demonic forces, a motif one also finds in Dostoevskij. The theme of man's various passions (*zadory*) is treated humorously at the beginning of the novella.

10. Even as a boy, Gogol' had been a talented actor. He was unsuccessful in his attempt to become an actor in St. Petersburg, but he is said to have been an incomparable reader of his own work. Early in his career, he tried his hand at writing plays; but

his efforts, of which we have only fragments, evidently failed because of Gogol's inexperience. He tried to put too much into his plays; and, for that matter, he seems always to have thought of the stage as a pulpit from which to preach.

His first complete play, *Revizor* [The Inspector General] (1836), was apparently written with the moralistic intention of improving people. The play has become a part of the repertoire of theaters all over the world. The story is not new: a man passing through town is mistaken for a high official. We know from Puškin's notes that he gave Gogol' the idea for the play, but the same idea had already been treated on the stage and in novellas. Later Gogol' interpreted his work as a symbolic representation of the city of the soul. The inhabitants are the passions and the inspector general whom they are expecting is death. One should not reject this interpretation offhand. The city of the soul is traditional and appears as early as the tenth century in Slavic literature, in a sermon of John Chrysostom translated from Greek. In Gogol's play, the corrupt officials of a small town receive word that an inspector general is to visit them. They mistake a petty official, Xlestakov, who happens to be passing through, for the inspector general. At first, Xlestakov does not understand all their attention; but since, as Gogol' says, he has "an unusually agile mind," he begins to play the part they expect of him without deliberately deceiving them. Deception comes as naturally to him as does the role of the inspector general. As an inspector general, he is actually only a figment of the bad consciences of the provincial officials. Working on this principle, Gogol' creates scenes in which the officials believe Xlestakov's incredible lies. The traditional love story associated with a comedy is present only in the form of a great parody. Xlestakov courts both the wife and daughter of the chief constable, becomes engaged to the daughter, and leaves town happy. Only then does the postmaster produce a letter he has intercepted, from Xlestakov to a friend in St. Petersburg; and the officials read it and discover their mistake. In the last sentence of the comedy, the arrival of the real inspector general is announced. The fact that the comedy is excellent on stage, though difficult to play, may be attributed to Gogol's ability to eliminate everything superfluous, even scenes that in themselves are good.

To some extent, the play goes back to Molière's tradition of exaggeration and grotesquery, but in Gogol' the grotesque nature of the characters and action is much greater than in Molière. The officials believe Xlestakov at once when he tells them that he is to become a field marshal, that 35,000 messengers were sent onto the streets of St. Petersburg to persuade him to accept a ministry, that at parties in St. Petersburg one is served watermelons that cost eight hundred rubles each and soup brought by steamer directly from Paris ("You lift the lid, and there's steam like nothing you've ever seen before!"). When Xlestakov asks the wife of the chief constable for her hand, she dares to say only, "I'm sort of married." The result of all this is that hackneyed theatrical effects, such as discovering a person's true identity from a letter, strike one as quite new. Actually, the role of Xlestakov is new; he is not an impostor. Although the subject matter of many scenes is old, they seem to be new. For instance, when Xlestakov and the chief constable first meet, they both are afraid of each other. In the final version, Gogol' eliminated much that he had borrowed from theatrical and anecdotal tradition and put into early drafts.

Although the première of the play in 1836 was rather well received, there was none of the moral rebirth of the audience that Gogol' had hoped for. Later, Gogol' portrayed the reaction of the audience and the critics in a brilliant scene, *The Departure After the Première of "The Inspector General."* The critics find fault with the comedy for having none of the usual love intrigues and no positive character. To the second objection, Gogol' replies that the positive character is laughter, an observation typical of all his writing.

Somewhat later, Gogol' wrote *Marriage, a Quite Improbable Event in Two Acts*, which was first published in 1842.[7] The play is about an official who becomes engaged but is so afraid of the changes in store for him that, just before the wedding, he leaps out the church window and escapes.

Gogol' reworked several fragments of an early play into separate one-act plays. He also wrote another one-act play, *Igroki*

7. [Gogol' started writing it in 1833, almost completely finished it in 1835, reworked it several times, and produced the final version in 1841.—EDITOR]

[The Gamblers], which is about the efforts of cardsharps to cheat one another and has no women's roles. All of Gogol's plays share the motif of the complete triviality of this world. In all of them, the audience is confronted with an illusory world of pseudobeing; and at the end of every play, this pseudobeing dissolves into nothing. The inspector general turns out to be a bad dream of the officials; the *Marriage* does not take place because the bridegroom is afraid of getting married; the fraternization of the cardsharps in *The Gamblers* is nothing more than mutual deception; and most of the characters are simply empty masks.

11. Soon after the première of *The Inspector General* in June 1836, Gogol' left Russia, without saying good-by even to Puškin. Although he returned to Russia several times on visits and came back for a longer stay toward the end of his life,[8] in effect Gogol' at this time left Russia forever. Abroad, he lived mainly in Rome and from there took trips about Europe. Later he went to spas, to seek relief from ailments and to see friends, especially Žukovskij, who was living in Germany.

When Gogol' went into voluntary exile, he took with him the plan for a trilogy, a poem, *Dead Souls*. He interrupted his work on it for a trip to Russia. In Vienna, he revised other works, wrote new ones, and, seriously ill, got far enough along in his poem for the first volume to appear in 1842. Gogol' is supposed to have been given the idea for this work, too, by Puškin. It is a picaresque novel about a hero, Čičikov, who buys dead souls, that is, serfs who have died since the last census and whom their owners are glad to sell cheaply to avoid paying taxes on them. Čičikov plans eventually to mortgage the dead serfs. The plan of the first part of the novel was suggested, naturally enough, by the subject matter. The hero travels about a provincial district, and the reader meets a number of human types. This is perhaps the definitive example of Gogol's typology. It is characteristic of the triviality of the world that Čičikov is trading in something that does not exist, dead serfs. The dead souls are a profound symbol of the essential thought in Gogol's view of the world. After Čičikov has visited

8. [Gogol' returned to Russia in 1848 and thereafter lived mostly in Moscow, where he died in 1852.—EDITOR]

various landowners, word of his strange business gets out, and, Čičikov is talked about. As in *The Inspector General*, grotesque and eerie rumors begin to circulate (that Čičikov is a forger, a thief, or even Napoleon escaped from St. Helena), and Čičikov manages to get away in time.

According to Gogol's friends and to suggestions that Gogol' himself made, his poem was evidently supposed to have been a kind of *Divine Comedy*. The first volume was to represent hell; the second volume, of which fragments survive, purgatory; and in the third volume at least some of the heroes were to be resurrected or born anew, the pietistic expressions for being converted to the faith. The principal characters of hell are wicked in their ways, but actually they are not criminals. The landowners do not abuse their serfs, for instance; and the dishonest officials are not really presented as lawbreakers—they practice only petty deceptions. They are better than the heroes of *The Inspector General*. One laughs at and feels sorry for the heroes of *Dead Souls* but is not frightened by them.

Previously, Gogol' had written short novellas and developed his stories swiftly and dynamically. In *Dead Souls*, his approach is slower and more expansive, but there are still many important images. Interspersed with descriptions of the unattractive features of the world are beautiful lyric passages, ranging from descriptions of nature to reflections on the two kinds of poets (the enthusiastic and the satirical) and prophetic views of the future of Russia. Even descriptions of the negative side of the world are relieved by metaphors, in particular, metaphors developed into complex images. The narrative method is generally grotesque and hyperbolic; lyric and pathetic passages interrupt the story and divert the reader with their far-ranging digressions.

Dead Souls was given a mixed reception. The grotesquery and caricature of the narration were particularly misunderstood and rejected. Only a few critics, like S.P. Ševyrev, noticed the two planes on which Gogol' had written his novel; and not until much later did one realize that Gogol' had been writing a psychological novel of much the same kind that Dostoevskij was to write. The first part of the poem gave rise to a new direction in literature, the Natural School (see sec. 16 below).

12. The two levels on which Gogol' was writing and the obvious ambivalence of his attitude toward reality are seen more clearly in the novellas that he wrote at about this time, *The Nose* (1836), *The Greatcoat* (1842), and *Rome* (1842).

The enormously grotesque *Nose*, a story that only Puškin dared to print in his magazine, and even then with an apologetic note, is a psychological, experimental story. The nose of a spiritually empty man goes its own way and wanders about St. Petersburg as an independent human being. Gogol' attempts to show what this unlikely occurrence causes to happen to the hero and his surroundings, which are just as spiritually impoverished as he is. This bold work is perhaps most closely related to Kafka's *The Metamorphosis*. To Gogol', the novella may have been an experiment in another sense. Like the novellas in *Evenings*, it is a stylistic exercise, a report delivered by someone who is apparently incapable of reflection.

The style of *The Greatcoat*, which is perhaps Gogol's most important novella, is again that of the *skaz* (see sec. 6 above); and the narrator is even less articulate than the narrator in *The Nose*. Gogol', the careful stylist, causes his narrator to stumble over his own bad conscience and constantly to use the word "even" (*daže*), after which one would expect some intensification but finds only triviality instead. The narrator views the world from below, as does the novella's hero, Akakij Akakievič Bašmačkin, a petty official who performs his duties like an automaton. The need to raise money for a new greatcoat so arouses him that he begins to show "something like character." But the greatcoat that he has worked so hard to pay for is stolen the first day he wears it, and his desperate efforts to get the coat back eventually lead him to the grave. After his death, he appears again, evidently simply to get the only object that has ever mattered to him while he was alive, the greatcoat. Gogol' originally called the story *Novella About an Official Who Stole Greatcoats*, a title that emphasized the ideological meaning of the story that is most often overlooked. Petty passions can lead men astray just as surely as can great and noble ones. To call attention to this, Gogol' speaks of Akakij's love for the greatcoat in the language of Eros. At the thought of the "eternal idea of the future greatcoat" "his existence (the hero's) became more complete, as though he had married . . . as though some dear woman-friend had been willing to travel with him over the path of life." Before he dies, "the radiant guest appeared before him in the guise of the greatcoat that for an instant brightened his miserable life."

At the same time that Gogol' published this story of a completely debased life, he also announced, apparently unwillingly, his plans for a novel, *Rome*, of a quite different kind. *Rome* is a fragment of a novel of which nothing else remains, as is the case with several of Gogol's works, even with some that appear to be complete. The fragment consists of a chapter, full of pathos and enthusiasm, and gives one an insight into Gogol's philosophy of culture. The novel was to have been about the love of a young Italian prince for a beautiful girl, Annunziata, whom he had seen at a carnival in Rome. Gogol' begins telling the story toward the end of the fragment, following an account of the life of the young prince. After a rather primitive upbringing in Rome, the prince is allowed to visit Paris. The contrast between the animated, brilliant, modern life of Paris, in which there are hints of a kind of socialism, and the calm, immobile, somewhat sad life of Rome is interpreted as a contrast between illusory splendor and existence rooted in profound and beautiful tradition. Like his hero, Gogol' decides in favor of the existence that is apparently insignificant but that bears the "seeds of eternal life," which may one day be important in some field or occupation (*poprišče*). The conclusion of the novella consists of wonderful scenes of the simple folk and of a description of Rome, the view of which causes the prince to forget "himself, the beauty of Annunziata, the mysterious fate of his people, and everything in the world." Several years later, Gogol' attempted to set down at least some elements of his philosophy of history in theoretical form. This was the subject matter of his last book, which has been justly called the strangest book in Russian literature.

13. This "strangest book" was *Selected Passages from a Correspondence with Friends*, a book consisting of letters written especially for it on Gogol's moral and social views. The letters on Gogol's philosophy of aesthetics and art have received less

attention than the "offensive" social-political letters, to which almost everyone has objected.

In the period immediately preceding the Revolution of 1848, any defense of absolutism and serfdom and any attitude that held them to be normal were considered incredible anachronisms. Gogol' does not think that conditions in Russia are good. They should be changed, but through the influence of men on their neighbors. Apparently, Gogol' saw potential good in every representative of his typology. He does not reject the world, no matter how low it may have fallen, but believes that it can and should be improved. It seems that even Čičikov's enterprising spirit could be the basis for a new order.

In his *Selected Passages*, Gogol' analyzes the possibility of transforming the detestable world (in Gogol's real letters, one can find parallels to almost all the theses held in *Selected Passages*, to which we shall confine ourselves here). Among the most important foundations of order is the economy. Gogol' sees the economy as existing in patriarchal forms, in which the landowner has charge not only of the material economy, but of the "spiritual" economy (*duševnoe xozjajstvo*) as well. In many respects, Gogol's presentation reminds one of Justus Möser's "patriotic fantasies," which appeared seventy years earlier. Gogol's attitude toward material possessions also reminds one of parallels in the "economic theology" of the Puritans and Benjamin Franklin. But in Russia, no one understood this. Gogol's contemporaries were even more perplexed at his political ideology, which assumed that the already compromised absolutism of Nicholas I was a normal political condition. Gogol' completely misunderstood the movements then current in Europe and believed that Europe would wish to return to the patriarchal life, which had been preserved only in Russia. In his naiveté, Gogol' did not, of course, reject the ideal of socialism, "that everything should be jointly owned, houses and land." But this ideal is the "Utopia of the past." In his view, a purgation could rid this past of its shortcomings, and art and the Christian religion were to bring about this transformation.

It was only now, in 1847, that Gogol' demonstrated to his contemporaries that he was actually behind the times. His ideology was more a part of the age of Alexander I than of his own day. It is from this earlier period that he acquired his interdenominational Christianity—which one also finds in his friend Žukovskij—and his indifference to the new ideology of the Slavophiles, with which he became acquainted after his return from Palestine in 1849.

Gogol' was deeply grieved by the failure of *Selected Passages* but continued work on the second part of *Dead Souls*. From late 1851 to early 1852, at least the greater part of the final version was finished; and Gogol' read it to his friends, some of whose notes on it survive. We know from the Aksakovs that, contrary to their expectations, the new part was poetically as perfect as the first. From people who heard the second part, we know something about the content, and their testimony has been substantiated by two small fragments recently discovered. The second part was not to be concerned with hell. The landscapes are delightful; and although the characters still have their faults, they are not at all like the grotesque figures of the first volume. In the poorly preserved fragments of the last chapter, there are heroes who seem intended to be positive, but who may or may not strike us as positive. Čičikov is unchanged. Gogol's illness and his spiritual suffering, the reasons for which we do not know (the widespread notion that he had had a religious crisis was circulated abroad and exaggerated into a fantastic account of his religious insanity), led him one evening to burn his old manuscripts, including the last version of the second part of *Dead Souls*. His mental and physical condition rapidly deteriorated, and he died on February 21, 1852.

14. In a brief description of Gogol's style, one cannot hope to encompass all the features of his art. His style is of such magnitude that, by and large, it determined the development of Russian literature for at least sixty or seventy years. All too many writers of widely differing schools have declared Gogol' to be their literary predecessor. There have also been a small number of important writers who have opposed the influence of Gogol'.

The realists have been the most insistent in tracing their genealogy from Gogol'. But Gogol's poetics differ from the realists' in that he does not try at all to make his manner of presentation resemble reality. Not only is the brown pig that defends his master's interests improbable; so is the landowner who wears a brown suit with blue sleeves, or the lady who has bitten off the nose of a court assessor. And the sale of dead souls is hardly plausibly presented. Gogol' echoes the doubts of his audience and readers at the improbability of his characters and events in the desperate cry of a gentleman in *The Departure after the Première of "The Inspector General"* (see sec. 10 above): "That's not the way to take a bribe!" But Gogol' was not interested in how bribes were actually given or taken.

His favorite artistic devices are hyperbole and oxymoron. Even his epithets are hyperbolic; and he speaks of things that are gigantic, monstrous, frightful, unprecedented, fantastic (*ogromnij, čudoviščnyj, strašilišče, nevidanny, nebyvalyj*). He writes of objects that "one cannot describe," that "no one has ever seen, even in a dream," "that one has never seen anywhere." There are even things "that bear no resemblance to anything else." Everything is "splendid," "brilliant," "unbearably bright." When Gogol' describes a city, he sees in it "thousands of sleighs," "a thousand kinds of hats"; "a million people" gather on a square; "millions of posters" decorate the walls of Paris; a waiter runs around with a tray on which there are as many cups as there are "birds on the seacoast"; smoke pours from a man's pipe "as though from the funnel of a steamship"; a man laughs as though "two oxen were bellowing simultaneously." The hyperboles are varied. The wide trousers of a Ukrainian are "like a barrel"; in the pocket of another man there is room for a watermelon; in the pocket of a third man, for an ox; in the pocket of a fourth, for a small store; if one were to spread out the pocket of a fifth man, there would be enough room on it for his farm with all its buildings; a sixth pocket is simply "as wide as the Black Sea." A carriage mentioned in a prosaic context is "the same one in which Adam rode.... Although we do not know how it was saved from the flood, we can assume that there was a special shed for it on Noah's Ark"—and this is the Gogol' from whom realism is supposed to have derived! In Gogol', a mouth is as big as the entrance to the St. Petersburg headquarters of the general staff, and this entrance is four stories tall!

Although in this respect the world may seem to have great dimensions and value, the objects of the world are of very dubious value. Gogol' preferred denigrating metaphors, which writers of the Natural School (see sec. 16 below) took over from him. Men are often described as monsters (*urody*) who have lost almost all their human qualities (cf. Edgar Allan Poe). A man looks like "a dog in a dress coat," others look like "a bear of medium size," "like an overfed pug," "like a turkey cock"; men move "like a goat," "like a cat that one scratches behind the ears," like "a poodle doused with water." One runs across animals unknown to zoology: "a pig with a cowl," "a tortoise in a bag," or even "the most natural beast" (*skotina preestestvennejšij*). A person can even be a samovar or a watermelon (*arbuz*); and since Gogol' is fond of turning metaphors into reality, he continues to call characters by their metaphoric names, such as watermelon, or, worse, he refers to them by their clothes instead of by their names.

Gogol' does not hesitate to join contradictory qualities, as in the "dynamic epithets" that he applies to immovable objects ("trees that roam about the plain"). One often finds a combination of attributes that cannot be combined. Gogol's liar knows a wine that is "at once burgundy and champagne"; the artisan Vasilij Fedorov is a foreigner; another craftsman is from both London and Paris; the chief constable in *The Inspector General* has two name days;[9] and although his name is Anton, he celebrates his second name day as Onufrij; a "fiery young mare" is seventeen years old; a hero in the novella about the feud of the two Ivans is introduced to us as a "nobleman and thief." In Gogol', it is not unusual for incongruous things to be joined in the course of fantastic events or dreams, so that a privy councilor is also a bassoon; or a nose that has run away prays piously in church in the guise of a high official.

One could mention other tropes, but perhaps it would be better to call attention to Gogol's language, which was at first deliber-

9. [Like others of the Greek Orthodox faith, Russians have only one "first" or "Christian" name, and they celebrate their "name day" on the same day that is celebrated in the memory of the saint bearing that name. Thus, two "name days" for the same person are impossible.—EDITOR]

ately filled with Ukrainian elements. Later, partly for the sake of rhythm and partly for no reason at all, Gogol' used forms that do not occur in Russian or in any other language. One is continually coming across forms such as *rebenki, kotenki, vorob'enki, doski nakladeny, bricka vykacana, ne proizvel izumlenija na obscestvo, ne poluciv uspexa, pesni s derevni, celujut gde-gde sumracnoe more, byl uzren, skladennye drova, ogloxlyj, stoskovalyj vzor, spokojsja, rastoskuet, vozdymilas', rozovaja dal'nost', menja predcuvstvie beret, vz"exal vo dvor, svet dosjagnul do zabora, na bjure*, and even *on menja ponravil*. There is much more one could say about Gogol's bold neologisms and the words that he collects from all walks of life. It is the sound of a word as well as its meaning that matters to Gogol', and he seems at times to seek out words for the oddness of their sound.

There is not space here to add to these brief remarks on Gogol's style, which released language from the bondage of grammatical norms and transformed everyday life into an illusory, fantastic, crumbling world that the reader had previously assumed to be real and firm.

15. In addition to the major Russian prose writers, there were in the period from 1820 to 1850 a number of other writers, some of whom have been forgotten and some of whom have an important place in the history of Russian literature.

Aleksej Alekseevič Perovskij (1787–1836), whose pseudonym was Antonij Pogorel'skij, wrote in the same vein as V. F. Odoevskij and E. T. A. Hoffmann and left two volumes of novellas, of which *Lafertovskaja makovnica* (1825) was the most successful. It is the story of a witch and is set in St. Petersburg, which is otherwise portrayed quite prosaically. When a suitor asks for a girl's hand in marriage, the witch's cat appears. The story has a happy ending, as does *Monastyrka* [The Nun] (1830–1833), which caricatures types taken from the social class of the small Ukrainian landowners.

The well-constructed novellas of Count Vladimir Aleksandrovič Sollogub (1813–1882), especially his *Tarantas* (1845), remind one in many respects of Gogol's "realistic" novellas. In *Tarantas*, a trip by two landowners through Russia serves as the background for various short scenes and finally for a dream that parodies the Slavophile utopia.

Aleksandr Fomič Vel'tman (1800–1870) was the author of a number of works, most of them based on episodes in Russian history. The poems he wrote in the 1820s were not especially successful, but his novel *Strannik* [The Wanderer] (1831–1832) made a name for him. He subsequently wrote many novels and novellas of various kinds, among them a parody on stories of wanderings. The structure of his novels, which is often paradoxical, and his colorful language, which is full of archaisms and argot, suggest that Vel'tman was a romantic who sought refuge in the past and in fantasy. But between 1846 and 1861, he published a major novel, *Priključenija počerpnutye iz morja žitejskogo*, [Adventures Drawn from the Sea of Life] with which he became one of the first Russians to write a psychological novel. It would appear, however, that he was too much affected by Western European literatures.

The popular journalist Osip Ivanovič Senkovskij (1800–1858), a Pole whose real name was Sękowski, was originally a professor of Oriental studies and later editor of the magazine *Biblioteka dlja čtenija*, in which he wrote a large number of essays and novellas under the pseudonym "Baron Brambeus." Senkovskij did not really contribute to the development of Russian literature and was opposed to the language of Puškin and to all of Gogol's writing. But he was unquestionably talented, and he had a considerable influence on the reading public.

Faddej Venediktovič Bulgarin (1789–1859) was also a Pole. Before 1825, he was close to the Decembrists; later he and N. Greč (1787–1867) published the very popular newspaper *Severnaja pčela*, and Bulgarin was also a secret agent of the police. He was opposed to both Puškin and Gogol'. Some of his novels were quite successful, especially the adventure novel *Ivan Vyžigin* (1829), which was translated into various European languages. Serious critics rejected the novel because of its classicism and its primitive moralism. But there is a certain vitality about Bulgarin's historical novels, such as *Dmitrij Samozvanec* (1830). Bulgarin also described the first technical utopia in Russian (1825).

Gogol's schoolmate, Nestor Vasil'evič Kukol'nik (1809–1868), wrote romantic, pathetic tragedies on the lives of Italian artists and poets (*Torkvato Tasso, Džulio Mosti* [Julio Mosti], *Džakobo Sanazaro* [Iacobo Sannazzaro], 1833 ff.), which enjoyed great success, and patriotic tragedies in the same elevated style, especially *Ruka Vsevyšnego otečestvo spasla* (1834). Kukol'nik's novellas are more substantial.

The most singular writer of Russian fiction in the 1830s was Nikolaj Filipovič Pavlov (1803–1864). Pavlov was born a serf but was freed while he was still a child. He began his career as an actor and poet and then published *Tri povesti* [Three Novellas] in 1835 and *Novye povesti* [New Novellas] in 1839. He was later a journalist and editor. All his novellas deal with "dangerous" themes—that is, with psychological and social subjects, such as the fate of a serf musician who is scorned by the girl he loves and, along with other serfs, is gambled away by his master in a card game. The hero joins the army and becomes an officer but is killed in a duel (*Imeniny*, [Name Day], 1835). In another story, *Jatagan* [Yataghan] (1835), a nobleman serving as an enlisted man in the army kills the colonel who has been persecuting him and is executed. Other novellas contain keen satire on high society. The characteristic feature of a number of Pavlov's novellas is the strong, unbridled passions of the heroes, who are portrayed in a style reminiscent of Marlinskij's (Bestužev's) society novellas. But in Pavlov, the characters do grow and develop. Pavlov seems to have been influenced by the French novella, possibly by Balzac.

16. The most important group in Russian narrative prose around the middle of the nineteenth century (from about 1842–1843 to 1855) was the Natural School or *Natural'naja škola*, as it was called by supporters and opponents. This school proved to be the bridge to realism. It was essentially still a romantic movement; but instead of contrasting the natural world with the supernatural world, it attempted to portray only the natural world and to portray it in all its ugliness. The aim was to awaken a desire for the other world, the supernatural world. This was certainly Gogol's intention in *Dead Souls* and that of many other novelists of the 1840s.

Several younger writers borrowed features from Gogol's style and used them to write grotesque and narrow literature. They

were influenced by other writers of the time, besides Gogol',
especially by French writers such as Jules Janin, and to some
extent by Dickens. A typical genre of the Natural School was the
semiliterary "physiological sketches" of the life of various social
classes. Of the older writers, Vladimir Ivanovič Dal' moved in
this direction. Other works, such as Vladimir Sollogub's *Tarantas*,
were reinterpreted from the point of view of the new school. A
number of promising young writers turned to this school. Among
them were Gogol's fellow Ukrainian, Evgenij Pavlovič Grebënka
(1812–1848: Hrebinka, in Ukrainian; he also wrote in Ukrainian);
Dmitrij Vasil'evič Grigorovič (1822–1899); Nikolaj Alekseevič
Nekrasov (1821–1878),[10] who later took up poetry; Ivan Ivanovič
Panaev (1812–1862); Fedor Mixajlovič Dostoevskij (1821–1881),
in his early works, and his brother Mixail; the Ukrainian writer
Pantelejmon (Pan'ko) Aleksandrovič Kuliš (1819–1897); the gifted
Ivan Timofeevič Kokorev (1825–1853); and a number of other
writers who soon disappeared from the scene. Even F. V. Bulgarin
published "physiological sketches" to attract the attention of
the public at the same time that he was attacking the new school.

The works of the Natural School have certain features in
common, most of which derive from Gogol'. Among the typical
features are the prevalence of grotesquery, paradoxical hyperbole,
the low-class origin of the principal characters, and the use of
low-class subject matter. The surroundings are dirty; the landscapes are prosaic and unattractive (like foggy, rainy St.
Petersburg); one calls attention to things behind which men hide
themselves—clothes, furniture. Much space is devoted to the
petty functions of man, eating, smoking, coughing, sneezing,
insignificant gestures and facial expressions. People are ridiculous, sick, poorly dressed; their language is awkward, hesitant,
and vulgar. The composition is made deliberately ungainly by
frequent digressions, a mixture of styles, and the emphasis of
unimportant details.

Among the most typical works of the Natural School are
Dostoevskij's early novellas, *Poor Folk* and *The Double* (both in
1846) and his early short novellas, which have almost all the

10. [Nekrasov died January 8, 1878, which would be December 27, 1877,
according to the nineteenth-century calendar.—EDITOR]

features of the new school in style and composition. Besides the favorite characters—petty officials—one finds descriptions of the everyday lives of vagabonds, janitors, wandering tradesmen, organ grinders, waiters, peasants, and small landowners.

Many of the writers mentioned above turned away from the "Natural" style once they had passed through the Natural School and made the transition to realism. This is particularly evident in Turgenev's development in the later stories of *A Sportsman's Sketches*, of which we shall speak again. One should not confuse the Natural School with the naturalism that later developed as a part of realism. The naturalness of the Natural School comes nearer being unnatural; that is, it is a caricature of reality, a quality which the writers themselves sensed and for which they strove. Many writers turned to realism within three or four years after they had contributed to such physiological anthologies as *Fiziologia Peterburga* (1844 and 1845), the almanac *Pervoe aprelja* [*April First*] (1846), *Peterburgskij Sbornik* (1846), and *Illjustrirovannyj Al'manax* (1848). Novellas and sketches by followers of the Natural School continued to appear until 1855.

V

Late Romantic Literature

1. It is difficult to establish exact dates for major literary periods and even more difficult to establish them for subperiods. The late romantic phase of Russian literature is distinguished, however, by conspicuous features, especially in verse; and these features enable one to set the period off. There are three of these features, which are not always present in every writer but which seem to characterize the period as a whole.

The features are (1) the reflective and philosophical character of many works—lyric poetry becomes more contemplative, less attention is paid to moods and personal experiences; (2) one often comes across a mood that literary historians around the turn of the century used to call *Weltschmerz*—that is, a kind of pessimism that has not yet acquired a philosophical character— and the optimistic and belligerent attitudes that were typical of early Russian romanticism tend to recede; (3) and, curiously, the influence of Byron becomes even stronger, although the generation of Vjazemskij and Puškin would seem to have exhausted it.

There are various explanations for this change in the tone of literature. Political reaction became more extreme, and writers saw what was happening to their friends. There were influences from the West, although the purely political radicalism that had played a part in the development of the Natural School contributed little to late Russian romantic literature (despite the excitement caused by the French Revolution of 1830). Western European romanticism, which was entering its Biedermeier phase, had a pronounced effect on Russian literature, especially on style.

135

It is significant that Puškin takes up the elegiac tone again after 1830 and cultivates new themes, such as escaping from the world (although this tendency could also have been influenced by events in his own life). One finds a distinct new note in the lyrics of Vjazemskij: in 1830, the thirty-eight-year-old poet wrote a poem, *The Parental House*, with a maxim from Žukovskij:

> The life of one alive is uncertain,
> the life of one dead (*otživšix*) is immutable.

The poem begins with a tribute to memories, which seem more precious to the poet than do the possessions and aspirations of his contemporaries (*Roditel'skij dom* [1830]). These new motifs are even more evident in the poems *Xandra* [Melancholy] (1831) and *Toska* (a difficult word to translate, *toska* combines the ideas of sadness, boredom, and yearning. The poem appeared in 1831). In the first poem, we read:

> Сердца томная забота,
> безымянная печаль!
> Я невольно жду чего-то,
> мне чего-то смутно жаль.

The heart's languid care, the nameless sorrow! Involuntarily I wait for something; I am sorry about something vague.

The characteristic words are *čto-to* (something indefinite that the poet cannot explain), "nameless," and "vague" (*smutno*). "Care," "sorrow," and "sorry" do not have any objects but, like anxiety, are whimsical moods that cannot be explained by the person affected by them. This is expressed even more clearly in the second poem:

> Не знаю я — кого, чего ищу,
> не разберу, чем мысли тайно полны;
> но что-то есть, о чем везде грущу,
> но снов, но слез, но дум, желаний волны
> текут, кипят в болезненной груди,
> и цели я не вижу впереди.

I don't know whom or what I am looking for; I can't make out with
what my thoughts are secretly filled. But there is something that I
yearn for everywhere. But the waves of dreams, tears, thoughts, desires
flow and boil in my morbid breast; and I see no goal before me.

At the sight of waves driven by an invisible force:

> мыслю я: "Прочь от земли постылой!
> Зачем нельзя мне к облакам прильнуть
> и с ними вдаль лететь куда-нибудь?"

I think: "Away from the hateful earth! Why can't I cling to the clouds
and fly with them somewhere into the distance?"

About the wind:

> темные нашептывает речи
> про чудный край, где кто-то из глуши
> манит меня приветом тайной встречи.

[The wind] whispers dark words about a wonderful land where from a
foresaken spot someone beckons me with the greeting of a mysterious
encounter.

> Я рвусь в простор иного бытия . . .

I long for the freedom of another existence . . .

> При блеске звезд в таинственный тот час,
> как ночи сон мир видимый объемлет
> и бодрствует то, что *не наше* в нас,
> что *жизнь души* — а *жизнь земная* дремлет.
> В тот час один сдается мне: живу,
> и сны одни я вижу наяву.

Beneath the splendor of the stars at a mysterious hour, when the sleep
of night envelops the visible world and that which is not ours is awake
in us, that which is the life of the soul, and earthly life is slumbering

—only in this hour does it seem to me that I am alive, and when I am awake I see only dreams.

> Все мнится мне: я накануне дня,
> который жизнь покажет без покрова;
> но настает обетованный день,
> и предо мной все та же, та же тень.

It always seems to me that I am on the eve of the day that will show life unveiled; but the promised day arrives, and before me there is always the same, same shadow.

One might assume that Vjazemskij has returned to the early romantic mood of Žukovskij; but if one examines the passages carefully, one finds a considerable difference between Žukovskij's mood, which is reassuring and optimistic in the certainty of its faith and hope, and this new mood, which is vague, hopeless in its search, and unsure of its goal.

Several new writers made their appearance in this period.

2. Andrej Ivanovič Podolinskij (1806–1886) was a member of this new generation. He was from a family of rich landowners in the Ukraine and was reared in St. Petersburg. Although he later held a secure position in the post office department, Podolinskij's poetry does not reflect his profession as an official. His first poem, *Div i Peri* (1827), treats the Oriental motif of the love of a male and female demon who bring happiness to mankind (Žukovskij had written about Peri). The poet's view of the world is pessimistic:

> Вот земное! Прах ничтожный!
> Ныне в блеске, завтра где?
> Дунет ветр неосторожный —
> и как тени на воде —
> все исчезнет! — все!

Here is that which is earthly! Worthless dust! Splendor today, where is it tomorrow? The careless wind blows—and like shadows on the water, everything vanishes, everything.

In the world one sees only ruins of old cultures, of life that has passed by.

At first, Podolinskij's work was welcomed by the *Literaturnaja gazeta* (Anton Del'vig and Aleksandr Puškin); but his subsequent poetry, which was much more nearly Byronic than Puškin's early poems, disappointed the Puškin circle. This poetry consisted of the narrative poems *Borskij* (1829),Niščij [The Beggar] (1830), *Zmij. Ukrainskaja byl'* [The Dragon] (1827), and a number of shorter poems. Podolinskij is a follower of the Byronic manner and an imitator of Žukovskij, although, as in the case of Vjazemskij, there is considerably more pessimism in his work after 1830. In 1837, Podolinskij published the poem *Smert' Peri* [The Death of Peri], which attracted less attention than did his previous work. In 1860, his collected poetry came out, at a time when romantic lyrics could expect only to be flatly rejected (in this case by Nikolaj A. Dobroljubov, chief critic of the literary quarterly *Sovremennik* [The Contemporary]). Some of Podolinskij's poetry first appeared posthumously.

The impetuous heroes of Podolinskij's epics correspond only partly to the thought of his poems, which do not seem to have any particular view of the world. The poet is a ruler in this world, a leader of the masses, or a man who suffers and is persecuted; above all he is an unhappy, inwardly torn creator—among Podolinskij's themes are the vocation and fate of the poet. Philosophical motifs in his work are equally unclear. The poet hears the "mysterious voice" of nature and understands its "rich and eloquent language"; he detects the harmony of distant worlds. On the other hand, the conjuration and temptation of nature are attractive only from a distance. If one comes close to nature, one is frightened at the sight of the abyss. Various motifs join to create a pessimistic picture of the world: the idea that the world is ruled by fate (*rok*), the view of history as a succession of ruins and of the great thoughtful and sensitive being as a "fallen seraph"— all these are motifs that one finds in lesser romantic poets.

Most of Podolinskij's shorter poems are written in stanzaic form. The language often contains prosaic terms, perhaps the provincialisms of a writer who lived outside the literary centers after 1831.

3. The pessimism and Byronism of Aleksandr Ivanovič Pole-žaev (1805–1838)[1] derive from different sources, and his life is perhaps more typical of his time than is his poetry. The illegitimate son of a rich landowner, Poležaev was educated at his father's expense at the boarding school connected with Moscow University. He became a student at the university in 1820 and graduated in 1826. Fellow students brought him into contact with circles that were opposed to the government. Poležaev's frivolous poem *Saška* proved to be fateful when, in the course of an investigation of hostile sentiment among students, it fell into the hands of Tsar Nicholas I. Poležaev paid for everyone's mistakes: "You must be punished as a lesson to the others," he was told. Poležaev was almost unknown as a poet, but the Tsar was certainly familiar with his political poems: he was assigned in 1806 as a noncommissioned officer to an infantry regiment, and every month the supreme commander of the general staff was to receive a report on his behavior.

In the army, Poležaev was frequently punished; and when finally he was absent from his regiment without leave, he was court-martialed, reduced in rank to private, and deprived of his title of nobility. With the loss of his title, he also lost various privileges connected with it, and the length of his service was extended to twenty-five years. He was transferred to remote Orenburg on the Asiatic border. Soon "seditious" poems by Poležaev were found in the possession of Moscow students who had been arrested; but at first this had no effect on Poležaev, since the poems had been written before he entered the army. Nevertheless, there were further arrests and trials. In 1829, Poležaev was sent to the war in the Caucasus with a new regiment to which he had been transferred. Around this time, he published a number of poems, under pseudonyms, of course. In 1833, he returned to Moscow; and in 1834, he went to Rjazan' province, where the same colonel who had denounced him eight years earlier sought to have him commissioned an officer. But once again Poležaev failed to return to his regiment from leave and he

1. [Polezaev's date of birth is uncertain. It is given variously as 1804, 1805, and even 1806.—EDITOR]

remained a private. Three weeks before he died of consumption, in 1838, he was promoted to the lowest officer's rank.

Poležaev's biography is almost unique, even by Russian standards (although the life of the Ukrainian writer T. Ševčenko was no easier—an artist by profession, Ševčenko served as a private in the Near East from 1847 to 1857 and was forbidden to write or to paint); and the events of Poležaev's life have a definite effect on his poetry. His poems are very uneven. Many of them are simply occasional poems in which the poet repeats the commonplaces of the day. It is the same with his narrative poems, in which stanzas do, however, sometimes rise above the level of mediocrity. The titles of his lyric poems suggest what they are about: *The Song of the Captive Iroquois*, *The Song of the Drowning Sailor*. The Iroquois yields to his tormentors proudly and without useless resistance. A sailor in a leaking boat waits resignedly for it to sink in a stormy sea. The symbol of life that has passed by is the waterfall. The first two of these themes are merely suggested later on; but the poems *Farewell to Life* (1835), *Otčajanie* [Desperation] (1835–1836), and *Ožestočennyj* [The Embittered One] (1828) evidence the principal moods in the poetry of Poležaev, who called himself a living corpse and is remembered more for his life than for his satirical and seditious poems.

Poležaev also wrote many poems on classical subjects (Brutus, Coriolanus, Marius) and on the Caucasian themes so typical of Russian romantic poetry. The Caucasian poems are colorful; in sometimes vulgar language, they tell of the prosaic life of the soldiers and mountaineers—a life for which the poet shows little understanding—and lament the senselessness of the whole military operation in the Caucasus.

4. The most typical poet of this period was Mixail Jur'evič Lermontov (1814–1841), who was long thought to be second only to Puškin in Russian poetry, an evaluation that we now find somewhat exaggerated. Lermontov's ancestors on his father's side are supposed to have come to Russia from Scotland in the seventeenth century, although this has never really been proved. His mother was from a prominent family, the Arsen'evs. Lermontov was born in Moscow and, after the death of his mother, was reared by his

grandmother. He began very early to write poetry prolifically. His splendid memory contributed to his productivity; and to some extent, his early poems are merely montages of lines taken from contemporary poets, Puškin, Jazykov, Kozlov, and others. Although Lermontov knew three European languages, they did not have much effect on his poetry, apart from his acquaintance with Byron. The melancholy of his youthful lyrics and the gloom and tragedy of the fifteen narrative poems that he wrote before he was eighteen (in which the demonic heroes destroy themselves and everyone around them) are more typical of Lermontov. He ruined his own life. From 1830 to 1832, he attended Moscow University but had no rapport with his fellow students, several of whom were to become important writers and thinkers. It is easier for us to understand that Lermontov was not interested in the lectures of his second-rate professors. In 1832, he left the university to go to the St. Petersburg cavalry school, where he spent, in his own words, two "terrible years" with primitive pleasure-seekers. He tried to keep pace with his comrades by writing pornographic verse, which was extremely dirty and poetically inferior. At the same time, he also wrote serious poetry, which was not made known until later. He did not really gain fame with the public until 1837, when he wrote a poem on Puškin's death, bitterly blaming for it the society and people he thought responsible. For writing this poem, Lermontov was transferred to a regiment in the Caucasus, a region that he already knew from visiting resorts there with his grandmother. While in the Caucasus, he wrote other works, some of which were published right away, including a section of the prose novel *Hero of Our Time*.

When he was allowed to return to St. Petersburg, Lermontov did not stay long. In 1840, he was exiled to the Caucasus again, this time for dueling with the son of a diplomat. Once again, he was able to write, and in 1840 a volume of twenty-eight of his best poems and the separate edition of the *Hero of Our Time* were published. In 1841, he was given a leave of absence but was unable to secure his discharge from the army and had to return to his combat unit. In the summer of 1841, while on leave at the resort town of Pjatigorsk, Lermontov seemed deliberately to taunt an officer whom he knew and provoked him to a duel, in which Lermontov was killed. His faithful servant, apparently afraid of legal action, is thought to havè burned all of Lermontov's papers. When the Tsar was told of the death of the poet, whom he especially hated, he is supposed to have said, "The dog died a dog's death."

5. Lermontov's poems were soon translated into German by Friedrich Bodenstedt, who also translated several short poems, the originals of which were not known and which are reported to have been found recently.

Lermontov's lyric poems are not all of the same high quality—understandably enough, since he wrote most of them between the ages of fourteen and sixteen. It is easy to demonstrate that they are montages of lines from other poets. Lines from Puškin occur frequently, especially in the early Caucasian narrative poems (*Čerkesy, Kavkazskij plennik*, and others). Even I. I. Dimitriev is borrowed from in the description of the battle in *Čerkesy*, in section nine. The second part of the Byronic *Korsar* ends with four lines from *Evgenij Onegin*; in the third part of the same poem (1.15 ff.), there are eight lines from an ode of Mixail Lomonosov (1746). Both poems were written in 1828, as was *Kavkazskij plennik*, in which one finds lines from Puškin, Kozlov, and Marlinskij (Bestužev). Even later, Lermontov wrote poems that somehow remind one of poems by Puškin and other poets. *Vetka Palestiny* [A Branch from Palestine] (1837) is an extension of a poem by Puškin; *Prorok* [The Prophet] (1841) is a continuation of Puškin's poem of the same title. But it is a mistake to believe, as Belinskij did, that Lermontov assumed that the Age of Puškin had solved all the problems of form and that he was concerned only with the content of his poetry. Actually, Lermontov introduced a great many formal features. For instance, he used dactylic rhyme, which had previously been considered a particular refinement, as in the poetry of Anton Del'vig. Like Podolinskij, Lermontov made free use of anacrusis, one or more unstressed syllables at the beginning of a verse before the normal meter begins. Ternary meters play a much more important part in Lermontov's poetry than in that of Puškin and his contemporaries. Lermontov wrote a light narrative poem, *Kaznačejša* [The Treasurer's Wife] (1838), in the *Evgenij Onegin* stanza and otherwise made frequent use of octaves, also in imitation of Puškin.

In contrast to the free forms of the early romanticists, Lermontov wrote his lyric poems in stanzas. Most of these poems have a definite plan that is carefully followed, as is evident in his short poems, such as the famous *Parus* [The Sail] (1832), *Angel* [The Angel] (1829), and *Plennyj rycar'* [The Captive Knight] (1840). In the last of these poems, the metaphors presented at the beginning are gradually clarified; the knight is enclosed in a stone coat of mail (the high walls of the prison); his shield is secure from swords and arrows (the iron door of his cell); his horse runs without being guided (that is, time), and so on. Often the two parts of a poem form a parallelism or antithesis, as in *Volny i ljudi* [Waves and People] (1831); or whole poems are long periods the individual parts of which are parallel to each other, as in the famous poems *Molitva* [Prayer] (1837), *Kogda volnuetsja želtejuščaja niva* [When the Yellow Cornfield Waves] (1837), and *Ona poet* [She Is Singing] (1838). The same thing is true of the structure of longer poems, as in *Poèt* (1838), which likens poetry to a dagger and to a bell and develops both metaphors extensively. This tendency toward carefully planned construction is evident even in poems that are apparently intimate, in occasional poems to society ladies, and in the lovely poem to the memory of A. I. Odoevskij (1839), who died in the Caucasus.

The themes of Lermontov's poetry are equally typical; there is no poet of the Age of Puškin who uses the word "death" and the theme of it as often as does Lermontov. In his poetry, one also reads of imprisonment, a theme that may well be connected with the poet's own experience, of a yearning for faraway places, no matter where the poet is, and of a demon who has become identified with the poet. Two historical figures, Byron and Napoleon, are often mentioned; and sometimes poems are written about them. A number of poems are devoted to the poet's pessimistic view of the times. The poet is not only a persecuted prophet; he does not expect from his generation any fruitful thought or works of genius. He finds the times gloomy and empty and his generation indifferent to good and evil, incapable of fighting, and marked by a "fortuitousness in love and hate" that is connected with a "secret coldness in the blood." Although Lermontov expected answers to the problems of his time from the "word born of fire and light," this hopefulness seems to derive from an inconsistency in his basic view of the world, the same contradiction that accounts for all the optimistic notes in his poetry.

As a stylist, Lermontov valued the epithets with which he characterized his substantives as few poets before him had done. He makes careful use of imagery and creates the same poetic jewels as do the other romantic poets, in language that is just as unlikely to become proverbial as is that of Lermontov's romantic predecessors, Puškin not excepted (contrast this language with the familiar quotations of Aleksandr Griboedov).

6. Lermontov wrote a great many longer poems, some of which are incomplete. At least fifteen of these are among his youthful works, which, as we have mentioned, amount in part to poetic compilations and which, despite the variety of their themes, all portray men with strong passions who destroy themselves and everyone around them. There is an interesting occasional use of the first-person narrator, such as Puškin had employed in *The Robber Brothers*.

There are at least six complete or partly complete narrative poems from Lermontov's mature period. Two of them are quite different from the poems of his youth; the light poem *Kaznačejša* (see above), the improbable story of an official's wife who has been gambled away at cards, and the important poem *Pesnja pro carja Ivana Vasil'eviča, molodogo opričnika i udalogo kupca Kalašnikova* [Song of Tsar Ivan Vasil'evič, His Young Bodyguard, and the Bold Merchant Kalašnikov] (1837), the folk style and meter of which Lermontov had acquired from Kirša Danilov's collection of *byliny*, published in 1818. This poem is a further step by the romanticists toward the use of genuine folklore. The story is about an *opričnik*, a member of Ivan the Terrible's guard, who insults the wife of the merchant Kalašnikov and is challenged to a duel and killed in front of the Tsar by Kalašnikov. For killing the *opričnik*, Kalašnikov is executed.

Other poems related to *Kalašnikov* include, in 1839, *Mcyri* (Georgian for a novice in a monastery), the confession of a young man who has escaped from a monastery and is roaming about in the freedom of the Caucasus; and *Saška* (1835–1836), the story of the youth of an imaginary contemporary of Lermontov, a "super-fluous man"—who deserves to be called that more than does Onegin—told in ottava rima. Another poem, which was just begun, seems intended to have been a similar story of youthful development, this time of a young woman as seen through the eyes of a demon: *Skazka dlja detej* [A Fairy Tale for Children] (1840). The plot of the poem *Demon*, of which Lermontov wrote various versions, was apparently of great importance to him. The demon was supposed to undergo an inward change as the result of the love of a Georgian girl. The plot was changed several times; and in the final version, the Byronic demon at least comes to understand his loneliness, for which he is to blame, although he does not change for the better. It is possible that Lermontov was still not satisfied with the story told in the poem, which could not be published until 1856 and then only abroad.

7. Lermontov also wrote several plays. Four of them, including *Two Brothers* (1836), may be thought of as products of his youthful fermentation. Once more, the plots revolve around men with great, unbridled passions. The completed tragedy *Maskarad* [*The Masquerade*] (1834?–1835) is an eerie drama of jealousy. The demonic hero Arbenin has unfounded suspicions, kills his wife, and, when he discovers that she was innocent, goes mad. The verse form reminds one of *Woe from Wit* by Griboedov—some passages sound like an imitation of Griboedov's verse. The complex intrigue depends on chance happenings but is clearly developed. The principal characters are stiff. Some of the characters and details of the intrigue remind one of *Ispytanie* by Marlinskij (Bestužev) and of a novella, *Predubeždenie* [Prejudice] by O. I. Senkovskij. Although Lermontov added the element of retribution, Arbenin's madness, in the hope of persuading the censorship to reconsider its refusal to pass the play, the censorship did not change its mind; and the play was not produced until 1862.

8. The principal innovation contributed by Lermontov to Russian literature is his prose. Of his incomplete youthful works, one should mention his novel on the Pugačev Rebellion, *Vadim* (1833–1834?), with its monster-hero and demonic villain Vadim,

who harasses the family of a landowner. His novel on society, *Princess Ligovskaja* (probably 1836–1837), remained unfinished.

The great prose work of Lermontov's mature period is *Geroj našego vremeni* [A Hero of Our Time] (1837–1839). When the work came out in a single volume in 1840, Lermontov said that it was a novel, not a collection of novellas. But the novel is made up of four separate narratives. The first part of the novel consists of *Bèla*, and a sketch of a character, Maksim Maksimyč, who later passes on to the narrator the diary of the hero of the novel, Pečorin. The second part of the novel consists of *Taman'*, *Knjažna Meri* [Princess·Mary], and *Fatalist*. Pečorin's death is reported in the introduction to his diary.

Evidently, Lermontov regarded Pečorin as a typical representative of an unhappy and uncreative generation. In the manuscript of the novel, there is a characterization of Pečorin that does not appear in the printed text:

If one believes that every person bears a resemblance to some animal, Pečorin can be likened to a tiger. Strong and supple, tender and brooding, magnanimous and cruel, according to the mood of the moment, always ready for battle but often put to flight, still unwilling to submit, not bored in solitude, but in the company of his equals demanding complete obedience—this is what it seems to me his physical character should be like.

But the soul "either submits to inclinations from nature or struggles with them or overcomes them. This is what sets apart villains, the mass of people, and people of great virtue. In this respect Pečorin is one of the broad mass of people; and if he is neither a villain nor a saint, I am convinced that it is only because of his laziness."

Pečorin's struggle with his nature is one of the subjects of the love novellas *Bèla* and *Princess Mary*. Bèla is Pečorin's Caucasian mistress, whom he abducts and whom one of her countrymen, the Circassian Kazbič, steals back and kills. The story is told by a simple army officer, Maksim Maksimovič, who is described in a brief supplement to the novella. Here Lermontov has to contend with the difficulties involved in introducing a fictitious narrator who is to report on events in the life of someone else and who must largely depend on chance observations and on conversations overheard. In *Bèla*, one recognizes Marlinskij's theme of the relationship between two views of the world, that of a primitive people and that of "civilized" men. In *Princess Mary*, Lermontov allows Pečorin to speak for himself, and one realizes that he can have only a destructive effect on the people around him. In the Caucasian resort Pjatigorsk, Pečorin meets a former friend, Vera, who is still in love with him. Once more, without returning her love, he causes her to suffer. Above all, he wishes to win the young Princess Mary. Although he does not love her either, he wishes to destroy the happiness she has found with Grušnickij, who is in love with her and is a kind of parody of the Byronic hero. Grušnickij is killed in the subsequent duel; and Pečorin, for whom the whole adventure is over, goes to a "dull fortress" in the mountains. In various passages of Pečorin's diary, his characterization of himself corresponds to the lines by Lermontov quoted above, even though the wording is different. The short narrative *Taman'* is about an adventure Pečorin has when he runs across smugglers in the town of Taman'.[2] *Fatalist* tells of an incident that confirms Pečorin's fatalistic views. Before a group of officers, one of Pečorin's fellow officers attempts to shoot himself to prove his belief in fate. The loaded pistol does not go off, but on the same evening the "fatalist" is murdered by a drunken Cossack.

Of Lermontov's other prose narratives, one should mention the incomplete novella *Štos* (Štos is the name of a character in the work and of a card game), which is written in the style of E. T. A. Hoffmann and V. F. Odoevskij, although recent scholarship may not agree that the styles are similar.

Lermontov's prose continued the tradition of Puškin. His task was simplified by the fact that he rejected stylization, although the stylization in Puškin is modest. Lermontov's prose style is closest to the language of *The Captain's Daughter*. Lermontov did not completely share Puškin's reticence to use ornamental devices, especially epithets; but the purity, clarity, and simplicity of Lermontov's language certainly influenced the best prose of

2. [Taman' is located on the Strait of Kerch, which connects the Black Sea and the Sea of Azov.—EDITOR]

Russian realism, in particular the early work of Lev Tolstoj and the late work of Ivan Turgenev.

9. Stepan Petrovič Ševyrev (1806–1864) appeared rather early in literature, as a writer of reflective and philosophical lyrics. He was the son of a landowner and went to the boarding school for young noblemen at Moscow University. He came into contact with the "Ljubomudry" circle and in 1825, along with two friends, published a translation of *Outpouring of the Heart of an Art-loving Lay Brother*, by the German Romantic author W.H. Wackenroder (1797).[3] In the translation, the lay brother became a hermit. Ševyrev then published a number of essays in Pogodin's *Moskovskij vestnik*, including works on aesthetics and an analysis of the second part of *Faust*. From 1829 to 1832, Ševyrev was in Italy as tutor to the son of Princess Z. Volkonskaja, who was on friendly terms with many Russian writers and with the Polish poet Adam Mickiewicz. Ševyrev took advantage of his stay in Italy to write and publish a number of poems. On returning to Russia, he was appointed professor of poetry at Moscow University. There he published works on the history of Western European literature and a four-volume *History of Russian Literature* (1846–1860), pages of which are still of interest, since Ševyrev made use of original manuscripts in his research. He saw Puškin and Gogol' socially; and his essays on the works of the latter contain many pertinent observations on Gogol's style, most of them original. Later, Ševyrev was decried as a reactionary, and justifiably so; but this attitude toward him has prevented critics from becoming adequately acquainted with his work. His writings were not collected until the Soviet period, and his complete works have not yet been published.

The themes of Ševyrev's poems are strikingly close to those of the important Russian philosophical poet, Fedor Ivanovič Tjutčev. Various motifs of Ševyrev are also to be found in the work of Baratynskij and other romantic poets. Ševyrev shares with Tjutčev the motif of night, as in two poems entitled *Noč'*,

3. [This work was written by Wackenroder in collaboration with Ludwig Tieck, and it revolutionized art criticism, elevating art almost to a religion.—EDITOR]

written in 1828 and 1829, and in other poems. Although one does not see as well at night, one's soul is better able to perceive then (*"no vse dušoju dozrevaeš"*); in the night, sparks of thought illuminate the darkness, which is filled with spirits. The epithets that characterize the night are related to or identical with those in Tjutčev: "sublime," "mysterious," "prophetic," "holy." In contrast to Tjutčev's view of the "night side of the world" as an abyss and chaos, Ševyrev considers the night to be predominantly harmonious and tranquil. Both poems mentioned above contain the invocation to the night typical of romanticism. These motifs, which are beautifully and originally developed, are traditionally romantic; and Ševyrev could easily have acquired them from the literature and philosophy of German romanticism, for instance from Schelling, whom he later rejected. The symbol of a germinating seed for the development of a thought in the human consciousness and the idea of the "mute voices of nature" remind one of several poems by Baratynskij. Finally, Ševyrev deals on a number of occasions with the vocation and the task of the poet. As early as 1824, he wrote of poetry as a great power related to nature (*Sila pesnopenija*). In several poems, among them two addressed to Puškin, Ševyrev turns to specific problems of verse technique. Not only does he defend his own "dark verse," but, under the influence of his acquaintance with Italian poetry, he attempts to revise the Russian system of versification.

Ševyrev's early poems are closely connected with those of Vasilij Žukovskij (see *Pesn' starca* [1823]); but he developed his own "heavy" or "dark" style, relying on Homer, Dante, and Shakespeare, and in some cases introduced themes that were later taken up by other poets. His poem on the St. Petersburg flood, written in 1829, was a source of Puškin's *Bronze Horseman.* His poem *To the Unlovely* [*neprigožaja*] *Mother* (1829), in which he praises Russia as an "unlovely mother," is an early statement of a thought that recurs in other poets—for example, Tjutčev and Nekrasov.

In any case, Ševyrev's poetry deserves no less attention than do his better-known critical works and works on literary history.

10. Fedor Ivanovič Tjutčev (1803–1873) is one of the most

important Russian poets. Although Russian writers and critics of different leanings, such as Ivan S. Turgenev and Nikolaj A. Nekrasov, dedicated enthusiastic essays to him during the age of realism, he was long overlooked. Even today, sophistic arguments are used to separate Tjutčev from the literary school to which he is undoubtedly closest, symbolism. Tjutčev is the most genuine romanticist in Russian literature and, as such, is related to the symbolists, although he is distinguished from most of the symbolists by the profound seriousness of his view of life and the world. Tjutčev's view of life is by no means purely aesthetic, in contrast to that of many symbolists, especially those of the first or older generation.

· Tjutčev was from an old noble family. In his early years, he was tutored by the significant writer and translator S. E. Raič. Later, he went to the boarding school for young noblemen at Moscow University and there called attention to himself with his poems, the first of which was published in 1818. He was a member of V. F. Odoevskij's circle. In 1821, Tjutčev broke off his studies at the university, became an official in the Foreign Office, and in 1822 went to the Russian embassy in Munich, where he remained until 1837, when he was transferred to the diplomatic mission in Turin. In 1839, he was dismissed from the service for having left Turin for a short time without permission. He then returned to Munich, where he stayed on as a private citizen until 1844— his second wife was from the Bavarian nobility, as had been his first wife, who died in 1838. We do not know much about Tjutčev's relations with the Germans. He knew Schelling personally, and Schelling spoke well of him. He saw Heine, who repeated several of his witticisms. He visited Goethe and was related by marriage to the von Maltitz brothers, Friedrich and Apollonius, German writers in the Russian diplomatic service. He had other acquaintances among the Bavarian nobility. In 1844, Tjutčev returned to Russia, where he became a rather high official. Later, he often traveled abroad. We shall not go into his rather complicated family life, although there are overtones of it in his poetry. On the surface, Tjutčev's success as a poet was rather modest. Before 1837, he had published only a few poems in Russian magazines and almanacs. From 1836 to 1840, over the initials "F. T.," *Poems*

Sent from Germany appeared in the periodical *Sovremennik* which was founded by Puškin. These poems received little critical attention, and no one connected the poet with the almost forgotten Fedor Tjutčev. We do not know what Puškin thought of these poems: they were first mentioned in 1846—ten years after they had come out—by the critic V. N. Majkov, who called Tjutčev "a poet whom no one remembers." In 1850, Nikolaj Nekrasov published an essay in which he praised Tjutčev, but said that he was not understood by the reading public. Tjutčev, who had not published since 1840, began in 1850 to bring out a few of his poems. In 1854, his first collection of poems was published; and in 1868, his oldest son and his son-in-law, I. S. Aksakov, published a more complete volume of his poetry. After a long illness, Tjutčev died in 1873, and I. S. Aksakov wrote his biography. From this time on, as has been mentioned, Tjutčev was almost forgotten. The well-known authority among Russian critics, A. M. Skabičevskij (1838–1911), who is still occasionally read by German and American students, said of the great poet: "He is difficult to read (*čitaetsja s trudom*) and is valued only by zealous and incorrigible aesthetes." The philosopher Vladimir Solovev spoke well of Tjutčev, and finally the symbolists "discovered" him. Recent literature on Tjutčev has made worthwhile contributions to our knowledge of his life and to textual criticism of his work, but his poetry has not been evaluated objectively. In order to make him more topical, one writer has maintained that Tjutčev, who was a Christian and a Slavophile, "moved toward atheism." In the United States, an otherwise unknown émigré authority has declared that Tjutčev was a Buddhist; and in a selected edition of Tjutčev's poetry published in New York, his "reactionary" poems, which are included even in Soviet editions, have been entirely omitted.

11. Tjutčev is a master of short forms, in which there is something reminiscent of the long forms of the eighteenth century (as L. V. Pumpjanskij[4] points out, with considerable exaggeration).

4. [L. V. Pumpjanskij (1894–1940) was a leading Russian literary critic and historian. See his article on Tjutčev in *Uranija-Tjutčevskij Almanax*, Leningrad, 1928.—EDITOR]

Tjutčev did not write many poems; apart from occasional poems and epigrams, there are barely three hundred and fifty of them. The poems that are of the greatest philosophical and poetic importance are usually from twelve to twenty lines in length; and some poems, especially the incomparable landscapes, are only eight lines. In addition, Tjutčev's work includes several political essays and many rather interesting letters, which have not yet been collected.

We need not be surprised that in the style of his youthful poems Tjutčev was close to the Žukovskij of 1800 to 1810. But he soon easily abandoned this style and, about 1820, when he was seventeen, reached his poetic maturity and acquired a different tonality in his verse from that of Puškin or Baratynskij. In Tjutčev's poems, which are sometimes all too short, one finds a distant similarity in style to the odes of the eighteenth century, because his thought and manner of expression are unusually concentrated. This tendency often accounts for his "difficult" words, which sound archaic without really being antiquated. In his poetry, the poet seems often to be talking to someone or to himself; but this light rhetorical note is not enough to make his poems "miniature odes," as L. Pumpjanskij has suggested. Tjutčev's pithy aphorisms can hardly be compared with those of the classicists; on the other hand, they do not lend themselves, any more than do the aphorisms of Puškin and Baratynskij, to proverbial use, because they are too difficult. Only the archaist Aleksandr Griboedov and the belated classicist Ivan A. Krylov were able to coin proverbs. The classical reminiscences and mythological names often found in Tjutčev's early poems are entirely absent from his later poetry.

Tjutčev has a vocabulary and set of themes all his own. His treatment of a theme is usually bipolar; that is, he speaks of the same theme in both light and dark colors, in bright and sad tones. This bipolarity is evident in every phase of his development, but in his images and symbols one can detect an increasing disenchantment, perhaps a progression to a Biedermeier or even realistic phase. One should not forget that Tjutčev's last poems, which were not influenced by the effect on his mind of his fatal disease, were written in 1871.

Tjutčev's first theme, one that is particularly striking in its bipolarity, is nature. Some of his poems portraying spring, fall, storms, and the harmonious beauty of southern landscapes are among the most beautiful poems about nature in Russian—of course, the nature that he presents is often that of Bavaria. The miniature form of his poems led Tjutčev to work with nuances and minute strokes. With a reference to the dying off of nature, he can make a charming picture of autumn seem melancholy. Or a night landscape, which could be lovely, since it brings peace and cool air after a busy day, becomes eerie when Tjutčev mentions distant summer lightning that flashes ominously as though monstrous eyes were opening and reminds one of a conversation between deaf-mute demons who can communicate only by signaling with light.

Tjutčev is fascinated with nature at night and describes night landscapes as often as does Eichendorff.[5] One seldom notices that all Russian romanticists, including Puškin and Gogol', set their scenes at night extraordinarily often. To Tjutčev, the night is a time of revelation of the "night side of the world." One sees the "living carriage of the universe rolling freely in the sky." One hears the "sources of existence audibly flowing." Although life is always surrounded by the "ocean of dreams," at night these waves break on the threshold of consciousness; and the "enchanted boat" bears us into the infinity of these dark waves. The visible world disappears like a dream. The splendor of the stars causes the poet to call out to the night, although the night is not just wonderful; it also submerges man, in the person of the poet, into the depths of abysmal being and allows man, who is as pale in the day as is the moon, to shine down on the world like a luminous god. In dealing with the night, Tjutčev makes use of a broad semantic field, the elements of which one finds seldom in other Russian poets but often in the German romanticists. The night reveals the abyss, the celestial sphere, that stands before us or the "mysterious world of spirits." The strange voices in the night, the din, the

5. [Joseph von Eichendorff (1797–1857), important German romantic poet and literary critic.—EDITOR]

roar ("*gul*"), and the howling of the wind seem to the poet wonderful, incomprehensible ("*nepostižimyj*"), mysterious, unspeakable, undiscovered ("*nerazgadannyj*"), strange, and fateful ("*rokovoj*"). The abyss and chaos that man perceives at night are also the home of man's soul ("*rodimyj xaos*") since the forces of the night reveal the deeper levels of the soul, where one finds chaos just as in the night. Thoughts "conceal themselves" in the "chaos of the night." The "world of the night soul" listens eagerly for voices from chaos. Although this is a time of indescribable sadness and yearning ("*toska*") and although the voices of night sound "like the terrible laughter of madness," the soul strives to unite with the infinite or to lose itself in it. Despite the variety of these phrases we have quoted from Tjutčev, one can easily see that they are all part of a single semantic field. These central thoughts and images in Tjutčev's poetry illuminate all reality.

Let us turn first to the soul of man. The fact that chaos is concealed in the soul, even though deeply, explains the abysmal character of the life of the soul, the dream, in a similar sense as in Puškin. Poetry and love are also dreams. Tjutčev's love poems show the importance he would like to attribute to love. But perhaps love is only transitory. Perhaps the entire life of the soul is only a "restless, empty apparition." The poet makes use of impressive imagery to clarify the thought of the eternal and insurmountable boundaries of the existence and striving of the soul. Like the drops of a fountain, the efforts of the soul can go only so high. The soul cannot find adequate expression for itself, not even in words, since "a thought once uttered is a lie." Perhaps our life is only smoke or merely the shadow that smoke drifting through the moonlight casts on the earth.

It is no wonder that what Tjutčev has to say about poetry and the poet is so ambivalent. On the one hand, poetry is a force that descends amid thunder and lightning from heaven to the warring elements and stills the raging sea with oil. On the other hand, the poet, who is as powerful as a natural force, can only burn the living human soul. "Maiden, do not believe the poet! ... And fear the love of a poet more than his fiery rage, for he does not bite in the heart like a snake, but sucks from it, like a bee." In Tjutčev, too, who had much to say about the destructive power of love, the poet is a demonic being. In this respect, Tjutčev shares the view of some of his contemporaries.

History is also an ambiguous area of man's life. Some of Tjutčev's political poems are pure occasional poetry and have been preserved perhaps for the fortunate turns of phrase they contain. Others of these poems present the poet's basic views, which are again bipolar. On the one hand, Tjutčev sees the entire historical process as something that happens so that the observer can relish the "fateful hours" of it, the revolutions and the like—this comes in connection with a quotation from Cicero's *Brutus*. Like most Russian writers, Tjutčev thinks that Napoleon was a great man, despite all the trouble that he caused Russia, presumably because he was part of a "fateful hour" in history. On the other hand, Tjutčev often emphasizes that, when one considers eternal being and nature, "our years" are "illusory" ("*prizračnye gody*"), and men are perhaps but "dreams of nature." Nature does not know history and is indifferent to both the good and the bad of historical events.

Tjutčev's attitude toward Russia was equally bipolar, although it was probably the crisis of the Crimean War that shook his original politically conservative optimism, which held that Russia was "the eternal pole" in European politics. Like Stepan Ševyrev, Tjutčev regarded Russia as "unlovely" and as an impoverished mother. On returning home, he called the estate of his fathers "unlovely ('*nemilye*') places but my own" (1849); Russia seemed to him to consist of "miserable villages, the bare necessities of nature . . . humiliating nakedness" (1855). Nevertheless, in a special way, Russia had been shown the grace of God; Tjutčev had wandered through Russia, like a slave, with the burden of the cross on his shoulders (1855). In his later years, Tjutčev appropriated the ideas of the Slavophiles on the mission of Russia among the Slavs. During the festivites connected with the coronation of Tsar Alexander II in 1855, Tjutčev experienced a vision of the future greatness of Russia as he was standing on the steps of a Moscow cathedral; later he described the vision in a letter. Many of Tjutčev's poems testify that he was a visionary. Among these poems are adaptations and other verse, such as *Bessonnica* [Insomnia] and *Problesk* [Ray of Light], both written shortly after 1820.

It is entirely possible that Tjutčev did not learn about German idealistic philosophy from books. He seems to have been influenced mainly by Schelling (it has been maintained that he was also influenced by Schopenhauer, but I do not find sufficient evidence of this); and his poems are reminiscent of Schelling's *Systems of Transcendental Idealism,* in some respects of the *Investigation of the Nature of Human Freedom,* and even of *The Philosophy of the Arts,* which was not published until later.

One should not overlook Tjutčev's occasional poems, which are distinguished by an abundance of strange, weighty words. Among these occasional poems are verses on the death of Goethe (1832), on the death of Žukovskij (1852, and a four-line poem on his death in 1867), on the death of Count N. Bludov, a politician (1864), and on the Vjazemskij celebration (1861). Tjutčev also reacted to his personal experiences with the same keenness and refinement of expression. During a business meeting, he succeeded in writing a beautiful poem that another participant in the meeting happened to preserve for us (*Kak ni tjažel poslednij čas* [1867]). In his translations, Tjutčev did not have Žukovskij's ability to enter into a work. He translated Goethe (but destroyed the greater part of his translation of *Faust*), Schiller, and Heine, the last of these especially well. Sometimes he borrowed particularly appealing thoughts from Goethe, Schiller, and Shakespeare. For example, there is an image from Goethe in *Pesok sypučij*, from Schiller in *Fontan*, and from *Hamlet* in *O veščaja duša moja.*

12. Among the popular poets of this late romantic period was Vladimir Grigor'evič Benediktov (1807–1873). Although from modest circumstances, Benediktov joined the guard and was an official in the Ministry of Finance from 1832 to his retirement in 1860. His first volume of poetry came out in 1835 and was extraordinarily successful. His verse was hailed by important writers, such as Vjazemskij, Žukovskij, Tjutčev, and Ševyrev. Although he was not very active in literary circles, Benediktov was well educated—for instance, we have parts of works on

mathematics that he wrote. After 1845, his popularity seemed to wane, but he continued to write; and his work from this period includes translations of Adam Mickiewicz and of Serbian poets. His attempts at political lyrics in the 1870s were unsuccessful.

Benediktov's poetry is distinguished primarily by a lavish use of poetic ornamentation. The essential elements of romantic philosophical imagery serve him as decorative metaphors. A waterfall, the night, stars, the universe, the abyss, world spheres, eternity, and so on, are used to ornament everyday people and things, such as the eyes and curls of a pretty girl, a waltz, a girl riding, and pretty landscapes. Unlike Baratynskij, Tjutčev, and even Podolinskij, Benediktov rarely associates philosophical thoughts with his landscapes. His philosophical poems (*No dolgo*, *Priroda*, and others) contain at best traditional images ("but the entire abyss of heaven is reflected in a drop," "do not damage with your hypotheses that which is concealed in the darkness of holy mysticism") that sometimes remind one of the conceits of the baroque, which Benediktov perhaps knew from his broad reading.

The themes of Benediktov's poetry are the curls of a young enchantress, which he calls "splendor and aroma, rings, streams, snakes, waterfall of silk," dark eyes as contrasted with blue (something one could have read in V. I. Tumanskij), the bold "amazon Matil'da," the steppe, the sea, rocks, a rose, the polar star, and so forth. It is not until one reads the work of Konstantin Bal'mont that one again encounters such a variety of themes. The important aspect of Benediktov's poetry is the use of unusual and surprising metaphors, which had largely been forgotten since the baroque. A saber is a beautiful woman; poetic enthusiasm is a miraculous horse (neither metaphor is explained, and the name "Pegasus" is not used); a rose that has been plucked is a "glowing harvest"; to bathe is to embrace a water sprite; rocks are the "contemporaries of the creation", the "mighty uprisings ('*vosstanija*') of the earth," and the "sprouts of dust reaching to heaven." Poetic enthusiasm is a sturdy shield or a meteor; clouds are dark curls; raindrops are tears; the breast of a man who is suffering is "a temple of unhappiness"; a ship is "a warrior against the waves," "a swimming temple"("*volnoborec,*" "*xram plovučij*"), and "Bedouin of the watery desert" ("*pustyni vlažnoj beduin*"); the heart of a beautiful woman is "an abyss at the bottom of which a crocodile lies in repose"; the waltz is "a demon of circular motion"; at night, the world rests on the breast of a god. The epithets are also surprising: "*smertel'nyj poceluj,*" "*zamorožennyj vostorg,*" the infinitely capricious ("*beskonečno prixotlivaja*") waist of a woman; and in Benediktov, one finds a black sky and black flames seen by the lover of a dark-eyed girl. Some of Benediktov's images, such as "the wave-like world" ("*volnoobraznyj mir*"), "the angry flame of the sea" ("*gnevnyj ogon' morja*"), and "the fire of thundering inspirations" ("*ogon' gremučix vdoxnovenij*") are not altogether obvious. One also finds neologisms used as epithets: "*predbitvennyj meč,*" "*navstrečnaja tolpa,*" "*bezjakornyj*" (sailor), "*bezpredmetnyj*" ("*objectless,*" in the sense of barren: "*bezpredmetnaja step'*"), "*xval'nyj venec,*" "*bezot"ezdnaja kolesnica*" of Ursa Major, which never goes down in our part of the world, "*začašnyj privet,*" and so on. Noun neologisms are not infrequent: "*vlastelinka,*" "*predosveščenie,*" "*bezverec,*" "*črezoblačnyj,*" "*privetnost'*"; and one finds the verb neologisms "*koketstvovat',*" "*ničtožestvovat',*" "*uletučit',*" "*otstradat'sja,*" "*zapancyrit'sja,*" and others. Some of Benediktov's usages appear to be unjustifiable— for instance, why does "innocence shine silver"?—and some of his turns of phrase make us think that we should perhaps call Benediktov a romantic mannerist. Examples of this tendency are "the snake-beauty shone hellishly" ("*adski blistala zmeja-krasota*"); the snake is also a symbol of hope, as in "a beautiful snake" ("*i radostno zmeju— nadeždu sčast'ja/nosil v grudi—prekrasnaja zmeja*") and in "and the profound folds of their agitated garments whisper with the rustle of hope" ("*i šepčut šoroxom nadežd/glubokomyslennye skladki/ee vzvolnovannyx odežd*"). But this is perhaps understandable in a poet who wrote:

чтоб выразить таинственные муки,
чтоб сердца огнь в словах твоих изник,
изобретай неслыханные звуки,
выдумывай неведомый язык!

To express mysterious torments, in order that the fire of the heart will
rise up in your words, invent sounds that have never before been heard,
devise an unknown language!

It would be a mistake to call all Benediktov's "inventions"
successful. Nevertheless, his verse flows smoothly and is usually
resonant. His vocabulary is rich in neologisms and overlong
words, and as a result the rhythm of his verse is peculiar. His
vocabulary is also unusually colorful and contains vulgarisms,
especially in his images and symbols.

Benediktov's ideology is confined to the idea of the lonely
poet, who is persecuted and despised. He dreams of a strong,
proud man who will rise above the masses. The symbols for such
a man are the rock (*utes*) and the eagle. But there is no doubt
that Benediktov himself was not one of these men and did not
believe himself to be.

13. Another late romantic poet, Aleksej Vasil'evic Kol'cov
(1809–1842), enjoyed a reputation that was not entirely deserved.
Kol'cov was the son of a rich merchant of Voronezh and was
forced to leave school early to help his father with his business. In
1825, he happened to come across some poetry, oddly enough by
Ivan I. Dmitriev, and he realized that he wished to write poetry
himself. In 1829, he met the unimportant but not untalented poet
A. P. Srebrjanskij, who was the moving spirit among the students
at the theological seminary in Voronezh. Srebrjanskij taught
Kol'cov something about poetic technique and aesthetics. By
1829, a publisher had brought out several poems by Kol'cov,
without mentioning his name. In 1830, Kol'cov met the young
Hegelian Nikolaj Vladimirovič Stankevič and, in 1831, the
critic Vissarion Belinskij, who was a member of Stankevič's
circle. These two were yearning for an expression of the Russian
national spirit. They were delighted with Kol'cov, placed poems
by this "poet of the people" in various magazines, and, in 1835,
published eighteen of his poems in a small volume. Kol'cov also
met Puškin and other writers. Unfortunately, his friends "improved" his poems before publishing them. What is even more
regrettable, Kol'cov began to reflect on "nature, the fate of man,
and the mysteries of life and death." The result of this reflection

was poems written in an undigested vocabulary. After a long illness, Kol'cov died in 1842. A larger collection of his poems was published in 1846.

The significance of Kol'cov in the history of literature and culture is certainly greater than his modest achievement. He proved to his contemporaries and to following generations that great intellectual forces lay dormant in the "simple Russian masses."

Even before Kol'cov, there had been imitations of Russian folk songs. In this connection, one should mention the late-classicist professor of poetics at Moscow University, Aleksej Fedorovič Merzljakov (1778–1830), and Nikolaj Grigor'evič Cyganov (1797–1831), who was from a family of freed serfs and about whom we still know rather little. Cyganov's first poems came out in 1830, at the same time as Kol'cov's. F. N. Slepuškin (1783–1848), M. D. Suxanov (c. 1801–1843), and E. I. Alipanov (1800–1860), who came on the scene at the same time as Kol'cov, acquired a reputation as peasant poets but were actually insignificant imitators of literary verse. Kol'cov succeeded, however, in approaching the folk song in at least some of his poems. But even in these poems, one finds words and phrases taken from literary poetry: "silent forests" ("*lesa molčalivy*"), "Fragrant May" ("*blagovonnyj maj*"), "the dreams of ardent youth" ("*pylkoj junosti mečty*"), "merciful Providence" ("*vseblagoe providenie*"), "lilywhite breast" ("*lilejnaja grud'*"), and words such as *vkušat', lobzanie, vostorgi, lanity* (Church Slavonic). There are, to be sure, popular words in Kol'cov, such as *talanliv* ("happy"), *moč'* ("power"), *pesni igryvat'* ("to sing songs"); there are popular ornamental adjectives, such as *zolotaja kazna, solnce krasnoe, vetry bujnye*; there are paired words, such as *ptašečki-kasatočki, grust'-toska*, and words paired in the fashion of folk pairs, such as *kon'-paxar'* and *borona-soxa*. The most characteristic feature of Kol'cov is the meter of his verse, which is closely related to that of the folk song and has short lines with a fixed distribution of stresses—for instance:

$$\text{X } \acute{\text{X}} \text{ X X } \acute{\text{X}} \text{ or } \acute{\text{X}} \text{ X } \acute{\text{X}} \text{ X X,}$$

but is divided into stanzas, which are not required in the Russian folk song. Of Kol'cov's approximately one hundred and thirty poems, only thirty-five can be called songs; eleven others may be thought of as songs with the reservations about literary usages mentioned above. This is not much, especially when one considers that Kol'cov also wrote a number of awful pseudophilosophical poems called *dumy*.

In any case, Kol'cov did succeed in creating a certain tradition, even if his songs are, by and large, no more popular than those of Puškin, Merzljakov, or Cyganov.

14. The poetry of the talented and original Karolina Karlovna Pavlova ([1807–1893] née Janisch, wife of Nikolaj Pavlov, the writer of novellas discussed in chapter IV, sec. 15) also belongs to the late romantic period. The daughter of a German doctor who became a professor at Moscow University, Karolina Pavlova knew three European languages perfectly and in 1833 published a collection of excellent translations of Russian poetry into German, *Das Nordlicht: Proben der neueren russischen Literatur*. In 1839, she published a group of French translations (*Les préludes*, printed in Paris) from Russian, English, Italian, and Polish literature. Her Russian poems began to appear, in magazines, toward the end of the 1830s. They are mostly examples of reflective poetry and are formally perfect. The subject matter is somewhat heavy, as the poetess herself conceded in contrasting herself with the great or "immediate" poets (*Est' ljubimcy vdoxnovenij*, 1839). She felt that she was to remain an unknown nightingale. But every poet was in a sense the owner of the world, which delighted him with its sweet sounds (*Poèt*, 1839). She dedicated some of her poems to young girls, who were confronted with quite different problems from those today. Her unusual story *Dvojnaja žizn'* [Double Life] (1848) tells of the experiences of a young girl. At the end of each chapter, the author changes from prose to poetry, as though her waking life were changing to dreams. Pavlova's poems are original in their rhythm. She was especially fond of original rhymes (in a letter to Petr Pletnev, she pointed out that Puškin had used unusual rhymes), and she experimented with them, as in her poem *Vezde i vsegda* (1850).

Although Pavlova saw the most important Russian writers socially and her literary salon was for a time a center for discussions between Westernizers and Slavophiles, as a poet she was rather lonely. She was close to the Polish writer Adam Mickiewicz while he was in exile in Russia. Later, Nikolaj Jazykov and the young Slavophiles K. S. Aksakov and Ju. F. Samarin were fond of talking with her. Little is known about her life after 1858, when she left her husband and moved to Dresden. Her papers seem to have disappeared. In Germany, she was on friendly terms with an epigone of romanticism, Count Aleksej K. Tolstoj, and made a German translation of his dramatic trilogy that was produced on the German stage. Pavlova was rediscovered by the symbolist V. Ja. Brjusov.

15. The poems of three Slavophile poets are thematically close-ly related, since all three deal with religious and political subjects.

Aleksej Stepanovič Xomjakov (1804–1860), the acknowledged leader of the Slavophile movement, began writing poetry in the 1820s (see chapter VII, sec. 3). In their tight construction and rhetorical tone, Xomjakov's poems are reminiscent of those of Lermontov. He even treats the same themes, such as a dagger used as an extended metaphor for poetry (*Klinok* [The Blade], 1829). In Xomjakov, too, the eagle is a symbol of the poet (*Žavoronok, orel i poèt* [The Lark, the Eagle, and the Poet], 1833). Xomjakov also writes about Russia, which he thinks should lead the Slavic world (*Orel* [The Eagle], 1832, a poem in which he likens the gospel to a starry sky). Xomjakov repeatedly wrote poems (1839, 1854) in which he rebuked Russia for its sins, since he did not believe that Russia could fulfill its mission without penitence.

A more important poet was Ivan Sergeevič Aksakov (1823–1886), who wrote rather little. In addition to mentioning his reflective lyrics, one should call attention to Aksakov's incom-plete poem *Brodjaga* [The Vagabond], excerpts from which were published in 1852. Several pages of *The Vagabond* are among the best-known poetry in Russian. Aksakov also made use of the romantic form of the mystery play, as Wilhelm Küchelbecker and A. V. Timofeev had done, but with a prosaic subject, the life of an official.

Ivan Aksakov's older brother Konstantin (1817–1860) wrote rather weak poetry when he was still quite young but later com-posed a number of reflective and philosophical poems that share with the poems of Mixail Lermontov and Aleksej Xomjakov a tight and almost logical construction. His metaphors are traditional, such as a rock, a storm, and an eagle (*Orel i poèt*, written around 1833). Among his philosophical poems is an enthusiastic letter of farewell to Mixail Bakunin, who was going to Berlin to study Hegelian philosophy. Konstantin Aksakov likens Bakunin to a crusader. Several years later, when Konstantin was no longer a Hegelian, he wrote a poem, *A. Popovu v Berlin* (1842), that contains a poetic description of abstract philosophy and warns against it. At the same time, he argued against empiricism (*Tolpe èmpirikov* [1842]); and later he wrote a poem against literary realism (*Literatory-naturalisty* [1856]). He was the rhetorical herald of the Slavophile ideology, especially in his famous and pathetically pointed work *Svobodnoe slovo*, in which he defended freedom of speech. K.S. Aksakov also wrote several novellas and two historical dramas.

16. The poets who belonged to Nikolaj Stankevič's circle (see chapter VII) were also closely connected with late romanticism. There is hardly a trace of Hegelianism in their poetry, since Hegel's philosophy does not go well with romanticism. Among these poets are the following.

Vasilij Ivanovič Krasov (1810–1854), was the son of a Northern Russian priest. While at Moscow University, he was a member of Stankevič's circle; and from 1837 to 1839, he was a docent at Kiev University. Beginning in 1832, Krasov published poetry rather often; in 1859, his poems were brought out in a collected edition. He wrote ballads and songs, in some of which he imitated Kol'cov, and he treated typical romantic themes, such as the grandeur of poetry and the poet and the demonic character of the poet (*A Warning to a Girl against the Love of a Poet* [1838]). His own sad life presumably accounts for the melancholy tone of his poems. Ivan Turgenev later quoted Krasov's poem *Klara Movraj* [Clara Mowbray].

Ivan Petrovič Kljušnikov (1811–1895) was the son of a Ukrainian landowner. He was also a member of Stankevič's circle and later taught in Moscow, where Ivan Turgenev was one of his students. For a short time, between 1838 and early 1840, Kljušnikov published a number of poems, but afterward he was seldom heard from. Most of his poems are pessimistic; he dwells on his doubts and failures, curses the world, and calls it a "barren desert" and "a world begotten with a curse by the Creator."

In his youth, Nikolaj Vladimirovič Stankevič (1813–1840) wrote several poems and a tragedy. His work contains philosophical motifs on the merging of the individual with the universe.

The most talented poet among the members of Stankevič's circle was certainly Ivan Sergeevič Turgenev (1818–1883). During the 1840s Turgenev wrote several narrative poems, which anticipate the themes of his later prose narratives, ballads, and pretty mood and nature poems. Turgenev's verse will be discussed together with his prose in volume II of this history.

17. One should mention several other poets, who did not become well known until later; these poets will be treated in another connection, but their early work, often modest, belongs to romanticism: Nikolaj Platonovič Ogarev (1813–1877), Jakov Petrovič Polonskij (1819–1898), Afanasij Afanas'evič Fet (a pseudonym for Afanasij Šenšin [1820–1892] taken from his German mother Foeth), Nikolaj Alekseevič Nekrasov (1821–1878),[6] and Count Aleksej Konstantinovič Tolstoj (1817–1875).

18. There are poems by Vladimir Benediktov that can be called products of romantic mannerism. Poems by several other poets can be called manneristic with greater justification, and among these poets is Aleksej Vasil'evič Timofeev (1812–1883). Timofeev studied at Kazan' University, went to St. Petersburg to work in 1831, and in 1833 published his first book, *Twelve Songs*. *Pesni* [Songs] followed in 1835 (this is called the second edition, but nothing is known about the first edition). In 1837, Timofeev's collected works (*Opyty*) were brought out in three volumes. Later, several works by Timofeev appeared in magazines, and others came out in book form—among his works were two mystery plays and several novellas. In 1834, he interrupted his career as an

6. [As previously noted, Nekrasov died December 27, 1877, according to the prerevolutionary Russian calendar, thus January 8, 1878.—EDITOR]

official to go abroad for an extended period, and it is there that a great many of his poems were written. Later, he rose to a high position in the civil service. Some of his poems have become widely popular and several have been set to music by prominent composers.

Most of Timofeev's poems sound like parodies, however, on the metaphors and vocabulary of the romantic lyric. The titles are indicative: *Otveržennyj* [The Outcast] (almost all undated poems are from the 1835 edition of *Pesni*); *The Misanthrope, The Dagger, To My Demon, The Hermit, The Sailor, Goremyka* [Unlucky Devil], *The Criminal, Loneliness,* and *Mertvec* [The Dead Man]. *Lullaby* even has the subtitle *To the Lover of a Very Terrible Man.* In *Happy Moment*, Timofeev tells the reader:

> Что все почести? — игрушка;
> слава — дым, любовь — хандра,
> дружба — маска, счастье — призрак,
> люди — куклы, случай — бог.

What are all honors? A toy. Fame? Smoke. Love? Melancholy. Friendship? A mask. Happiness? An apparition. People? Puppets. Chance? God.

The poet calls out to those accompanying him, "Caw, you raven; croak, toad; / sing, sing, you spirits of hell . . . / the owl hoots, toads croak," and so on. In "one draft he drained the cup with the sweet drink, and on the cold, sad ground only gall was left." Only the dagger is his "true friend," whom the poet reveres "in a fit of rage, with a wandering gaze . . . with a mad and ardent prayer." Timofeev's poems dwell on storms, fire, murder, destruction, ruins, corpses (described in detail in *Lullaby*), incest, suicide, and so forth. When Moscow is in flames in 1812, a Russian can only cry, "Rage on, you angel of destruction, / Russia is being destroyed; there is no saving it; / let everything be destroyed!"

Timofeev's language is rich, and his meters are varied. At times, he attempts to imitate the form of the folk song, and, like Kol'cov, writes in short lines. Some of his songs have lived on into the twentieth century, particularly as favorites of Philistines. But one should remember that, besides the romantic horror lyric, there was also romantic horror prose, to which Gogol' and authors of historical novels—Ivan Lažečnikov could not do without such scenes—were indebted (see Gogol's *The Bloody Bandore Player*.)

VI

Classicism in the Romantic Period.

1. Russian romantic literature demonstrated that Russian classicism had been unable to establish a stable tradition, in contrast, for instance, to that of Polish literature. Nevertheless, various classicist authors went on writing for a long time and rarely took a militant attitude toward the new romanticism. Some of these classicist writers lived in the provinces, where the new literary currents had not yet arrived; others were of the clergy, which was culturally conservative. It will be enough to name a few of these writers.

Aleksandr Efimovič Izmajlov (1779–1831) was an official. In 1799, he brought out his novel on character development, *Evgenij ili pagubnye sledstvija durnogo vospitanija i soobščestva* [Evgenij or the Pernicious Effect of Bad Upbringing and Company] (1799–1801). Afterward, he published other prose works, fables, and epigrams, in which he used many vulgarisms. Izmajlov was an active journalist, and from 1818 to 1826 he published the magazine *Blagonamerennyj* [Well-Minded]. He was on friendly terms with the younger generation.

The Ukrainian Vasilij Trofimovič Narežnyj (1780–1825), whose name in Ukrainian is spelled *Narižnyj*, was a strange and lonely man. He wrote several novels that anticipate the plots of Gogol's work. The material of his novels is taken partly from the life of the Ukrainian landowners and partly from Ukrainian history, although the treatment is unhistorical. In 1814, Narežnyj published a novel, *Rossijskij Žil-Blas* [A Russian Gil-Blas],[1] but the work was soon banned because of its daring scenes and obvious references to actual persons. Narežnyj's novel on the Caucasus, *Gorskie knjaz'ja* [Mountain Princes], did not appear until after his death. In composition, Narežnyj's novels go back to the eighteenth-century novel of adventure. His style is little better than that of the pre-Karamzin period.

The Ukrainian Grigorij Fedorovič Kvitka-Osnov'janenko (1778–1843) is of importance only as a writer of Ukrainian novellas. His Russian works, which are much weaker, include the novels *Žizn' i Poxoždenija Petra Stepanova, Syna Stolbikova* [The Life and Adventures of Peter Stepanov, Son of Stolbikov] and *Pan Xaljavskij* [Mr. Xaljavskij] (1839) and the play *Priezžij iz stolicy* [The Visitor from the Capital] (1827), the plot of which reminds one of Gogol's *The Inspector General*. These works in Russian are nothing more than vividly related collections of anecdotes.

Prince Aleksandr Aleksandrovič Šaxovskoj (1777–1846) is another late classicist. Like many other writers, Šaxovskoj attended the boarding school at Moscow University and later served in the guard. In 1795, he began a career as a playwright. After studying theater in Paris, he held an administrative position in the St. Petersburg theater. He was an able teacher of actors and was long acknowledged to be the leader in Russian theatrical life. Šaxovskoj wrote approximately a hundred plays, most of them in verse; and because of his position, he had no trouble in getting them staged. At times, his relations with the Karamzin School were strained; and one of his comedies attacking Žukovskij led to the founding of the society of innovators, Arzamas (see chapter II, sec. 8). Nevertheless, Šaxovskoj collaborated with Aleksandr Griboedov; and Puškin and others of his contemporaries had a good opinion of his work. The level of Šaxovskoj's comedies is uneven. They treat a wide range of subjects, and some of the plots are interesting from a cultural-historical point of view. His satires and his serious plays, largely

1. [The first three parts of this novel were published in 1814. The complete edition appeared much later, in 1938.—EDITOR]

adaptations for the stage of well-known literary works, were less successful.

Vladimir Ivanovič Panaev (1792–1859) began in 1817 to publish idylls, an unusual genre in Russian literature. His poetry was soon forgotten. In his prose, V. I. Panaev wrote in the same vein as Karamzin.

The nephew of Ivan Dmitriev (see chapter II, sec. 9), Mixail Aleksandrovič Dmitriev (1796–1866), was a late classicist who published collections of poems in 1831 and 1835 and *Moskovskie èlegii* in 1858, but his language was close to that of the newer poetry. His valuable memoirs, *Meloči iz zapasa moej pamjati* (second edition, 1869), bring back many forgotten episodes from the literary wars of the time.

2. Ivan Andreevič Krylov (1769–1844) was the most important classicist who wrote in the romantic period. He had already passed through several stages of development in the eighteenth century, writing odes, comedies, epigrams, and prose satires and publishing a satirical magazine. But his lasting fame is due to his fables, which were written in the nineteenth century. He was on good terms with the romanticists. His activity, or rather inactivity, as librarian at the Imperial Public Library gave him time for writing. Attempts by some official circles to set him up in opposition to the innovators, especially to Puškin, were unsuccessful. His fables were soon read in the schools and have remained a traditional part of Russian education. Many of his maxims have become proverbial.

A true son of the eighteenth century, Krylov was an enlightener. After overcoming the radical political tendencies of his youth, he became a conservative, a change to which the Napoleonic Wars and other successes of Russia in world politics contributed considerably. He was sometimes able to express his own thoughts in original fables. But, as with all the fabulists of more recent times, most of Krylov's fables are adaptations of traditional material, often used by Russian writers in the past. Although there were many Russian fabulists in the eighteenth century, they are now forgotten, with the possible exception of Ivan Xemnicer and Ivan Dmitriev.

The Russian word for fable is *basnja*, which is connected with the verb *bajat'*, often used in the sense of "to chat" or "to gossip." Perhaps for this reason, the Russian fable is often a leisurely, chatty tale with a transparent moral, which is often added in a brief observation at the end, sometimes in the form of a maxim. Krylov retains this structure. The main charm of his fables is in his language. In the course of his life, Krylov had occasion to learn the popular language of various regions of Russia. As a result, his language is incomparably rich; he introduced many words and expressions from the popular language into the literary language or at least preserved them from neglect. It is true, however, that most of Krylov's original and attractive expressions survive in modern Russian only in quotations, as, for example, "*emu by ruku priložit'*," "*glaza prodrat'*," "*udarili v smyčki*," "*na volka tol'ko slava*," "*prošibli slezy*," "*net ugomonu*," "*vkos' i vprjam*," "*stavit' v malost'*," and "*net priliki voru*." Curiously, there are a number of Krylov's fables that require explanatory footnotes in school or for the average reader because of the mythological references (Parnassus, Juno, Juno's bird, Achilles, Jupiter, Zeus, Aeolus's sons, Hercules, Homer—even in the obsolete form "Omir"). Krylov also wrote many fables with historical references.

In content, the morals of Krylov's fables are quite varied. Some of them deal with contemporary events. For instance, an admiral who is supposed to have made strategic mistakes on land during Napoleon's retreat is likened to a pike that joins a cat in catching mice. Other fables contain general observations on the corruptibility of officials, on the impossibility of obtaining justice from the mighty, on the poor advisers of rulers, and so forth. There are even fables that were said to allude to the shortcomings of the tsars. In judging the tsar, Krylov was more skeptical of Alexander I than of Nicholas I.

One should remember that the older Krylov had become as conservative as he had once been radical and had long ago set aside his free thinking. The morals of his fables are not always traditional but are often too conservative. He is critical of foreign countries and even attacks traveling abroad—here he may have been thinking of the many trips abroad taken by Alexander I. He does not believe that one should doubt the wisdom of Providence. The lower classes grumble only because they do not understand the good intentions of the authorities. Krylov also criticizes, in his "Vodolazy," the "audacious intellect" (*derzkij um*) that is brought to ruin by striving after knowledge. Freedom without "sensible moderation" seemed dangerous to Krylov, a view that did not need to be emphasized during the reign of Nicholas I. Philosophy, too, seemed dangerous. This thought is expressed somewhat vaguely in *Ogorodnik i filosof*, but more precisely in *Filin i osel*. The dangerous writer, by which Krylov certainly means Voltaire, should be more severely punished in hell than a harmless thief, since the works of the writer can "fill a land with murder, discord, and revolt and lead it to destruction" (*Sočinitel' i razbojnik* [1817]).

But, of course, few readers have turned to the fables of Krylov for ideological instruction. His fables have had their greatest influence as poems to be studied in school.

VII

Notes on the Cultural History of the Romantic Period

1. Literature is intimately connected with cultural history. One's view of man, history, and the world is expressed in works of art, particularly in literature. In the first years of disputation, some Russian formalists denied that the content of literature had any significance. This is, of course, an exaggerated view that no one today would take seriously. On the other hand, works on purely theoretical and ideological matters should not be considered belles-lettres. Here we shall deal briefly with developments in cultural history that were of importance to belles-lettres in Russia during the romantic period.

In the eighteenth century, two currents from Western Europe were received in Russia with only minor variations. On the one hand, there was the Enlightenment, which was also called "Voltairianism"; and its proponents were sometimes called "Voltairians." On the other hand, there was a movement that derived from Western European Pietism and that was carried on in eighteenth-century Russia by the Freemasons, who rallied around Nikolaj Ivanovič Novikov. Disappointed by the results of the French Revolution, some of the enlighteners eventually gave up their cause. The Freemasons never really recovered from the ban placed on them by Catherine II and her destruction of their organization. But for a short time, both of these eighteenth-century movements were revived in the early decades of the nineteenth century. Then the Enlightenment gave way to romanticism, even though the first generation of romanticists sometimes reverted to Voltairianism. There was only a small group of

Freemasons left; they were joined by the Pietists and visionaries who came to Russia and the court of the tsar after the Napoleonic Wars. This group and the Bible Society, which was not at all visionary, were disbanded by Alexander I after his sudden conversion to an orthodox religious view in 1820, and some of their members were exiled. Both of these currents, that of the Enlightenment and of Pietism, continued to exist in Russia, but in different forms.

2. In addition to isolated seekers after truth, mystical and idealistic philosophical interests were pursued by the group of young men who gathered around Prince Vladimir Fedorovič Odoevskij. These were the *ljubomudry*, or philosophers, who were at first concerned, not with the mystical tradition, but with Schelling and his school of thought. (For earlier discussion of the *ljubomudry*, see Chapter IV, sec. 1.) Besides Prince V. F. Odoevskij, they included Stepan Ševyrev, Fedor Tjutčev, Mixail Pogodin, I. V. Kireevskij, and Wilhelm Küchelbecker. In this circle, the emphasis was on German philosophy and on philosophical literature in general. But it would be a mistake to assume that all members of the circle knew Schelling's philosophy really well. Later, most of them went over to other ideological points of view, but to some extent they were still influenced by the aesthetics and by the philosophy of nature and history of German idealism. Some of the members of the Odoevskij circle became Slavophiles, and others of them were skeptical of Western European philosophy in general; they did not notice how much they were still influenced by elements of German idealism.

While the *ljubomudry* were occupied with Schelling, various secret societies were meeting that were later to become known as Decembrists; their members were by no means in agreement in their philosophical views or in their political program. But many of them were still close to the eighteenth-century tradition of Enlightenment and to the political radicalism of Aleksandr Nikolaevič Radiščev (1749–1802), whose opposition to the monarchy and to serfdom was related to the Enlightenment. In these circles, there was more interest in politics and the national economy than in purely philosophical matters. The suppression of the Decembrist Revolt in 1825 removed a large number of important men from Russian intellectual life, but did not eradicate their views. Consequently, several currents of thought were joined together; vestiges of Enlightenment were mixed with some skepticism, materialism, and atheism. As we have mentioned, one finds traces of Voltairianism even in some romanticists; and this tendency to combine features of different periods was increased by the unfortunate Russian domestic policy of the 1830s and 1840s and by the influence of Western European revolutionary movements, the French Revolution of 1830, so-called Utopian Socialism, and the period preceding the Revolution of 1848. Around 1830, the most important influences were the new Western European radicalism and socialism. It was not until the 1840s that original Russian movements with radical political and social programs began to make themselves felt. The thoughts of these movements were expressed by some of the writers of the Natural School.

3. Of greater importance for the cultural development of Russia was the emergence of two philosophically opposed groups, the Slavophiles and the Westernizers. Aleksej S. Xomjakov (see chapter V, sec. 15), Ivan Vasil'evič Kireevskij (1806–1856), and Jurij Fedorovič Samarin (1819–1876) joined the first group of Konstantin S. Aksakov (also discussed in chapter V, sec. 15). One should not overestimate the extent of agreement among the Slavophiles. K. S. Aksakov and Samarin were for a long time proponents of Hegel, but Xomjakov was opposed to him. I. V. Kireevskij had taken a great interest in Schelling's philosophy. There were only two points on which the early Slavophiles agreed in their philosophical views. They regarded the Orthodox Church as a firm foundation for Russian national culture, and they believed that Russia's historical way was different from that of Western Europe. Thinking as they did, they took a skeptical view of the reforms of Peter I and saw in the Russia before Peter, or even before Ivan the Terrible, the germ of a great native culture that had subsequently been preserved only by the simple Russian folk. Actually, one should call the first group of Slavophiles *Russophiles*. The name Slavophile came from the idea of several of their partisans, such as Mixail Pogodin, that the other Slavic

peoples were spiritually close to the Russians. In literature, Slavophile motifs are obvious in only a few poets: in addition to the Slavophile writers already mentioned, perhaps in the late work of Fedor Glinka. Russian literature is indebted to the Slavophiles for their interest in the Slavic folk song, although Aleksandr Vostokov had already published the Serbian epics and Puškin had written *Pesni zapadnyx slavjan* [Songs of the Western Slavs] (1834). (Incidentally, Puškin's *Songs* are based, by and large, on a "forgery" by the French poet Prosper Mérimée.) The Slavophiles also contributed to Russian literature occasional treatments of peculiarly Russian themes; for example, they praised Moscow as opposed to St. Petersburg, which was thought to be an alien city. The early Slavophiles were by no means blindly hostile to European culture. To Xomjakov, the West was "the land of holy wonders"; by wonders, he had in mind the cultural achievements of the West.

The Westernizers spoke out against the high opinion of Russian cultural values, but they were even less unified than the Slavophiles. Although the Slavophiles saw in Russian culture the germ for an independent development, the Westernizers thought that Russia would have to go the same way that Europe had already gone. There were three groups of Westernizers. The first of them agreed with Tsar Nicholas I that Russia was not essentially different from the countries of Western Europe; to be sure, Russia was a little backward in some respects; but, all in all, Russia was superior to the weak, politically unstable West. Many liberals felt the same way; and although they rejected the government's policy, they wished to follow the example of "progressive" Western Europe. The second group of Westernizers were the political radicals, who were actually opposed to the first group. They did not look to the ruling classes in the "progressive" West, but to the socialists and radicals. This was the way of the future for Russia, they thought, whether or not these movements won out in the West. It was this group of Russian radicals that became strong in the last half of the nineteenth century. In the forties, as the period in Russian intellectual history from 1835 to 1845 is called, this group included the critic and publicist Vissarion Grigor'evič Belinskij (1811–1848), who is important more for his political influence than for his dubious literary opinions; Aleksandr Ivanovič Herzen (in Russian, *Gercen* [1812–1870]), who also made a contribution to Russian literature as a stylist and writer of novellas; and several of their friends.

The third group of Westernizers was represented by the original thinker Petr Jakovlevič Čaadaev (1793–1856), who looked for guidance to the Catholic West. He thought that Russia would have to join the Western Catholic tradition in order to overcome its isolated position in world history and to develop into a really cultured country. Most Westernizers had a low opinion of Russia before the time of Peter the Great. Only members of official circles, who sometimes assumed a pseudo-Slavophile manner of expressing themselves, thought that the Russian past had been altogether splendid.

In literature, there were few spokesmen of Western thought. Before 1855, radical and socialistic ideas seldom found their way into printed works. But there was no difference between Slavophiles and Westernizers in regard to the influence of Western literature. Among the Slavophiles, there were those who revered Schiller; and Xomjakov relied on French and German theological sources, not only in his prose work but also in his poems.

4. One should not overlook an important aspect of Russian cultural history in the forties, the interest in the philosophy of Hegel. In this connection one should think not only of the circle of the talented Nikolaj Vladimirovič Stankevič (1813–1840), but also of those influenced indirectly by the circle, such as Vissarion Belinskij, Aleksandr Herzen, Nikolaj Ogarev, I. S. Turgenev, Mixail Bakunin, K. S. Aksakov, and the late romantic poets Vasilij Krasov and Ivan Kljušnikov, who have already been mentioned (see chapter V, sec. 16). For that matter, Stankevič himself wrote poetry (also chapter V, sec. 16).

The importance of Hegelianism for Russian literature lies not so much in the fact that it contributed to supplanting romanticism, as one might have expected from the antiromantic philosophy of Hegel. Rather, Hegelianism was important because the writers who embraced it, whether only for a time or for all their lives, were influenced by its aesthetic doctrine and its philosophy of history. Hegelian philosophy was of great importance to the development of scholarly Russian and, to some extent, of literary Russian. Many Hegelians, who should not be taken seriously, appear as characters in literature, in Apollon Grigor'ev, Afanasij Fet, I. S. Turgenev, Jakov Polonskij, and others. In comedies of the period, there are often caricatures of Hegelians. And there were attempts to set forth the thought of Hegel in poetry, as in the verse of Konstantin S. Aksakov.

Bibliography of Russian Romanticism

Editor's note: The original bibliography on the Romantic period of Russian literature, compiled by Professor D. I. Čiževskij and included in the German edition of this work, was so extensive that, at the request of the publisher, I have revised it.

In order to avoid any biased approach in the revision of this bibliography, I was guided by the following principle: I excluded, first of all, the references to the original texts of Russian writers and poets of this period. The number of editions of these texts is extensive and is augmented by new publications almost every year. Thereafter, in most cases, the German works on Russian Romanticism were excluded. However, the works of Professor Čiževskij and some other publications which, in my opinion, were of paramount importance, were retained. In order to facilitate the work of the English and American readers of this volume, I added the most important research in English on Russian Romanticism as well as on the individual writers and poets of this era. In several cases, recent Russian publications pertaining to the topic of this book were also added. The most complete bibliography in Russian can be found in AN SSSR *Istoriia russkoi literatury XIX veka, Bibliograficheskii ukazatel,* edited by K. Muratova (Moscow-Leningrad, 1962).

Those persons who would like to use primarily English translations of Russian texts are advised to consult *The Literature of the World in English Translation,* Richard Lewanski, compiler, vol. II: *The Slavic Literatures: Beginnings to 1960* (New York: New York Public Library, 1967). For the publication of books after 1960, we suggest that the reader consult *American Bibliography of Slavic and East European Studies* (Bloomington, Indiana: Indiana University Press, 1957 –). A general survey of bibliographies on Russian literature can be found in *A Guide to the Bibliographies of Russian Literature,* by Serge A. Zenkovsky and David L. Armbruster (Nashville: Vanderbilt University Press, 1970). It will also be helpful to consult the book review section and the list of books recently received in the *Slavic Review, Slavic and East European Journal,* the *Russian Review, Russian Literature Triquarterly,* and the *Slavonic and East European Review.*

We remind our readers that the bibliography, both in the original German edition of Professor Čiževskij's book and in the present American edition, has not been organized alphabetically by the writers' and poets' names, but according to the chapters of this text. It might also be helpful to readers not familiar with the Russian language to remember that there is no single, all-purpose method of transliterating Russian words from the Cyrillic into a non-Cyrillic alphabet. Several different systems have been developed to meet the needs of varied types of readers and publications. That adopted for the general reading public is different from that used by specialists in various fields; and both of these systems often differ from that used by the Library of Congress and many other American libraries. As Professor Čiževskij mentions in his preface, the system used in the text of this translation is the international system preferred by linguists and literary scholars whose field is Russian and Slavic studies. For the convenience of readers who may wish to do further research in the field, however, this bibliography uses a different system, that followed by the Library of Congress. Thus the names of many authors, including that of Professor Čiževskij himself, are spelled differently within the text from the way they appear in the bibliography. We may add that Professor Čiževskij's name may often be seen in several different spellings, depending on the system of transliteration used: *Čiževskij, Čyzevskyj, Tschizhevskii,* and *Chyzhevs'kyi.*

S.A.Z.

List of Abbreviations

The following abbreviations are used throughout this bibliography.

ACICS   American Contributions to the International Congress of Slavists

AfsP   *Archiv für slavische Philologie* (periodical)

AN   Akademiia Nauk SSSR

ASEER   *American Slavic and East European Review* (periodical)

BBP   Biblioteka poeta, bol'shaia seriia

CL   *Comparative Literature* (periodical)

FZ   *Filologicheskie zapiski* (Voronezh) (periodical)

IORIa   *Izvestiia otdeleniia russkogo iazyka* (periodical)

IpRIa   *Izvestiia po russkomu iazyku* (periodical)

IRK   *Istoriia russkoi kritiki* (AN SSSR)

IRL   *Istoriia russkoi literatury*

IRL OK   *Istoriia russkoi literatury XIX veka,* edited by D. N. Ovsianiko-Kulikovskii

IRP   *Istoriia russkoi poezii* (AN SSSR)

IRR   *Istoriia russkogo romana* (AN SSSR)

ISS   Indiana Slavic Studies

IV   *Istoricheskii vestnik* (periodical)

KLE   *Kratkaia Literaturnaia Entsiklopediia*

KUI   *Kievskie universitetskie izvestiia* (periodical)

LE   *Literaturnaia entsiklopediia*

LN   *Literaturnoe nasledstvo* (serial)

MBP   Biblioteka poeta, malaia seriia

MIRLIa   *Materialy i issledovaniia po istorii russkogo literaturnogo iazyka* (serial)

NZ   *Novyi Zhurnal* (New York)

OSP   Oxford Slavonic Papers

PI   Pedagogicheskii Institut

RA   *Russkii arkhiv* (periodical)

RBS   Russkii biograficheskii slovar'
RFV   *Russkii fililogicheskii vestnik* (Warsaw) (periodical)
RL   *Russkaia literatura* (periodical)
RLT   *Russian Literature Triquarterly* (1971 –)
RM   *Russkaia mysl'* (periodical)
RR   *Russian Review*
RSt   *Russkaia starina* (periodical)
RV   *Russkii vestnik* (periodical)
Sl   Slavia (Prague)
SEEJ   *Slavic and East European Journal* (periodical)
SEER   *Slavic and East European Review* (periodical)
SPRL   *Studies in Russian and Polish Literature in Honor of Woclaw*
           Lednichi
SR   *Slavic Review* (periodical)
SZ   *Sovremennye Zapiski* (Paris) (periodical)
TONRL   *Trudy otdela novoi russkoi literatury* (serial)
Un.Iz.   *Universitetskie Izvestiia* (periodical)
UZ   Uchenye Zapiski
VE   *Vestnik Evropy* (periodical)
WdS   *Die Welt der Slaven* (periodical)
WSJ   *Wiener slavistisches Jahrbuch* (periodical)
ZfS   *Zeitschrift für Slawistik* (periodical)
ZfsP   *Zeitschrift für slavische Philologie* (periodical)
ZMNP   *Zhurnal Ministerstva Narodnogo Prosveshcheniia* (periodical)
Ukr. Q   *Ukrainian Quarterly* (periodical)

CHAPTER I

Among the most important general works we should mention are the following.

Sections 1–5:

In Russian

AN SSSR. Institut russkoi literatury. *Istoriia russkoi poezii*. Vols. I–II. Moscow-Leningrad, 1968, 1969.

AN SSSR. Institut russkoi literatury. *Istoriia russkogo romana*. Vols. I–II. Moscow-Leningrad, 1962, 1964.

AN SSSR. Institut russkoi literatury. *Istoriia russkoi kritiki*. Vols. I–II. Leningrad, 1958.

AN SSSR. Institut russkoi literatury. *Istoriia russkoi literatury*. Vols. 5–9. Moscow-Leningrad, 1941–1956.

Bitsilli, P. *Etiudy po russkoi poezii*. Prague, 1925.

Bagrii, A. *Russkaia literatura 19—pervoi chetverti 20 veka*. Baku, 1926.

Bulich, N. *Ocherki po istorii russkoi literatury i prosveshcheniia*. Vols. I–II. St. Petersburg, 1902–1905, 1912.

Eikhenvald, Iu. *Siluety russkikh pisatelei*. Vols. I–III. Moscow, 1906. Last revised edition, Berlin, 1922.

Kirpichnikov, A. *Ocherki po novoi russkoi literature*. Vols. I–II. Moscow, 1903.

Kratkaia literaturnaia entsiklopediia. Vols. I–VII—. Moscow, 1962—.

Ovsianiko-Kulikovskii, D.N. *Istoriia russkoi intelligentsii*. Moscow, 1906–07.

Ovsianiko-Kulikovskii, D.N., editor. *Istoriia russkoi literatury 19 veka*. Vols. I–VI. Moscow, 1908–10.

Pypin, A. *Istoriia russkoi literatury*. Vol. IV. Petersburg, 1899.

———. *Kharakteristika literaturnykh mnenii ot 20-kh do 50-kh godov*. Istoricheskie ocherki. St. Petersburg, 1873. Last edition, 1909.

Razumnik, R.I. *Istoriia russkoi obshchestvennoi mysli*. Vols. I–II. St. Petersburg, 1907. Revised edition, Petrograd, 1918.

Russkie pisateli—Biobibliograficheskii slovar'. Compiled by A.P. Spasibenko, and N.M. Gaidenkov. Moscow, 1971.

Rozanov, I. *Russkaia lirika*. Vols. I–II. Moscow, 1914–25.

Sakulin, P. *Russkaia literatura*. Vol. II. Moscow, 1929.

———. "Russkaia literatura vo vtoroi chetverti veka." In *Istoriia Rossii 19 veka*. Moscow: A. and I. Granat, publishers, circa 1912.

Sokolov, A., editor. *Lektsii po istorii russkoi literatury*. Vols. I–II. Moscow. 1951.

Sovetskaia literaturnaia entsiklopediia. Vols. 1–9, 11. Moscow, 1929–39.

Tkhorzhevskii, I. *Russkaia literatura.* 2nd edition. Paris, 1950.

Vengerov, S. *Ocherki po istorii russkoi literatury s epokhi Belinskogo do nashikh dnei.* St. Petersburg, 1907.

IN WESTERN LANGUAGES

Lettenbauer, W. *Russische Literaturgeschichte.* 2nd edition. Wiesbaden, 1958.

Lo Gatto, Ettore. *Histoire de la littérature russe des origines á nos jours.* Bruges-Paris, 1965.

Luther, A. *Geschichte der russischen Literatur.* Leipzig, 1924.

Mercereau, John, Jr. "Yes, Virginia, there Was a Russian Romantic Movement." *RLT* III (1972), 128–148.

———. "Normative Distinction of Russian Romanticism and Realism." *ACICS* VII (1973).

Mirsky, D.S. *A History of Russian Literature.* Abridged and edited by Francis J. Whitfield. New York: Alfred A. Knopf, 1949.

———. *Contemporary Russian Literature (1881–1925).* New York: Alfred A. Knopf, 1926.

Slonim, Marc. *The Epic of Russian Literature.* New York: Oxford University Press, 1950.

Stender-Petersen, A. *Geschichte der russischen Literatur.* Vols. I–II. Munchen, 1957.

Varneke, B. *History of the Russian Theatre, Seventeenth through Nineteenth Century.* New York: Macmillan, 1951.

CHAPTER II

Section 1

Blagoi, D. "Karamzin." In *LE*, vol. V.

Dewey, H.W. "Sentimentalism in the Historical writings of N.M. Karamzin." *ACICS* 47 (1958).

Eikhenbaum, B. *Skvoz' literatury.* Petrograd, 1924. 2nd edition, 1962.

Gukovskii, G. Chapter on Karamzin. In *IRL.* Vol. V. Moscow-Leningrad: AN SSSR, 1945.

Iatsimirskii, A. "N.M. Karamzin." In *IRL-OK.* Vol. I. Moscow: Mir, 1908.

Kucherov, A. Chapter on Karamzin. In *IRL.* Vol. V. Moscow-Leningrad: AN SSSR, 1945.

———. "N.M. Karamzin." In *Karamzin i Dmitriev.* Leningrad, 1953.

Pipes, R., editor. *Karamzin's Memoirs on Ancient and New Russia.* Cambridge, Mass.: Harvard University Press, 1959.

Piksanov, N. "Bednaia Aniuta i Bednaia Liza." In *XVIII vek*, Sbornik. Vol. III. Moscow: AN SSSR, 1958.

Skipina, K. "Chuvstvitel'naia povest'." *Russkaia proza*. Leningrad, 1926.

Section 2:

Desnitskii, V.; A. Kucherov; E. Kupreianova; A. Maksimovich. Articles on "Karamzin and Sentimentalism." In *IRL*. Vol. V. Moscow-Leningrad: AN SSSR, 1941.

Gukovskii, G. Chapter on Karamzin. In *Russkaia literatura 18 veka*. Moscow, 1939.

Kotliarevskii, N. *Literaturnye napravleniia Aleksandrovskoi epokhi*. Petrograd, 1917.

Maslov, V. "Interes k Sternu v russkoi literature." *Sbornik v chest' V. Sreznevskogo*. Leningrad, circa 1930.

———. *Ossian v Rossii*. Trudy Pushkinskogo doma, 1928.

Pumpianskii, L. "Sentimentalism." In *IRL*. Vol. IV. Moscow-Leningrad: AN SSSR, 1947.

Vinogradov, V. *Ocherki po istorii russkogo literaturnogo iazyka*. Moscow, 1934, and reprints.

Vvedenskii, D. *Etiudy o vliianii ossianovskoi poezii*. Nezhin, 1918.

Section 3:

Bulakhovskii, L. *Russkii literaturnyi iazyk pervoi poloviny XIX v.* Vol. I. Moscow, 1954. Vol. II. Kiev, 1957.

Efimov. A., T. Ivanova, and N. Shvedova, Articles on Karamzin. In *MIRLIa* I (1959).

Section 6:

Sipovskii, V. *Karamzin kak avtor pisem russkogo puteshestvennika*. St. Petersburg, 1899.

Section 8: *The Arzamas*

Borovkova-Maikova, editor. *Arzamas i arzamasskie protokoly*. Leningrad, 1933.

Sidorov, E. "Literaturnoe obshchestvo Arzamas." *ZMNP* VI, VII (1901).

Section 9: *I. I. Dmitriev*

Kucherov, A., editor "I.I. Dmitriev." In *Karamzin i Dmitriev*, pp. 7–242. Moscow: BBP, 1953.

Kupreianova, E. "Dmitriev." In *IRL*. Vol. V. Moscow-Leningrad: AN SSSR, 1941.

Vinogradov, V. "Nabliudenie nad iazykom i stilem Dmitrieva." *MIRLIa* I (1949).

Section 10: *V. L. Pushkin*

Khalanskii, M. "O vliianii V. L. Pushkina na poeticheskoe tvorchestvo
A.S. Pushkina." *Kharkovskii Univ. Sbornik v pamiat' A.S. Pushkina.*
Kharkov, 1900, and separately.
Kupreianova, E. "Dmitriev." In *IRL*. Vol. V. Moscow-Leningrad: AN
SSSR, 1941.
Piksanov, N. "V. L. Pushkin." In *RBS*. St. Petersburg, 1900.

Section 11: *V. Ozerov*

Maikov, L. "Viazemskii i Pushkin ob Ozerove." In *Starina i Novizna* I
(1897).
Maksimovich, N. "Ozerov." In *IRL*. Vol. V. Moscow-Leningrad: AN
SSSR, 1941.
Potapov, P. *Iz istorii russkogo teatra. Zhizn' i deiatel'nost' Ozerova.*
Odessa 1915. Also in *Zapiski Novorossiskogo Universiteta* II (1915).

Iu. A. Neledinskii-Meletskii

Rozanov, I. *Russkaia lirika.* Moscow, 1914.

M. V. Milonov

Bitner, G., editor. "Poety-satiriki kontsa 18 nachala 19 v." *BBP*, 1959.
Longinov, M. "Materialy dlia pol. sob. soch. Milonova." *RA* 1864, 3.
Mochul'skii, V. "Milonov." In *FZ* (1908), 1.
Rozanov, I. *Russkaia lirika.* Moscow, 1914.

N. I. Gnedich

Kukulevich, A. "Russkaia idilliia Gnedicha . . . Rybaki." *UZ Leningrad-
skogo Universiteta.* 1939, 46, 3.
Orlov, V., and A. Kukulevich. "Gnedich." In *IRL*. Vol. V. Moscow-
Leningrad: AN SSSR, 1941.
Rozanov, I. *Russkaia lirika.* Moscow, 1914.
Tikhonravov, N. "Gnedich." In *Sochineniia*, by N. Tikhonravov. Vol. III.
Moscow, 1898, 2.

A. X. Vostokov

Orlov, V. "Vostokov." In *Poety-radishchevtsy.* Moscow, 1952.
———. *Russkie prosvetiteli*, 1790–1800. Moscow, 1950, 1953.
Rozanov, I. *Russkaia lirika.* Moscow, 1914.

Section 12: *K. N. Batiushkov*

Alekseev, M. *Vestnik Leningradskogo Universiteta.* 1955, VI.

Eliash, N. "K voprosu o vliianii Batiushkova na Pushkina." In *Pushkin i ego sovremenniki*. 19–20, 1914.

Ivask, Iu. "Batiushkov." *NZ* 46 (1914).

Gershenzon, M. "Pushkin i Batiushkov." *Atenei*. Petrograd-Moscow, 1924, 1–2.

Nekrasov, A. "Batiushkov i Petrarka." In *IORIa* XVI (1911), 4.

Rozanov, I. *Russkaia lirika*. Moscow, 1914.

Section 13: *G. P. Kamenev*

Bobrov, E. "Kamenev." In *Varshavskie Univ. Izvestiia*. 1905.

Lotman, Iu., editor. "Kamenev." In *Poety nachala 19 veka*. *MBP*, 1961.

Orlov, V., editor. *Poety-radishchevtsy*. *BBP*, 1935.

Zalkina, G. *Kamenev, 1772–1803*. Kazan, 1926.

I. P. Pnin

Orlov, V., editor. "Poety-radishchevtsy." In *BBP*. Moscow-Leningrad, 1935.

Orlov, V., editor. *Russkie prosvetiteli*. Moscow, 1950.

Zapadov, V. A. "Pnin i Derzhavin." *RL* I. (1965).

V. V. Popugaev

Orlov, V., editor. "Poety-radishchevtsy." In *BBP*. Moscow-Leningrad, 1935.

Orlov, V., editor. *Russkie prosvetiteli*. Moscow, 1950.

A. F. Merzliakov

Ivanov, I. *Istoriia russkoi kritiki*. Vol. II. St. Petersburg, 1898. (Also in *Mir Bozhii*, 1897, 8.)

Mordovchenko, N. "Merzliakov." In *Russkaia kritika pervoi chetverti 19 v*. Moscow-Leningrad, 1959.

Rozanov, I. "Merzliakov." In *Russkaia lirika*. Moscow, 1914.

N. F. Ostolopov

Berkov, P. Article in *LE*, vol. VIII.

Orlov, V., editor. "Poety-radishchevtsy." In *BBP*. Moscow-Leningrad, 1935.

Ostolopov, N. *Slovar' drevnei i novoi poezii*. I–III. St. Petersburg, 1821.

A. F. Voeikov

Bitner, G. "Poety-satiriki kontsa 18—nachala 19 veka." In *BBP*. Moscow-Leningrad, 1959.

Mordovchenko, N. *Russkaia kritika pervoi chetverti 19 veka*. Moscow-Leningrad, 1959.

Veselovskii, A. *Zhukovskii, poeziia chuvstva i serdechnogo voobrazheniia*. St. Petersburg, 1904. 2nd edition, Petrograd, 1918.

CHAPTER III

There are not many general surveys on Russian Romanticism which deserve to be mentioned. The following are useful.

Section 1:

Beletskii, A., editor. *Russkii romantizm.* Leningrad, 1927.

Kozmin, N. *Ocherki po istorii russkogo romantizma.* St. Petersburg, 1903.

Sakulin, P. "Dvorianskie stili: Russkii romantizm." In *Russkaia literatura*, by P. Sakulin. Vol. II. Moscow, 1929.

Sokolov, A. *Ot romantizma k realizmu.* Moscow, 1957.

Tschizhevskii, D. *Einige Aufgaben der Romantikforschung WdS* I (1956), 1.

Zamotin, I. *Rannie romanticheskie vliianiia v russkoi literature.* Warsaw, 1900.

———. *Romantizm 20-kh godov 19 stoletiia v russkoi literature.* Vols. I–II. St. Petersburg, 1903–07. 2nd edition, Moscow, 1911–13.

Special problems of Russian Romanticism are discussed in several works:

Gerie, V. "Narodnost' i progress." In *Ideia narodlovlastiia*, by V. Gerie. Moscow, 1904.

Glan, M. "Iz istorii russkogo romantizma 30-kh godov." *Literaturnaia ucheba.* 1935, 7.

Gorodetskii, B. P., editor. *Istoriia russkoi poezii*, pp. 224–250. Leningrad: AN SSSR, 1968.

Gukovskii, G. In the collection: *Pushkin, rodonachal'nik novoi russkoi literatury.* Moscow-Leningrad, 1941.

———. "Pushkin i poetika russkogo romantizma." *Izvestiia AN. Otdelenie literatury i iazyka* (1940), 2.

———. Ocherki po istorii russkogo realizma. Vol. I. Pushkin i russkie romantiki. Saratov, 1946.

Korobka, N. "Gogol' kak romantik." *Vesy* IV (1909).

Mordovchenko, N. *Russkaia kritika pervoi treti 19 v.* Moscow-Leningrad, 1959.

Rodzevich, S. "K istorii russkogo romantizma." *RFV* (1917), 1–2.

Rusova, Z. "Romanticheskaia poema v dekabristkoi literature." *UZ Gor'kovskogo univ.* 39 (1957).

Sokolov, A. *Ocherki po istorii russkoi poemy.* Moscow, 1955.

Tschizhevskii, D. "Pushkin und die Romantik." *Slavische Rundschau*

2 (1937).

―――. "Pushkin und die deutsche Romantik." *Germano-slavica* (1937).

Vanslov, V. *Estetika romantizma*. Moscow, 1966.

See also Bibliography for Chapter IV, section 16.

Section 2: *V. A. Zhukovskii*

Durylin, S. "Russkie pisateli u Gete v Veimare." *LN* 4–6 (1932).

Eikhenbaum, B. *Melodika russkogo liricheskogo stikha*. Petrograd, 1922.

Galiun, I. "K voprosu o literaturnykh vliianiakh v poezii Zhukovskogo." *KUI* 4 (1916).

Petukhov, E. "Zhukovskii v Derpte." *UZ Iurevskogo Univ.* 5 (1904).

Rezanov, V. "Iz razyskanii o sochineniiakh Zhukovskogo." *ZMNP* (1906–16) and separate: Vols. I–II. St. Petersburg, 1906 and 1916.

Tikhonravov, N. *Sochineniia*, III, 1. Moscow, 1898.

Veselovskii, A. *Zhukovskii. Poeziia chuvstva i serdechnogo voobrazheniia*. St. Petersburg, 1904. 2nd edition, Petrograd, 1918.

Vol'pe, G. "Zhukovskii." In *IRL*. Vol. V. Moscow-Leningrad: AN SSSR, 1941.

Zagarin, P. *Zhukovskii i ego proizvedeniia*. Moscow, 1883.

Zaitsev, B. *Zhukovskii*. Paris, 1951.

Zeidlits, K. *Zhizn' Zhukovskogo*. St. Petersburg, 1883.

Zhirmunskii, V. *Gete v russkoi literature*. Leningrad, 1937.

Section 3:

Boborov, S. "O stikhotvornom perevode" (Zhukovskii i Tiutchev). *Inostrannaia literatura* 7–8 (1940).

Cheshikhin-Vetrinskii, V. *Zhukovskii kak perevodchik Shillera*. Riga, 1895.

Tschizhevskii, D. "J. P. Hebel in der russischen Literatur und Schule." *Ruperto-Carola* XII, 28, (1960).

Section 5:

Eiges, I. "Zhukovskii." In *Sofiia* 1 Moscow, 1914.

Sections 6–7: *A. V. Viazemskii*

Ginzburg, L. "Viazemskii." In *IRL*. Vol. VI. Moscow-Leningrad: AN SSSR, 1953.

Kul'man, N. "Kniaz' Viazemskii kak kritik." *IORIa* IX (1904), 1.

Kutanov, N. *Dekabristy i ikh vremia* II (1932).

Wytrzens, G. *Prinz A. W. Wjazemskij*. Vienna, 1961.

Section 8: *K. F. Ryleev*

Bazanov, V. *Poety-dekabristy.* Moscow-Leningrad, 1950.

Gofman, V. "Ryleev." In *Russkaia poeziia 19 v.* 1929.

Maslov, V. *Literaturnaia deiatel'nost' Ryleeva.* Kiev, 1912. Also in *KUI* (1912); *KUI* (1916), 2.

Neiman, B. *Ryleev. Zhizn' i tvorchestvo.* Moscow, 1946.

Rozanov, I. *Poety 20-kh godov 19-go veka.* Moscow, 1925.

Sirotin, A. "Ryleev." *RA* 6 (1890).

————. "Ryleev i Nemtsevich." *RA* 1 (1898).

Tseitlin, A. *Tvorchestvo Ryleeva.* Moscow, 1955.

Section 9: *A. S. Griboedov*

Blagoi, D. "Griboedov." In *LE*, vol. II.

Blok, A. *Sobranie sochinenii.* Vol. XI. Moscow, 1934.

Goncharov, I. "Mil'on terzanii." In Goncharov's *Polnoe sobranie sochinenii.* Vol. VIII. Moscow, 1958.

Kleiner, B. Zagadka "Gore ot uma." *Scandoslavica* VII (1961).

Narkov, N. "Dva Chatskikh." *NZ* 53 (1958).

Nechkina, M. *Griboedov i dekabristy.* Moscow, 1951.

Orlov, V. *Iazyk russkikh pisatelei.* Moscow-Leningrad, 1948.

Ovsianiko-Kulikovskii, D. *Istoriia russkoi intelligentsii.* Vol. I. Moscow, 1961.

Piksanov, N. *Griboedov i Molier.* Moscow, 1928.

————. *Griboedov.* Leningrad, 1934.

————. *Tvorcheskaia istoriia Gore ot uma.* Moscow-Leningrad, 1929.

Rozanov, I. "Griboedov i Pushkin." *Pushkinskii sbornik.* Moscow, 1900.

Tomashevskii, B. "Stikh Gore ot uma." In *Stikh i iazyk*, by B. Tomashevskii. Moscow-Leningrad, 1959.

Tynianov, Iu. *Arkhaisty i novatory.* Leningrad, 1929.

————. *Smert' Vazir-Mukhtara* Moscow, 1929. (A novel.)

Vinokur, G. Gore ot uma kak pamiatnik russkoi khudozhestvennoi rechi. *UZ Moskovskogo Univ.* 128 (1948), 1.

Section 10: *A. S. Pushkin*

GENERAL:

Alekseev, M., editor. *Pushkin. Issledovaniia i Materialy.* Vols. I–III. Moscow-Leningrad, 1956–62.

Bakhtin, Nicholas. "Pushkin." *OSP* XI, 38–45.

Bitsilli, P. "Iz zametok o Pushkine." *Sl* X (1931), 3; *Sl.* XI (1932), 4.

Blagoi, D. *Tvorcheskii put' Pushkina.* Moscow, 1967.

Bowra, W. Pushkin. *OSP* I (1950).

Briusov, V. *Moi Pushkin*. Moscow-Leningrad, 1929.

Costello, D. P. "Pushkin and Roman Literature." *OSP* XI 46–55.

Gershenzon, M. *Mudrost' Pushkina*. Moscow, 1919.

———. *Stat'i o Pushkine*. Moscow, 1926.

Greene, M. "Pushkin and Sir Walter Scott." *Forum for Modern Language Studies* I, 3 (July 1965), 207–215.

Gregg, Richard, A. "Pushkin and Shenstone: The Case Reopened." *CL.* XVII (1965), 109–116.

Grossman, L. *Etiudy o Pushkine*. Moscow, 1928.

Gukovskii, G. A. *Pushkin i russkie romantiki*. Moscow, 1965.

Hope, A. D. "Pushkin's Don Juan." Melbourne Slavic Studies, vols. 5–10. Melbourne, Australia: Melbourne University, 1967.

Ivanov, V. "O Pushkine." *SZ* 64 (1937).

Johnson, C. C. "Pushkin: A Personal View." *Contemporary Review* CCVII 1198 (November 1965), 254–60.

Karlinsky, Simon. Two Pushkin Studies. California Slavic Studies, vol. II. Berkeley: University of California Press, 1963.

Kostka, E. "Pushkin's Debt to Schiller." Riv. di Letterature Moderne e Comparate, Firenze 20 (1967), 85–100.

Lednitski, W., editor. *Puszkin*. Vols. I–II. Krakau, 1937.

McConnell, A. "Pushkin's Literary Gamble." *ASEER XIX* (1960), 577–593.

Meilakh, B. S. *Pushkin i russkii romantizm*. Moscow-Leningrad, 1937.

Mirsky, D. *Pushkin*. New York: Dutton, 1963.

Modzalevskii, B. *Pushkin*. Leningrad, 1929.

New York Public Library. *Bulletin* (Slavonic Division), pp. 530–559. New York: New York Public Library, 1937.

Peace, R. *Pushkin. Vremennik Pushkinskoi kommissii*. Vols. I–VII. Moscow-Leningrad, 1936–1941.

Simmons, E. J. *Pushkin*. Gloucester, Mass.: P. Smith, 1965.

Tomashevskii, B. *Pushkin*. Vols. I, II. Moscow-Leningrad, 1956———.

Tsiavlovskii, M., editor. *Moskovskii pushkinist*. Vols. I–II. Moscow, 1927–1930.

———. *Stat'i o Pushkine*. Moscow, 1962.

Tsvetaieva, M. *Moi Pushkin*. Moscow, 1967.

Tynianov, Iu. *Arkhaisty i novatory*. Leningrad, 1929.

Vengerov, S., editor. *Pushkin i ego sovremenniki*. Vols. I–XXXVI. St. Petersburg-Leningrad, 1903–1934.

Vickery, W. N. "Parallelizm v literaturnom raxvitii Bairona i Pushkina." *ACICS* II (1963), 371–402.

———. *Pushkin: Death of a Poet*. Bloomington, Ind.: Indiana University Press, 1968.

———. *Alexander Pushkin*. New York: Twayne, 1970.

Sections 11–12:

POETRY UP TO 1825

Blagoi, D. *Tvorcheskii put' Pushkina*. Moscow-Leningrad, 1950.

Borshch, A., editor. *Pushkin na iuge*. Kishinev, 1958.

Dolinin, A. "Tsygane." *Pushkinist. Sbornik* I. St. Petersburg, 1914.

Grossman, L. "Ruslan i Liudmila." *UZ Moskovskogo gorodskogo PI* 48 (1955), 5.

Gudzii, N. "Brat'ia-razboiniki." *Izvestiia AN, Otdelenie obshchestvennykh nauk*, 1937, 2–3.

Gustafson R. F. "The Upas Tree (Anchar): Pushkin and Erasmus, Darwin." *PMLA LXXV* (1960), 101–109.

Iakovlev, N. "Tsygane." *Pushkin i ego sovremenniki* XXXVI (1934).

Nekrasov, A. "Kavkazskii plennik." *Sbornik v chest' A. Orlova*. Leningrad, 1934.

Pachmuss, T., and Victor Terras. "The Shift of the Image of Napoleon in the Poetry of A. Pushkin." *SEEJ* V (1961), 311–330.

Sipovskii, V. "Ruslan i Liudmila." *Pushkin i ego sovremenniki*, IV, 1906.

Vygodskii, D. "Iz evfonicheskikh nabliudenii (Bakhchisaraiskii fontan)" *Pushkinist*. Sbornik IV. Moscow-Petrograd, 1922.

Zhirmunskii, V. *Bairon i Pushkin*. Leningrad, 1924.

Section 13: Pushkin, *Boris Godunov*

Bazilevich, K. "Boris Godunov v izobrazhenii Pushkina." *Istoricheskie Zapiski* 1 (1937).

Bernshtein, D. *LN* 16–18 (1934).

———. "Boris Godunov." In *Pushkin rodonachal'nik novoi russkoi literatury*. Sbornik. Moscow-Leningrad, 1941.

Derzhavine, G. R. "Tragediia Pushkina Boris Godunov i russkie istoricheskie povesti nachala 17 veka." *UZ Moskovskogo PI* 43 (1954), 4.

Slonimskii, A., editor. "Boris Godunov." In *Boris Godunov, A. S. Pushkina (Sbornik statei)*. Leningrad, 1936.

Varneke, B. "Istochniki i zamysel Borisa Godunova." In *Pushkin. Stat'i i materialy*, edited by M. Alekseev. 1925.

Verkhovskii, N. "Zapadnoevropeiskaia istoricheskaia drama i Boris Godunov Pushkina." *Zapadnyi Sbornik*, edited by V. Zhirmunskii. Moscow-Leningrad, 1937.

Section 14: Pushkin, *Evgenii Onegin*

Bitsilli, P. "Smert' Evgenina i Tat'iany." *SZ* 64 (1937).

Bondi, S. "Ob'iasnitel'nye stat'i." In A. Pushkin's *Evgenii Onegin*, pp. 235–321. Moscow: Detizdat, 1936.

Brodskii, N. *Kommentarii k romanu Pushkina Evgenii Onegin.* Moscow, 1932. Revised edition: *Evgenii Onegin.* Moscow, 1957.

Degtiarevskii, I. "O nekotorykh osobennostiakh stilia Evgeniia Onegina." *UZ Moskovskogo PI* 48 (1955), 5.

Gibian, G. "Narrative Technique and Realism: Evgeny Onegin and Madame Bovary." *Langue et litterature*, 1962, 339.

Gustafson, R. F. "The Metaphors of the Seasons in Evgenii Onegin." *SEEJ* VI, no. 1, Spring 1962, 6–20.

Matlaw, R. E. "The Dream in *Evgenii Onegin* with a Note on *Gore ot uma.*" *SEER* XXXVII (1959), 487–503.

Meilakh, B. "Evgenii Onegin." In *Istoriia russkogo romana.* IRL. Vol. I. Moscow: AN SSSR, 1962.

Pletnev, R. "Negoch, Pushkin i Mitskevich." *NZ* 68 (1962).

Tschizhevskii, D. *Pushkin. "Evgenii Onegin": A Novel in Verse.* With Introduction and Commentary. Cambridge, Mass.: Harvard University Press, 1953.

Vickery, W. N. "Byron's *Don Juan* and Pushkin's *Evgenii Onegin.* The Question of Parallelism." Indiana Slavic Studies, vol. 4. Bloomington, Ind.: Indiana University Press, 1967.

So-Called Tenth Chapter Of Evgenii Onegin

Gessen, S. "Istochniki 10-oi glavy". *Dekabristy i ikh vremia.* Vol. II. Moscow, 1932.

Morozov, P. *Pushkin i ego sovremenniki* XIII (1910).

Sokolov, D. *Pushkin i ego sovremenniki* XVI (1913).

Tomashevskii, B. *LN* 16–18 (1934).

Section 15:

Pushkin, Narrative Poems

Alekseev, M., editor. "Pushkin." *Trudy tret'ei Pushkinskoi konferentsii.* Moscow-Leningrad, 1953.

Aronson, M. "Mednyi Vsadnik." *Pushkin. Vremennik* I (1936).

Bitsilli, P. *Etiudy o russkoi poezii.* Prag, 1925.

Blagoi, D. "Poltava." In *Moskovskoi Pushkinist* II (1953).

Eikhenbaum, B. "Graf Nulin." *Pushkin. Vremennik* II (1937).

Iakobson, R. "Sokha v simvolike Pushkinove." *Slovo i slovesnost'* III (1937).

Komarovich, V. "O Mednom Vsadnike." *Literaturnyi sovremennik* 2 (1937).

Oksenov, I. "O simvolike Mednogo Vsadnika." In *Pushkin 1833 god.* Leningrad, 1933. (Miscellaneous.)

Pauls, J. P. "Historicity of Pushkin's Poltava." *Ukr Q.* XVII (1961), 230–246, 342–361.

———. "Pushkin's Poltava." *Shevchenko Scientific Society.* New York, 1963.

———. "Pushkin's Dedication of Poltava and Princess Mariya Volkonskaia." *Marquette University Slavic Institute Papers*, no. 12. Milwaukee, Wisc.: Marquette University, 1961.

Pumpianskii, L. "Mednyi Vsadnik i poeticheskaia traditsiia 18. v." *Pushkin. Vremennik* IV–V (1939).

Vernadskii, G. "Mednyi Vsadnik." *Sl*, II (1923), 4.

Zhdanov, I. *Pamiati Pushkina.* Miscellany on "Rusalka." St. Petersburg, 1900.

Zhinkin, N., editor. "Poltava Pushkina." *Sl* XII, 1932, 4.

Pushkin, Fairy Tales

Akhmatova, A. "Posledniaia skazka Pushkina." (Skazka o zolotom petushke). *Zvezda* I (1933).

Azadovskii, M. "Pushkin i fol'klor." *Pushkin. Vremennik* I (1936) and III (1937).

Kirtley, Bacil, F. "National Character and Folklore in Pushkin's Skazki." West Virginia University Philological Papers, vol. XI. Morgantown, West Va.: West Virginia University, 1958.

Section 16:

Pushkin, Little Tragedies

Akhmatova, A. "Kamennyi gost' Pushkina." In *Pushkin. Issledovaniia i materialy*, edited by M. Alekseev. Vol. II. Moscow-Leningrad, 1958.

Berkov, P. "Ob odnom otrazhenii Kamennogo gostia Pushkina i Dostoevskogo." In *Pushkin. Issledovaniia i materialy*, edited by M. Alekseev. Vol. II. Moscow-Leningrad, 1958.

Bliumenfel'd, V. "K problematike Motsarta i Salieri." *Voprosy literatury*, 1958, 2.

Darskii, D. *Malenkie tragedii Pushkina.* Moscow, 1915.

Druzhinina, N. "K voprosu o traditsiakh antichnoi dramaturgii v malen'kikh tragediakh Pushkina." *UZ Leningradskogo PI* (1957), 2.

Frantsev, V. "K tvorcheskoi istorii Motsarta i Salieri" *Sl*, X (1931), 2.

Gefford, H. "Pushkin's Feast in Time of Plague." *Slavic Review.* (New York) VIII (1949).

Gregg, Richard A. "Pushkin and Shenstone: The Case Reopened." *Comparative Literature* (Skupoj rycar') XVII (1965), 109–116.

Iakovlev, N. "Ob istochnikakh Pira vo vremia chumy." *Pushkinist* IV (1922).

Seeley, F. F. "The Problem of Kamennyi Gost'." *SEER* XLI, no. 97 (June 1963), 345–367.

Tomashevskii, B. "Malen'kie tragedii Pushkina." *Pushkin. Vremennik* I (1936).

Section 17:

PUSHKIN, PROSE

Alekseev, M. "Istoriia sela Goriukhina." *Pushkin.* Vol. II. Odessa, 1926.

Al'tman, M. "Videnie Germana." *Sl* IX (1930), 4.

———. "Baryshnia-krestianka." *Sl* X (1931), 4.

Bogorodskii, B. "O iazyke i stile romana Arap Petra Velikogo." *UZ Leningradskogo PI*, 1956.

Fokht, U. P. "Proza Pushkina." In *Pushkin rodonachal'nik russkoi literatury.* Moscow, 1941.

Gippius, V., and I. Kroll'. *Pushkin i teatr.* Sbornik statei. Leningrad, 1937.

Gregg, Richard, "Scapegoat for all Seasons: The Unity and the Shape of the *Tales of Belkin.*" *SR* XXX (1971).

———. "Balzac and the Women in *The Queen of Spades.*" *SEEJ* X (1966).

Grossman, L. "Vystrel." *Novyi Mir* 5 (1929).

Gukasova, A. "Istoriia sela Goriuchina. *UZ Moskovskogo PI*, 1954, 4.

Iakubovich, D. "Pikovaia dama." *Pushkin. 1833 god.* Leningrad, 1933.

———. "Dubrovskii." *Pushkin. 1833 god.* Leningrad, 1933.

Karlinskii, Simon. "Two Pushkin Studies: I. Pushkin, Chateaubriand, and the Romantic Prose; II. The Amber Beads of Crimea (Pushkin and Mickiewicz)." California Slavic Studies, vol. II. Berkeley: University of California Press, 1963.

Lerner, N. *Proza Pushkina.* Moscow, 1923.

Lezhnev, I. *Proza Pushkina.* Moscow, 1937.

Loppatto, M. "Povesti Pushkina." *Pushkinist* III (1918).

———. "Kapitanskaia dochka." *Pushkinist* III (1918).

Pedrotti, L. "Sekowski's Defense of Pushkin's Prose." *SEEJ* VII, no. 1 (Spring 1963), 18–25.

Proffer, C., editor. *The Critical Prose of A. S. Pushkin*, with Critical Essays by Four Russian Romantic Poets. Bloomington, Ind. University of Indiana Press, 1969.

Shaw, J. T. "The Conclusion of Pushkin's Queen of Spades." *SPRL*, 1954.

———. "Form and Style in the Letters of Aleksandr Pushkin." *SEEJ* IV (1959), 147–157.

———. "Pushkin's *The Shot.*" Indiana Slavic Studies, vol. 3. Bloomington, Ind.: Indiana University Press, 1963.

———. "The Problem of Persona in Journalism: Pushkin's Feofilakt Kosičkin." *ACICS* V (1963).

Slonimskii, A. "Pikovaia dama." *Pushkinist* IV (1922).

Tschizhevskij, D. Nachwort zu *A. Pushkin. Erzhälungen.* Munich, 1957.

Vinogradov, V. "K izucheniiu iazyka i stilia pushkinskoi prozy: Stantsionnyi smotritel'." *Russkii iazyk v shkole* VIII (1949), 3.

Section 18:
PUSHKIN, CRITICAL AND HISTORICAL WORKS

Bogoslovskii, N. V., editor. *Pushkin kritik.* Moscow-Leningrad, 1934. Revised edition. 1950.

Bondi, S. "Istorikoliteraturnye opyty Pushkina." *LN* 16–18 (1934).

Chicherin, A. "Put' Pushkina k istoricheskomu romanu." In *IRR.* Vol. I. Moscow, 1962.

Gippius, V. "Pushkin i zhurnal'naia polemika ego vremeni." *Pamiati Pushkina.* St. Petersburg, 1900.

Izmailov, N. "Kapitanskaia dochka." In *IRR.* Vol. I Moscow, 1962.

Komarovich, V. *Pushkin. Vremennik* III (1937).

Lerner, N. "Novootkrytye stat'i." *Pushkin i ego sovremenniki* XII (1909).

Oksman, Iu. "Pushkin v rabote nad Istoriei Pugacheva." *LN* 16–18 (1934).

Tynianov, Iu. "Puteshestvie v Arzrum." *Pushkin. Vremennik* II (1936).

Section 19:
PUSHKIN, LANGUAGE AND POETICS

Bitsilli, P. *Etiudy o russkoi poezii.* Prag, 1925.

Bobrov, S. *Novoe stikhoslozhenie Pushkina.* Moscow, 1915.

Chernyshev, V. "Stikhotvoreniia Pushkina v stile narodnykh pesen." *Sl* II (1930), 3.

Grossman, L. "Oneginskaia strofa." In *Pushkin,* edited by N. Piskanov. Vol. I. Moscow-Leningrad, 1924.

Gudzii, N. "Prozopopeia u Pushkina." In *Pamiati P. N. Sakulina.* Moscow, 1931.

Gukovskii, G. *Pushkin i problemy realisticheskogo stilia.* Moscow, 1957.

Khodasevich, V. *Poeticheskoe khoziastvo Pushkina.* Paris, 1934.

Nechaeva, V. "Pushkin." In *LE* IX (1935), 378–450.

Orlov, A. *Iazyk russkikh pisatelei*. Moscow-Leningrad, 1948.

Poeticheskaia frazeologiia Pushkina, edited by V. Levin. Moscow, 1969.

Shcherba, L. "Opyt lingvisticheskogo tolkovaniia stikhotvorenii." *Russkaia rech'* I (1933). Also in Shcherba, L. *Izbrannye raboty*. Moscow, 1957.

Slonimskii, A. *Masterstvo Pushkina*. Moscow, 1959.

Tomashevskii, B. "Ritmika 4-khstopnogo iamba." *Pushkin i ego sovremenniki* XXIX–XXX (1927).

———. "Piatistopnyi iamb Pushkina." *Ocherki po poetike Pushkina*. Berlin, 1923. Also in *O stikhe*, by B. Tomashevskii. Petrograd, 1920.

Tschizhevskij, D. *Solange Dichter leben*. Krefeld, 1949.

Vinogradov, V. *Iazyk Pushkina*. Moscow-Leningrad, 1935.

———. *Stil' Pushkina*. Moscow, 1941.

Vinokur, G. "Pushkin i russkii iazyk." In *A. S. Pushkin 1837–1937*. (Misc.) Moscow, 1937.

Section 20: *Anton Del'vig*

Kiselev, N. "Razmery Del'viga." In *Trudy i dni* VIII (1916).

Koehler, Ludmila. *Anton Antonovič Del'vig*. The Hague: Mouton, 1970.

Modzalevskii, B. *Pushkin*. Leningrad, 1929.

Rozanov, I. *Poety 20-kh godov 19 veka*. Moscow, 1925.

Shervinskii, S. "Baron Del'vig i russkaia narodnaia pesnia." *RA*, 1915, 6.

Uspenskii, V. "O Del'vige." *Russkaia poeziia*. Leningrad, 1929.

Vinogradov, I. *Bor'ba za stil'*. Leningrad, 1937.

Vinogradov, V. "Pushkin" *Vremennik* IV–V (1939).

Section 21: *Wilhelm Kiukhelbeker* (Küchelbecker)

Arkhipova, A. "O tragedii V. K. Kiukhelbekera Argiviane." *UZ Leningradskogo PI*, 1958, l.

Bazanov, V. *Poety-dekabristy*. Moscow-Leningrad, 1950.

Durylin, S. N. "Russkie pisateli u Gete v Veimare." *LN* 4–6 (1932). *Literaturnoe Nasledstvo* 59 (1954).

Mordovchenko, N. *Russkaia kritika pervoi chetverti 19 veka*. Moscow-Leningrad, 1959.

Tomashevskii, B. "Vorlesungen uber die russische Literatur." *LN* 59 (1954).

Tynianov, Iu. "Prokopii Liapunov." *Literaturnyi sovremennik*. 1938, l.

———. "Kiukhelbeker." *Literaturnyi sovremennik*. 1938, 10.

———. *Arkhaisty i novatory*. Leningrad, 1929.

———. "Kiukhelbeker." In *LN* 16–18 (1934); *LN* 33–34 (1939).

Section 22: *E. A. Baratynskii*

Briusov, V. "Baratynskii i Salieri." *RA*, 1900, 8.
———. "K stoletiu so dnia rozhdeniia Baratynskogo." *RA*, 1900, 4.
Dees, Benjamin. *E. A. Baratynsky*. New York: Twayne, 1972.
Filippovich, P. *Zhizn' i tvorchestvo Baratynskogo*. Kiev, 1917. Also in *KUI*, 1917.
Griftsov, B. "Dve otchizny v poezii Baratynskogo." *RM*, 1915, 6.
Ivask, Iu. "Baratynskii." *Novyi zhurnal* L (1957).
Kjetsaa, A. *Evgenij Baratynskii*. Oslo, 1973.
Kotliarevskii, N. *Starinnye portrety*. St. Petersburg, 1917.
Sadovskoi, B. *Ledokhod*. St. Petersburg, 1916.
Stammler, Heinrich. *E. A. Baratynski: Introduction*. Munich: Winkler-Verlag, 1948.
Struve, Gleb. "Evgeny Baratynsky." *SEER* XXIII (1945).
Verkhovskii, Iu. "O simvolizme Baratynskogo." *Trudy i dni*, 1912, 3.

Section 23: *N. M. Iazykov*

Azadovskii, M. *Literatura i fol'klor*. Leningrad, 1938.
Orlov, V. *Puti i sud'by*. Moscow-Leningrad, 1963.
Sadovskoi, B. *Ledokhod*. St. Petersburg, 1916.
Shenrok, V. "Iazykov." *VE*, 1897, pp. 11–12.

Section 24: *D. V. Venevitinov*

Ginzburg, L. "Opyt filosofskoi liriki." *Poetika* V (1929).
Kotliarevskii, N. *Starinnye portrety*. St. Petersburg, 1907.
Mordovchenko, N. *Russkaia kritika pervoi chetverti 19 veka*. Moscow-Leningrad, 1950.
Nekrasov, F. "Venevitinov kak poet i kritik." In *Pushkinskii sbornik*, edited by A. Kirpichnikov. Moscow, 1900.
Sadovskoi, B. *Russkaia kamena*. Moscow, 1910.

A. I. Odoevskii

Bazanov, V. *Poety-dekabristy*. Moscow-Leningrad, 1950.
Kotliarevskii, N. *Dekabristy*. St. Petersburg, 1907.

F. N. Glinka

Bazanov, v. *Poeticheskoe nasledie F. Glinki*. Petrozavodsk, 1949.
———. *Ocherki dekabristkoi literatury*. Moscow, 1953.
Bochkarev, V. *Russkaia istoricheskaia dramaturgiia nachala 19 veka*. Kuibishev, 1959.
Kliuev, S. "Kol'tsov i Glinka." *Voprosy russkoi literatury. Sbornik statei*. Moscow, 1959.

Rozanov, I. *Russkaia lirika.* Moscow, 1914.

P. A. Pletnev

Grot, K. "Pletnev." *RBS*, 1905.

Kaminskii, V. "Pletnev." *RSt*, 1904, 9.

———. "Gogol' i Pletnev." *IORIa* XVII (1912).

———. "Pletnev kak kritik i publitsist." *RSt*, 1906, 11.

Krukovskii, A. "Pletnev kak kritik." *FZ* (1916), 1.

Rozanov, I. *Russkaia lirika.* Moscow, 1914.

———. *Pushkinskaia pleiada.* Moscow, 1923.

D. V. Davydov

Literaturnoe Nasledstvo 19–21 (1935).

Leighton, L. G. "Denis Davydov's Hussar Style." *SEEJ* XII (1968), 4.

Orlov, V. *Puti i sud'by.* Moscow-Leningrad, 1936.

Rozanov, I. *Russkaia lirika.* Moscow, 1914.

———. *Poety 20-kh godov 19 veka.* Moscow, 1925.

Section 25: I. I. Kozlov

Maslov, V. *Nachal'nyi period baironizma v Rossii.* Kiev, 1915. Also in *KUI*, 1915.

Neiman, B. "Otrazhenie poezii Kozlova v tvorchestve Lermontova." *IORIa*, 1914, 19.

Orlov, V. "Kozlov." In *IRL.* Vol. VI. Moscow-Leningrad: AN SSSR, 1963.

Section 26: P. A. Katenin

Bertenson, S. "Katenin." In *Literaturnye materialy.* St. Petersburg, 1909.

Bitner, G. "Dramaturgiia Katenina." *UZ Leningradskogo Univ.* 1939, 33.

Orlov, V. *Puti i sud'by.* 1963.

Piskanov, N. "Zametki o Katenine." *Pushkin i ego sovremenniki* XII (1909).

Rozanov, I. *Russkaia lirika.* Moscow, 1914.

———. *Pushkinskaia pleiada.* Moscow, 1923.

Tynianov, Iu. *Arkhaisty i novatory.* Leningrad, 1929.

CHAPTER IV

Section 1: V. F. Odoevskii

Chertkov, L. "Odoevskii." *KLE* V (1968).

Gippius, V. "Uzkii put'." *RM*, 1914, 12.

Kotliarevskii, N. "Odoevskii." *IORIa* IX, (1904), 2. Also in *Starinnye portrety*, by N. Kotliarevskii. St. Petersburg, 1907.

Lezin, B. *Ocherki iz zhizni i literaturnoi deiatel'nosti kn. V. F. Odoevskogo.* Kharkov, 1907.

Sakulin, P. *Iz istorii russkogo idealizma.* Vol. I Moscow, 1913.

Stammler, H. Introduction to *Russische Nächte* by W. F. Odoevskii. Ellermann, München, 1970.

Section 2: *A. A. Bestuzhev-Marlinskii*

Alekseev, M. *Etiudy o Marlinskom. Sbornik trudov Irkutskogo Univ.* 1928, 15. And separately: Irkutsk, 1920.

Bazanov, V. *Ocherki dekabristkoi literatury.* Moscow, 1953.

Kovarskii, N. "Rannii Marlinskii." *Russkaia proza.* Leningrad, 1926.

Mordovchenko, N. *Russkaia kritika pervoi chetverti 19 veka.* Moscow-Leningrad, 1959.

Tsetlin, A. "Bestuzhin-Marlinskii." *LE* VII (1934).

Vinogradov, V. *O iazyke khudozhestvennoi literatury.* Moscow, 1959.

Section 3: *M. N. Zagoskin.*

Grushkin, A. "Roslavlev." In *Pushkin*, by A. Grushkin. Published in *Pushkin. Vremennik* VI (1941).

Nikulin, L. "Roslavlev Zagoskina." In *Roslavlev*, by M.N. Zagoskin. Moscow, 1955.

Pavsha, A. "Istochniki romana Zagoskina Iurii Miloslavskii." *Izvestiia Voronezhskogo PI* (1940), 6.

Petrov, S. "Zagoskin." In *IRR*. Vol. I. Moscow-Leningrad: AN SSSR, 1962.

Vinogradov, V. "Iurii Miloslavskii." *Doklady i soobshcheniia Filolog. Fak. Moskovskogo Univ.* (1948), 5.

I. I. Lazhechnikov

Iliinskaia, N. "Roman Lazhechnikova, Ledianoi dom." *UZ Leningradskogo PI* (1959), 189.

Litvinova, G. "Roman Lazhechnikova, Basurman." *UZ Moskovskogo gorodskogo PI* (1959), 98.

Modzalevskii, B. *Pushkin.* Leningrad, 1929.

Petrov, S. "Lazhechnikov." In *IRR*. Vol. I. Moscow-Leningrad: AN SSSR, 1962.

Pinchuk, A. "Russkii istoricheskii roman." *FZ* (1914), 1.

Section 4: *N.A. Polevoi*

Berezina, V. "N. Polevoi v Moskovskom Telegrafe." *UZ Leningradskogo*

Univ. 173 (1954), 20.

Bernshtein, D. "Polevoi." In *LE*, Vol. 9.

——. "Khudozhestvennoe tvorchestvo N. Polevogo." *Literatura i marksizm.* 1929, 5.

Dubrovin, N. "N.A. Polevoi i ego storonniki i protivniki." *RSt,* 1903, 2.

Kogan, P. *Ocherki po istorii russkoi kritiki.* Vol. I. Moscow-Leningrad, 1929.

Kozmin, N. *Ocherki iz istorii russkogo romantizma.* St. Petersburg, 1903.

Kupreianova, E. "Polevoi." *IRR,* I.

Orlov, V. *Ocherki po istorii russkoi zhurnalistiki i kritiki.* Leningrad, 1950.

Orlov, V., editor. "N. Polevoi" *Materialy po istorii russkoi literatury i zhurnalistiki.* Leningrad, 1934.

Section 5: *M. P. Pogodin*

Barsukov, N. *Zhizn'i trudy Pogodina.* I–XXII. St. Petersburg, 1888–1910, 1–22.

Kirpichnikov, A. "Pogodin i Gogol'." *RSt,* 1901, 1. Also in *Ocherki po istorii novoi russkoi literatury.* Moscow, 1903, 1.

Stepanov, N. "Pogodin." In *IRL.* Vol. VI. Moscow-Leningrad, 1953.

Toibin, I. M. "Pushkin i Pogodin." *Uchenye Zapiski Kurskogo PI* (1956), 5.

Section 6: *V. I. Dal'*

Barkova, E. "Dal' kak belletrist." *Voronezhskii istorichesko-arkheologicheskii vestnik,* 1921, 1–2.

Gofman, V. "Fol'klornyi skaz Dalia." *Russkaia proza.* Leningrad, 1926.

Mironov, G. "Dal'." *KLE* II (1964).

Myshkovskaia, L. "Dal'." *LE,* 3.

Prokhorova, V. *Dialektizm v iazyke khudozhestvennoi literatury.* Moscow, 1957.

Section 7: *N. V. Gogol'*

GENERAL:

Alekseev, M., editor. *Gogol': Stat'i i materialy.* Leningrad, 1954.

Belyi, A. "Gogol'." *Vesy* IV (1909). Also in *Lug Zelenyi.* Moscow, 1909. Reprint. New York: Johnson Reprint Corp., 1967.

Briusov, V. *Ispepeplennyi.* Moscow, 1909. Also in English translation in *RLT* III (1971).

Čiževskij, Dmitry, "The Unknown Gogol'." *SEER* XXX (1952).

Dashkevich, N., editor. *Pamiati Gogolia*; Istoricheskoe obshchestvo Nestora Letopistsa, Kiev, 1902.

Debreczeny, P. N. *Gogol and his Contemporary Critics.* Philadelphia: Amer. Phil. Society, 1966.

Driessen, Frederick, C. *Gogol as a Short Story Writer.* Slavistic Printings and Reprintings, 57. Mouton, The Hague.

Ermilov, V. *Gogol'.* Moscow. Different editions, 1952–56.

Fanger, Donald. *Dostoevsky and Romantic Realism: A Study of Dostoevsky in Relation to Balzac, Dickens, and Gogol'.* Cambridge: Harvard University Press, 1965.

Gippius, V. *Gogol'.* Petrograd, 1924. Reprint, Ann Arbor, Michigan: University of Michigan Press, 1962.

Gippius, V., editor. *Gogol'*; *Materialy i issledovaniia,* I–II. Moscow-Leningrad, 1936.

Golubkova, V. V., editor. *Gogol' v shkole.* Moscow, 1954.

Gukovskii, G. *Realizm Gogolia.* Moscow-Leningrad, 1959.

Karlinsky, Simon. "Portrait of Gogol' as a Word Glutton, with Rabelais, Sterne, and Gertrude Stein as Background Figures." California Slavic Studies, vol. V. Berkeley: University of California Press, 1970.

Khrapchenko, M. *Gogol'.* Moscow, 1954.

Korobka, N. "Gogol' kak romantik." *Obrazovanie,* 1902, 2.

Kotliarevskii, N. "Gogol'." *Mir Bozhii,* 1902, 1–2.

Lavrin, J. *Nikolai Gogol: 1809–1852.* New York: Collier, 1962.

Magarschak, D. *Gogol, a Life.* London: Faber and Faber, 1957.

Mandelshtam, I. *O Kharaktere gogolevskogo stilia.* Petersburg-Helsingfors, 1902.

Merezhkovskii, D. *Gogol' i chort.* Moscow, 1906.

Mochulskii, V. *Dukhovnyi put' Gogolia.* Paris, 1934.

Nabokov, V. *Nikolai Gogol.* New York: New Directions Publishing Corp., 1944.

Ovsianiko-Kulikovskii, D. "Gogol'." In *Sobranie sochinenii,* by D. Ovsianiko-Kulikovskii. Moscow, 1912, and reprints.

Pamiati N. V. Gogolia. Kiev, 1911.

Pereverzev, V. *Tvorchestvo Gogolia.* Moscow, 1914.

Sadovskoi, B. "O romantizme Gogolia." *Vesy,* 1909, 4.

Sechkarev, V. *Gogol: His Life and Works.* New York: New York University Press, 1965.

Shambinago, S. *Trilogiia romantizma.* Moscow, 1911.

Stepanov, N. *Gogol'.* Moscow, 1955.

Troyat, H. *Gogol.* Paris, 1972.

Tschizhevskii, D. "Neizvestnyi Gogol'." *Novyi Zhurnal* 27 (1951). See also English translation: "The Unknown Gogol." *The Slavonic and East European Review* XXX, London, 1952, 75.

———. "Gogol, Artist and Thinker." *The Annals of the Ukrainian Academy in the U.S.* II. New York, 1952.

Vengerov, S. "Pisatel'—grazhdanin." In *Gogol': Sobranie sochinenii.* II. St. Petersburg, 1913.

Vlach, R. "Gogol and Hashek: Two Masters of Poshlost'." *Ètudes slaves et est-européens* VII, 239–242.
Zen'kovskii, V. *Gogol'.* Paris: YMCA Press, 1961.
———. In *ZfsP* 9 (1931), 2; and *ZfsP* 13 (1936).

Section 8:
GOGOL', UKRAINIAN STORIES AND SHORT NOVELS

Chudakov, G. "Otnoshenie tvorchestva Gogolia k zapadnoevropeiskim literaturam." *KUI*, 1907, 7–10.
Danilov, V. "Propavshaia gramota." *RA*, 1915, 2.
Galkina-Fedoruk, E. "O iazyke rannikh proizvedenii Gogolia." *Vestnik Moskovskogo Universiteta*, 1952, 4, 2.
Gippius, V. "Vechera na khutore bliz Dikan'ki." *TONRL* I (1948).
Kulish, P. "Gogol' kak avtor povestei iz ukrainskoi zhizni." *Osnova*, 1861, 4–5, 9, 11–12.
McLean, H. "Gogol's Retreat from Love: Towards an Interpretation of 'Mirgorod'." ACICS IV (1958).
Mashinskii, S. *Istoricheskaia povest' Gogolia.* Moscow, 1940.
Rozov, V. *Pamiati Gogolia.* (On the Ukrainian Theater). Kiev, 1911.
Sipovskii, V. *Ukraina v rossiiskom pysmenstvi.* Vol. I. Kiev, 1928.
Tschizhevskii, D. "Istoriia ukrainskoi literatury." Chap. VII B. New York: Ukrainian Free Academy of Sciences in U.S.A. 1956.
Vinogradov, V. "Iazyk rannei prozy Gogolia." *MIRLIa*, I (1948).

Section 9:
GOGOL', PETERSBURG STORIES

Annenskii, I. "Problema Gogolevskogo iumora" ("Nos", "Portret") In *Kniga otrazhenii*, by I. Annenskii, Vol. II. St. Petersburg, 1906.
Gustafson, R. "The Suffering Usurper: Gogol's Diary of A Madman." *SEEJ* IX, 3 (Fall 1965), 268–280.
Khrapchenko, M. "Peterburgskie povesti Gogolia." *Izvestiia AN. Otdelenie literatury i iazyka* XI (1952), 1.
Landry, H. "Gogol's *The Overcoat.*" *Explicator* XIX (1961), item 54.
Mordovchenko, N. "Gogol' v rabote nad Portretom." *UZ Leningradskogo Universiteta* 47 (1939), 4.
Shedova, N., and N. Tret'iakova. *MIRLIa* III (1953). (Article on the language of *Taras Bul'ba*").
Tschizhevskij, D. *Gogol' Studien* 2 ("The Overcoat").
Wilson, N. A. *Gogol et Péterbourg.* Stockholm, 1954.

Section 10:
GOGOL', THEATER

Danilov, S. *Gogol' i teatr.* Leningrad, 1936.

Gippius, V. "Revizor." In *Gogol'. Materialy i issledovaniia*. Vol. II. Moscow-Leningrad, 1936.

Gofman, V. "Iazyk Revizora." *Literaturnaia ucheba*, 1934, 6.

Gogol' i Meierkhold. Sbornik. Moscow, 1927.

Gogol' i teatr. Edited by N. Stepanov. Moscow, 1952.

Krestova, L. *Kommentarii k komedii N. V. Gogolia Revizor*. Moscow, 1933.

Slonimskii, A. "Istoriia sozdaniia Zhenit'by." In *Russkie klassiki i teatr*. Moscow-Leningrad, 1947.

Stanislavskii, K. "Rabota nad rol'iu." *Sochineniia*. Moscow, 1957.

Stepanov, N. "Rabota Gogolia nad iazykom Revizora." *Teatr* 3 (1952).

Section 11 (see also Section 12):

GOGOL', DEAD SOULS

Annenskii, I. "Estetika Mertvykh Dush." *Apollon* 8 (1911).

Bogolepov, P. *Iazyk poemy Gogolia Mertrye Duši*. Moscow, 1952.

Golovaniuk, N. "Materialy dlia slovaria poemy Mertvykh Dush." *UZ Zhitomirskogo PI* (1955), 2.

Khrapchenko, M. *Mertvye Dushi*. Moscow, 1952.

Kotliarevskii, N. "Mertvye Dushi i sovremennaia russkaia povest'." *Mir Bozhii*, 1903, 1–2.

Ovsianiko-Kulikovskii, D. "Liudi 40-kh godov (Tentetnikov)." In *Istoriia russkoi intelligentsii*, by D. Ovsianiko-Kulikovskii. Vol. I. Moscow, 1906.

Proffer, C. R. *The Simile in Gogol's Dead Souls*. The Hague. Mouton, 1967.

Shelegov, V. "Sintaksis Mertvykh Dush." *Literaturnaia ucheba*, 1937, 7.

Smirnova-Chikina, E. *Kommentarii k Mertvym Dusham*. Moscow, 1934.

Solertinskii, E. "O kompozitsii Mertvykh Dush." *Voprosy Literatury*. 1959, 3.

Stepanov, N. "Gogolevskaia povest' o Kapitane Kopeikine." *Izvestiia AN. Otdelenie literatury i iazyka* XVIII (1959), 1.

Tamarchenko, D. "Mertvye Dushi." In *Istoriia russkogo roman*, edited by G. M. Friedlander, 323–358. *IRL*, vol. I. Moscow-Leningrad: AN SSSR, 1962.

Toporkov, V. "Mertvye Dushi v MKhAt." In *K. S. Stanislavskii na repetitsii*, by V. Toporkov. Moscow-Leningrad, 1949.

Tschizhevskii, D. *Postword to the German Translation of Mertvye Dushi*. Munich, 1949.

Section 12 (see also Section 11):

GOGOL', LATER STORIES: THE NOSE, THE OVERCOAT, ROME

Annenskii, I. "Problema Gogolevskogo iumora" (Nos, Portret). In Kniga otrazhenii, by I. Annenskii, vol. II. St. Petersburg, 1906.

Eikhenbaum, B. "Kak sdelana Shinel'," in Skvoz' literaturu, by B. Eikhenbaum. Leningrad, 1924. Reprint, 1926. See also the English version: "The Structure of Gogol's The Overcoat." Russian Review XXII (1963), 377–399.

Gofman, V. "Iazyk i stil' povesti Nos." Literatura v shkole, 1936, 5.

Pedrotti, Louis. "The Architecture of Love in Gogol's Rome." California Slavic Studies, vol. VI. Berkeley: University of California Press, 1971.

Rozanov, V. "Kak proizoshel tip Akakiia Akakievicha." In Legenda o velikom inkvizitore. St. Petersburg, 1906. Reprint.

Spycher, P. C. "N. V. Gogol's The Nose: A Satirical Comic Fantasy Born of an Impotence Complex." SEEJ VII (Winter 1963), 361–374.

Tschizhevskii, D. Gogol'—Studien (The Overcoat). ZfsP 14 (1937).

Vinogradov, V. Gogol' i natural'naia shkola. Leningrad, 1925.

———. Evoliutsiia russkogo naturalizma (Gogol' i Dostoevskii). Moscow, 1929.

———. Etiudy o stile Gogolia. Moscow, 1926.

Section 13:
WORLD VIEW

Blagoi, D. "Gogol'—kritik." In Istoriia russkoi kritiki. Vol. I. Moscow, 1958.

Florovskii, G. Chapter on Gogol' in Puti russkogo bogosloviia. Belgrad, 1937.

Tschizhevskii, D. "Neizvestnyi Gogol'." NZ, 27, 1951.

Tynianov, Iu. Dostoevskii i Gogol' (K teorii parodii). Leningrad, 1929. Reprint, Munich, 1960.

Zeldin, J. Foreword to the English translation of Selected Passages from Correspondence with Friends. Nashville: Vanderbilt University Press, 1969.

Zen'kovskii, V. "Gogol' v ego religioznykh iskaniiakh." Khristianskaia mysl'. Kiev, 1916. I–III, V, VII–VIII, X, XII (not completed).

Zenkovsky, V. A History of Russian Philosophy. Vol. I. New York: Columbia University Press, 1953.

Section 14:
GOGOL, POETICS

Belyi, A. Masterstvo Gogolia. Moscow-Leningrad, 1934. Reprint.

Mandel'shtam, I. *O kharaktere Gogolevskogo stilia.* St. Petersburg-Helsinki, 1902.

Slonimskii, A. *Tekhnika komicheskogo u Gogolia.* Petrograd, 1923. Reprint, Ann Arbor, Michigan: University of Michigan Press, 1962.

Vinogradov, V. *Gogol' i natural'naia shkola.* Leningrad, 1925.

———. *Evoliutsiia russkogo naturalizma (Gogol'i Dostoevskii).* Moscow, 1929.

———. *Etiudy o stile Gogolia.* Moscow, 1926.

———. "Iazyk Gogolia." In *Gogol'. Materialy i issledovaniia,* edited by V. Gippius Vol. II. Moscow-Leningrad, 1936.

———. "Iazyk Gogolia i ego znachenie v istorii russkogo iazyka." *MIRLIa* III (1953).

———. "Iz istorii stilei russkogo istoricheskogo romana." *Voprosy literatury,* 1958, 12; also in *O iazyke khudozhestvennoi literatury,* by V. Vinogradov. Moscow, 1959.

Zundelovich, Ia. "Poetika Groteska." In *Problemy poetiki,* edited by V. Briusov. Moscow-Leningrad, 1925.

Section 15: *Antonij Pogorel'skii (pen name of Alexis Pervoskii)*

Fridlender, G. M. "Pogorel'skii." In *IRR,* Vol. I Moscow-Leningrad: AN SSSR, 1962.

Gorolenko, V. "Perovskii." In *Kievskaia starina,* 1888, 4.

Ignatov, S. "Pogorel'skii i E. Gofman." *RFV* 72 (1914), 3–4.

Kirpichnikov, A. "Pogorel'skii." In *RBS,* 1902.

———. "A. Pogorel'skii." In *Ocherki po istorii novoi russkoi literatury,* edited by L. F. Panteleev. St. Petersburg, 1896.

———. *Ocherki:* "Nemetskii istochnik odnogo russkogo romana." *RSt* 1900, 12.

V. A. Sollogub

Lotman, L. "Sollogub." In *IRL.* Vol. VII. Moscow-Leningrad: AN SSSR, 1955.

Prutkov, N. I. "Sollogub." In *IRR.* Vol. I. Moscow-Leningrad: AN SSSR, 1962.

A. F. Vel'tman

Bukhshtab, B. "Vel'tman." In *Russkaia proza.* Leningrad, 1926.

Efimova, Z. "Vel'tman." In *Russkii romantizm.* Leningrad, 1927.

Fridlender, G. M. "Vel'tman." In *IRR.* Vol. I. Moscow-Leningrad: AN SSSR, 1962.

Granin, Iu. "Vel'tman." In *Ocherki po istorii russkoi literatury pervoi poloviny 19 veka*. Baku, 1941.

Pereverzev, V. "Predtecha Dostoevskogo." In *U istokov russkogo real'nogo romana*. Moscow, 1937.

Pinchuk, A. "Russkii istoricheskii roman." *FZ* (1914), 4.

"Vel'tman," in *LE*, vol. II. Moscow, 1930.

Vinogradov, V. "O sviazi protsessov razvitiia khudozhestvennogo iazyka." In *O iazyke khudozhestvennoi literatury*. Moscow, 1959.

O. I. Senkovskii (Sekowski)

Dudyshkin, S. "Sekowski." In *Otechestvenny zapiski* 122 (1859).

Ginzburg, L. "Sekowski." In *Ocherki po istorii russkoi zhurnalistiki i kritiki*. Vol. I. Leningrad, 1950.

Kaverin, V. *Baron Brambeus*. Istoriia Osipa Senkovskogo, redaktora "Biblioteki dlia chteniia." Leningrad, 1929.

Pedrotti, Louis, *Genesis of a Literary Alien (Osip I. Senkovsky)*. Berkeley: University of California Press, 1965.

Soloviev, E.A. *Senkovskii*. St. Petersburg, 1891.

F. V. Bulgarin

Alkire, Gilman H. "Gogol' and Bulgarin's Ivan Vyzhigin." SR XXVIII (1969).

Dubrovin, N. D. "K istorii russkoi literatury." *RSt* (1900), 9.

Engel'gardt, N. "Gogol' i Bulgarin." In *IV* VII (1904).

Gippius, V. "Pushkin v bor'be s Bulgarinym. Pushkin." *Vremennik Pushkinskoi Komissii* VI (1941).

Kallash, V. "Pushkin, N. Polevoi i Bulgarin." In *Pushkin i ego sovremenniki* II (1904).

Pereverzev, V. "Pushkin v bor'be ..." In *U istokov russkogo real'nogo romana*. Moscow, 1937.

Stolpianskii, P. N. "Pushkin i Severnaia pchela." In *Pushkin i ego sovremenniki* XXXI–XXXII (1927).

Striedter, J. *Der Schelmen-Roman in Russland*. Wiesbaden, 1961.

N. V. Kukol'nik

Lotman, L. "Kukol'nik." In *IRL*. Vol. VII. Moscow-Leningrad: AN SSSR, 1955.

N. F. Pavlov

Granin, Iu. "Pavlov." In *Ocherki po istorii russkoi literatury pervoi poloviny 19 veka*, by I. Granin. Baku, 1941.

Sukhomlinov, M. "Epizod iz literatury 30-kh godov." In *Issledovaniia i stat'i*, by M. Sukhomlinov. Vol. II. St. Petersburg, 1889.

Vil'chinskii, V. "Kriticheskie stat'i Pavlova." In *Iz istorii russkikh literaturnykh otnoshenii 19–20 vekov*. Moscow-Leningrad, 1959.

Trifonov, N. "Povesti Pavlova." *UZ Kafedry russkoi literatury Moskovskogo oblastnogo PI* (1939), 2.

Section 16: *Natural'naia shkola*

ON V. G. BELINSKII

Mordovchenko, N. "Belinskii." In *LN* 55 (1948).

ON FEDOR DOSTOEVSKII

Vinogradov, V. "Bednye liudi." In *Tvorcheskii put' Dostoevskogo*, edited by N. Brodskii. Leningrad, 1924.

ON D. V. GRIGOROVICH

Tkebuchava, S. "Tvorchestvo Grigorovicha 40-kh godov." *Trudy Batumskogo PI* (1958), 6.

ON N. A. NEKRASOV

Gin, M. "Nekrasov kak kritik." In *Nekrasovskii sbornik*. Moscow-Leningrad, 1951.

Belkin, A. "Nekrasov i natural'naia shkola." In *Tvorchestvo Nekrasova*, edited by A. Egolin. Moscow, 1938.

ON A. F. PISEMSKII

Prutskov, N. "Tvorchestvo Pisemskogo 40-50-kh godov." *UZ Omskogo PI* (1941), 1.

ON M. E. SALTYKOV-SHCHEDRIN

Glagolev, N. "Saltykov-Shchedrin i natural'naia shkola." *Literatura v shkole* (1936), 3.

Koperzhinskii, K. "Rannie povesti Saltykova-Shchedrina." *UZ Irkutskogo PI* (1940), 5.

ON I. S. TURGENEV

Vinogradov, V. "Turgenev i shkola molodogo Dostoevskogo." *Russkaia literatura* (1959), 2.

Granin, Iu. "Literaturnye zametki." In *Literaturnyi Azerbaidzhan* (1938), 10–11.

The best works on "Natural'naia shkola" are:

Vinogradov, V. *Gogol' i natural'naia shkola.* Leningrad, 1925.
———. *Evoliutsiia russkogo naturalizma (Gogol' i Dostoevskii).* Moscow, 1929.
———. *Etiudy o stile Gogolia.* Moscow, 1926.

ON E. P. GREBENKA

LE, vol. II.

ON MIXAIL DOSTOEVSKII

Borozdin, A. "Dostoevskii." In *RBS* (1905).
LE, vol. III.

ON YAKOV BUTKOV

Bagirov, E. "Peterburgskie vershiny Butkova." In *UZ Moskovskogo PI* 115 (1957), 7.

CHAPTER V

Section 1:

On Byronism in Russian literature, partial bibliography is also to be found in Chapter III, sect. 6 of this bibliography.

Kotliarevskii, N. *Mirovaia skorb'.* St. Petersburg, 1898. 2nd edition, St. Petersburg, 1914.
Maslov, V. *Nachal'nyi period baironizma v Rossii.* Kiev, 1915. Also in *KUI*, 1915.
Storozhenko, N. *Poeziia mirovoi skorbi.* Odessa, 1895.
Veselovskii, A. *Etiudy i kharakteristiki.* Vol. I. Moscow, 1912. *Etiudy o baironizme*, S. 385–562.

(*See also bibliography in sections 4–8 of this chapter.*)

Section 2: *A. I. Podolinskii*

Kievskii, S. "Poslednii iz Pushkinskoi pleiady." *RV* (1886), 1.
Tiniakov, A. "Podolinskii." In *IV* (1916), 1.
Vitberg, F. "Podolinskii." In *RBS* (1905).
Zhdanov, V. "Podolinskii." In *LE*, vol. IX.

Section 3: *A. I. Polezhaev*

Bobrov, E. "Polezhaev kak perevodchik." *RFV* (1903), 49.

——. *Iz istorii zhizni i poezii Polezhaeva.* Warsaw, 1904.

——. "O baironizme Polezhaeva." *RFV* (1905), 51.

——. "Polezhaev o Pushkine." In *Pushkin i ego sovremenniki* V (1907).

——. "Etiudy o Polezhaeve." *Varshavskie universitetskie izvestiia.* Warsaw, 1909, 4. f.; 1913, 1. f.

Rozanov, I. N. "Dve povesti v stikhakh o moskovskom universitete." In *Sbornik statei k sorokaletneiuchenoi deiatelnosti akad. A. N. Orlova.* Moscow-Leningrad, 1934.

Sadovskoi, B. "Polezhaev." In *Russkaia Kamena.* Moscow, 1910.

Voronin, I. *Polezhaev.* Moscow, 1954.

Section 4: *M. Iu. Lermontov*

Dashkevich, N. "Motivy mirovoi poezii . . ." In *Stat'i po novoi russkoi literature,* by N. Dashkevich. St. Petersburg, 1914.

Debreczeny, Paul. "Elements of the Lyrical Verse Tale in Lermontov's *A Hero of Our Time.*" In *American Contributions to the Seventh International Congress of Slavists.* The Hague: Mouton & Co., 1973.

Dumnov, V. V. editor. *Venok Lermontovu.* Moscow-St. Petersburg, 1914.

Durylin, S. *Lermontov.* Moscow, 1944.

Eikhenbaum, B. *Lermontov.* Leningrad, 1924.

Ginzburg, L. *Tvorcheskii put' Lermontova.* Leningrad, 1940.

Kliuchevskii, V. "Grust'." *RM* (1891), 7. Also in *Ocherki i rechi,* by V. Kliuchevskii. Moscow, 1913.

Kotliarevskii, N. *Lermontov.* 5th edition. St. Petersburg, 1915.

Lelevich, G., editor. "Lermontov." In *LE,* vol. VI.

Literaturnoe Nasledstvo 43–44 (1935); *LN* 45–46 (1948); *LN* 58 (1952).

Maksimov, D. *Poeziia Lermontova.* Leningrad, 1959.

Manuilov, V. *Lermontov.* Moscow-Leningrad, 1950.

——. *Lermontov. Zhizn' i tvorchestvo.* Leningrad, 1939.

Merezhkovskii, D. *Lermontov kak poet sverkhchelovechestva.* St. Petersburg, 1909.

Mersereau, John Jr. *Mikhail Lermontov.* Carbondale, Illinois: Southern Illinois University Press, 1962.

——. "'The Fatalist' as a Keystone of Lermontov's *A Hero of our Times.*" ASEEJ (1960).

——. "Lermontov's *Shtoss:* Hoax or Literary Credo?" *SR* XXI (1962).

——. "Balazac and Lermontov." ACICS V (1963).

Neiman, B. *Pushkin i Lermontov. Iz nabliudenii nad stilem,* edited by A. Egolin. *Lermontov. Sbornik statei.* Moscow, 1941.

Ovsianiko-Kulikovskii, D. *Lermontov.* St. Petersburg, 1914.

Sadovskoi, B. "Tragediia Lermontova." *RM* (1912), 7.

Shaw, J. Thomas. "Byron: The Byronic Tradition of the Romantic Verse
Tale in Russian, and Lermontov's Mtsyri." *Indiana Slavic Studies*,
vol. 1. Bloomington, Indiana: Indiana University Press, 1956.
————. "Lermontov's *Demon* and the Byronic Oriental Verse Tale."
Indiana Slavic Studies, vol. 2. Bloomington, Indiana: Indiana
University Press, 1958.
Shuvalov, S. *Lermontov. Zhizn' i tvorchestvo*. Moscow-Leningrad, 1925.
Zhizn' i tvorchestvo Lermontova. Stat'i i materialy. Vol. I. Moscow, 1941.
Zonov, D., editor. *Lermontov v russkoi kritike*. 2nd edition. Moscow,
1955.

Section 5:

LERMONTOV, LYRIC

Eikhenbaum, B. *Melodika russkogo liricheskogo stikha*. Petrograd, 1922.
Ginzburg, D. *O russkom stikhoslozhenii*. St. Petersburg, 1915.
Maksimov, D. "O lirike Lermontova." *Literaturnaia ucheba*. (1939), 4.
————. "Obraz prostogo cheloveka v lirike Lermontova." *UZ Lenin-
gradskogo PI* 9 (1954), 3.
Neiman, B. *Vliianie Pushkina na Lermontova*. Kiev, 1914. Also in *KUI*
(1914).
————. "Lermontov i Zhukovskii." *Russkii Bibliofil'* (1914), 6.
————. "Otrazhenie poezii Kozlova v tvorchestve Lermontova." *IORIa*
XIX (1914), 1.
Rodzevich, S. ,'K voprosu o vliianii Bairona i A de Vigny na Lermon-
tova." *FZ* (1915), 2.
Shtein, S. "Liubov' mertvetsa." *IORIa* XXI (1916), 1.

Section 6:

LERMONTOV, EPIC

Babushkin, N. "Iz tvorcheskoi istorii Demona." *Uchenye Zapiski
Tomskogo Universiteta* (1915), 16.
Rodzevich, S. "K voprosu o vliianii Bairona i A de Vigny na Lermon-
tova." *FZ* (1915), 2.
Shaw, J. T. "Lermontov's Demon and Byronic Oriental Verse." Vol. II.
Indiana Slavic Studies. Bloomington, Indiana: Indiana University
Press. 1958.
————. "Byron . . . in Mtsyri." Vol. I. *Indiana Slavic Studies*. Blooming-
ton, Indiana: Indiana University Press, 1956.
Sokolov, A. "Lermontov i russkaia romanticheskaia poema." *UZ
Moskovskogo oblastnogo PI* XIII (1949), 1.

————. *Ocherki po istorii russkoi poemy.* Moscow, 1955.
Zhirmunskii, V. *Bairon i Pushkin.* Leningrad, 1924.

Section 7:

LERMONTOV, THEATER

Efimova, Z. *Russkii romantizm.* Leningrad, 1927.
Iakovlev, M. *Lermontov kak dramaturg.* Moscow-Leningrad, 1924.
Neiman, B. "Dramatugiia Lermontova." In *Lermontov: Dramy.* Moscow-Leningrad, 1940.
Novitskii, P. editor. *Maskarad Lermontova. Sbornik statei.* Moscow-Leningrad, 1941.

Section 8:

LERMONTOV, PROSE

Durylin, S. *Geroi nashego vremeni M. Iu. Lermontova.* Moscow, 1940.
Eikhenbaum, B. "O smyslovoi osnove Geroi nashego vremeni." *Russkaia literatura* (1959), 3.
Iakubovich, D. "Lermontov i Val'ter Skott." *Izvestiia AN. Otdelenie obshchestvennykh nauk* (1935), 3.
Nabokov, V. Foreword to Lermontov's *Hero of Our Time.* Garden City, N. Y.: Doubleday, 1958.
Neiman, B. "Elementy sentimentalizma v tvorchestve Lermontova." *IORIa* XXII (1918), 2.
Ovsianikov-Kulikovskii, D. *Istoriia russkoi intelligentsii.* Moscow, 1906. Also in *Sobranie sochinenii,* by D. Ovsianikov-Kulikovskii. Vol. VII. Moscow, 1912, and reprints.
Peterson, M. "Sintaksis Lermontova." In *SI* VI (1927), 2–3.

Section 9: *S. P. Shevyrev*

Dementev, A. "Bor'ba s Belinskim." *UZ Leningradskogo Universiteta* (1939), 47.
Durylin, S. "Russkie pisateli i Gete v Veimare." *LN* 4–6 (1932).
Ocherki po istorii russkoi zhurnalistiki i kritiki. Vol. I. Leningrad, 1950. (Articles on "Moskvitianin" "Moskovskii vestnik" and "Moskovskii nabliudatel'.")
Orlov, V. "Poety 20-30-kh godov. Poety-liubomudry." *Literaturnaia ucheba* (1940), 4–5.
Sokolov, Iu. "Mirosozertsanie Shevyreva." *Besedy Sbornik.* Vol. I. Moscow, 1915.
Vol'pe, C. "Shevyrev." In *Russkie poety—sovremenniki Pushkina.* Leningrad, 1937.

Sections 10–11: *F. I. Tiutchev*

Bernshtein, S. "Opyt analiza slovesnoi instrumentovki." *Poetika.* Vol. V. Leningrad, 1929.

Blagoi, D. "Turgenev—redaktor Tiutcheva." In *Turgenev i ego vremia.* Moscow-Petrograd, 1923.

———. *Tri veka.* Moscow, 1923.

Briusov, V. "Tiutchev." *RA* (1900), 3.

Chulkov, G. *Letopis' zhizni i tvorchestva Tiutcheva.* Moscow-Leningrad, 1933.

———. *Posledniaia liubov' Tiutcheva.* Moscow, 1928.

Darskii, D. *Chudnye vymysli.* Moscow, 1913.

Eikhenbaum, B. *Melodika russkogo liricheskogo stikha.* Petrograd, 1922.

Fet, A. "O stikhotvoreniiakh Tiutcheva." *Russkoe slovo* (1859), 2.

Frank, S. "Komicheskoe chuvstvo v poezii Tiutcheva." *RM* (1913), 11, and *ZfsP* III (1927).

Gregg, Richard A. *Fedor Tiutchev, Evolution of a Poet.* New York: Columbia University Press, 1965.

Grossman, L. "Tri sovremennika. Tiutchev, Dostoevskii, Grigor'ev." Moscow, 1922. Also in *Ot Pushkina do Bloka,* by L. Grossman. Moscow. 1926.

Gudzii, N. "Alliteratsiia i assonans u Tiutcheva." *Sl* VI (1927).

———. "Tiutchev v poeticheskoi kul'ture russkogo simvolizma." *IpRIa* III (1930), 2.

Lezhnev, A. *Dva poeta. Tiutchev, Geine.* Moscow, 1934.

LN 19–21 (1935); *LN* 31–32 (1937).

Merezhkovskii, D. *Dve tainy russkoi poezii. Nekrasov i Tiutchev.* St. Petersburg, 1915.

Nekrasov, N. "Russkie vtorostepennye poety." *Sovremennik* (1950), 19.

Soloviev, V. "Poeziia Tiutcheva." *VE* (1895), 4.

Stremoukhoff, D. *La poésie et l' idéologie de Tioutchev.* Paris, 1937.

Tschizhevskii, D. "Tiutchev." *ZfsP* IV (1927), 2.

Turgenev, I. "Neskol'ko slov o stikhotvoreniiakh Tiutcheva." *Sovremennik* 44 (1954).

Tynianov, Iu. "Tiutchev." *Arkhaisty i novatory.* Leningrad, 1929.

Section 12: *V. G. Benediktov*

Brandt, R. "Neskol'ko slov o Benediktove." *RFV* 78 (1918).

Bukhshtab, B. "Estetizm v poezii . . ." *TONRL* I (1948).

Ginzburg, L. "Pushkin i Benediktov." In *Pushkin. Vremennik. Sovremennik . . .* Vol. II. Moscow-Leningrad, 1936.

———. "Iz literaturnoi istorii Benediktova." *Poetika.* Leningrad, 1927.

Sadovskoi, B. "Poet-chinovnik." In *RM* (1909), 10. Also in *Russkaia kamena*. Moscow, 1910.

Shimkevich, K. "Benediktov, Nekrasov, Fet." *Poetika*. Vol. V. Leningrad, 1929.

Section 13: *A. V. Kol'tsov*

Denitskii, A. "Kol'tsov." In *UZ Leningradskogo PI* 14 (1938).

Iarmershtedt, V. "Mirosozertsanie kruzhka Stankevicha i poeziia Kol'tsova." In *Voprosy filosofii i psikhologii* (1893), 5; (1894), 2.

Kallash, V. "Kol'tsov." In *IRL OK*. Vol. II. Moscow: Mir, 1909.

Putintsev, A. "Kol'tsov kak sobiratel' russkikh narodnykh poslovits." *Trudy Voronezhskogo Un.* 3 (1926).

Rozanov, I. "Pesni russkikh poetov." *BBP*. 1936. (Also contains information on other songwriters.)

Sobolev, P. "Kol'tsov." In *LE*, vol. V.

Tonkov, V., editor. *Sovremenniki o Kol'tsove*. Voronezh, 1959.

Tonkov, V. *Kol'tsov. Zhizn' i tvorchestvo.* 2nd edition. Voronezh, 1958.

Tsitserov, V. *Voprosy teorii i istorii narodnogo tvorchestva.* Moscow, 1959.

Volynskii, A. "Kol'tsov." *Severnyi vestnik* XI (1892). Also in *Bor'ba za idealizm*, by A. Volynskii. St. Petersburg, 1900.

Zamotin, I. "Kol'tsov i russkie modernisty." *RFV* (1909), 3–4.

Section 14: *Karolina Pavlova*

Beletskii, A. "Pavlova." In *Izvestiia AN* XXII (1917), 2.

Griftsov, B. "Karolina Pavlova." In *RM* (1915), 11.

Pereverzev, V. "Salonnaia poetessa." *Sovremennyi Mir.* (1915), 12.

Rapgof, B. *Karolina Pavlova. Materialy dlia izucheniia zhizni i tvorchestva.* St. Petersburg, 1916.

Sadovskoi, B. *Ledokhod*. St. Petersburg, 1916.

Section 15: *A. S. Khomiakov*

Batiushkov, F. "Teatral'nye zametki." *Mir Bozhii* (1902), 12.

Berdiaev, N. *Khomiakov*. Moscow, 1912.

Florovskii, G. "Khomiakov." In *Puti russkogo bogosloviia*. Belgrad-Paris, 1937.

Kotliarevskii, N. "Khomiakov kak poet." *RM* (1908), 10.

Kuzmin, M. "Analogiia ili providenie." *Apollon* (1914), 6–7.

Liaskovskii, V. "Khomiakov." *RA* (1896), 11.

Radlov, E. *O poezii Khomiakova*. Sbornik v chest' S. F. Platonova. St. Petersburg, 1911.

Sirotinin, A. *Rossiia i slaviane*. St. Petersburg, 1913.

V pamiat' o Khomiakove. *Russkaia beseda* (1860), 2. (Mainly bibliography.)

Zavitnevich, V. *Khomiakov*. Vols. I–II. Kiev, 1902–1913.

Zenkovsky, V. *A History of Russian Philosophy*. Vol. I. New York; Columbia University Press, 1953.

K. S. Aksakov

Aksakov, I. "Materialy o literaturnoi deiatel'nosti Aksakova." *RV* (1888), 9.

Brodskii, N. *Rannie slavianofily*. Vol. I. Moscow, 1910.

Lotman, L. M. "Proza sorokovykh godov." In *IRL*. Vol. VII. Moscow-Leningrad: AN SSSR, 1955.

Section 16. *N. V. Stankevich*

Arkhangel'skii, K. "Stankevich. Iz istorii umstvennoi zhizni tridtsatykh godov." *Izvestiia Severo-Kavkazskogo Universiteta* I (1930).

Brodskii, N. "Poeziia Stankevicha". *Vestnik kruzhka Stankevicha*. IORIa XVII (1912), 4.

———. "Poeziia Stankevicha." *Vestnik vospitaniia* (1914), 3.

Chyzhevskyi, D. *Gegel' v Rossii*. Paris, 1938.

Iarmershtedt, V. "Mirosozertsanie krushka Stankevicha i poeziia Kol'tsova." In *Voprosy filosofii i psikhologii* (1893), 5; (1894) 2.

Gershenzon, M. *Istoriia molodoi Rossii*. Moscow, 1908.

Sakulin, P. "Idealizm Stankevicha." In *VE* (1915), 2.

I. P. Kliushnikov

Adrianov, S. "Zabytyi poet." *IV* (1898), 6.

V. I. Krasov

Brodskii, N. "Poety kruzhka Stankevicha." *IORIa* XVII (1912).

Tschizhevskii, D. *Gegel' v Rossii*. Paris, 1938.

Zhuravlev, A. I. "O poezii kruzhka Stankevicha." In *Vestnik Moskovskogo Universiteta* IV (1967).

Section 18: *A. V. Timofeev*

Rozanov, I. "Timofeev" in *Pesni russkikh poetov*. *BBP* (1936).

———. "Timofeev." In *LE*, Vol. XI.

CHAPTER VI

Section 1: *A. Izmailov*

Bitner, G., editor. "Poety-satiriki kontsa 18—nachala 19 veka." *BBP* (1959).

Brailovskii, S. "Izmailov." *FZ* (1891), 6.

Kubasov, I. "Izmailov." *RSt* (1900), 6-9; *RSt* (1901) 1-2; and separately, St. Petersburg, 1901.

Longinov, M. "Zaimstvovaniia russkikh basnopistsev u frantsuzskikh pisatelei." *RA* (1905), 1.

Manuilov, V., editor. "Russkaia epigramma." (18-19 vv.) *MBP* (1958).

Sipovskii, V. *Ocherki iz istorii russkogo romana.* Vol. I, pt. 2. St. Petersburg, 1910.

Stepanov, N. "Izmailov." In *LE*, vol. IV.

———. "Izmailov" Russkaia basnia XVIII-XIX vv." *MBP*, Leningrad, 1958; *BBP*, 1949.

Timofeev, L. "Izmailov." In *LE*, vol. IV.

V. T. Narezhnyi

Belozerskaia, N. *Narezhnyi.* Vols. I-II. St. Petersburg, 1896.

Bochkarev, V. "Russkaia istoricheskaia dramaturgiia nachala 19 v." *UZ Kuibyshevskogo PI* 25 (1959).

Budrin, V. "Poslednii roman Narezhnogo, Garkusha." *UZ Permskogo PI* 10 (1946).

Nazarov, L. "Narezhnyi." In *IRR* I (1962).

Pereverzev, V. *U istokov russkogo real'nogo romana.* Moscow, 1937.

Shaduri, V. *Pervyi russkii roman o Kavkaze.* Tblisi, 1947.

Sokolov, Iu. *Besedy.* Vol. I. Moscow, 1915.

Stepanov, N. "U" istokov russkogo real'nogo romana." *Literaturnaia ucheba* (1937), 7.

———. "Narezhnyi." In *IRL*. Vol. V, Pt. 1. Moscow-Leningrad: AN SSSR, 1941.

G. F. Kvitka-Osnovianenko

Aizenshtok, I. "K voprosu o literaturnykh vliianiiakh (Kvitka-Osnovianenko i Gogol')." *IORIa* XXIV (1922), 1.

———. "Kvitka-Osnovianenko." In *LE*, vol. V.

Chyzhevskyi, D. *Istoriia ukrainskoi literatury.* New York: Ukrainian Free Academy of Sciences in U.S.A., 1956.

Liashchenko, A. "Revizor Gogolia i komediia Kvitki." In *Pamiati L. N. Maikova.* St. Petersburg, 1902 (and separately).

Verbychka, Ie. *Kvitka-Osnovianenko.* Kiev, 1946.

Volkov, N. *Zavisimost' Revizora Gogolia ot komedii Kvitki-Osnovianenko.* St. Petersburg, 1899.

A. A. Shakhovskoi

Bulich, N. *Ocherki po istorii russkoi literatury i prosveshcheniia.* Vol. II. St. Petersburg, 1905.

Bochkarev, V. "Russkaia istoricheskaia dramaturgiia nachala 19 v." *UZ Kuibyshevskogo PI* 25 (1959).

Gozenpud, A. *Muzykal'nyi teatr v Rossii.* Leningrad, 1959.

Saitov, V. "Shakhovskoi." *RBS* (1902).

Tomashevskii, B. *Pushkin.* Vol. I. Moscow-Leningrad, 1956.

Section 2: *I. A. Krylov*

Gukovskii, G. *XVIII vek.* 2 (1940).

Krylov, A. *Issledovaniia i materialy.* Moscow, 1947.

Nechaev, V. "Krylov." In *LE*, vol. V.

Orlov, A. *Iazyk russkikh pisatelei.* Moscow-Leningrad, 1948.

Stepanov, N. *Masterstvo Krylova-basnopistsa.* Moscow, 1956.

————. *Krylov, Zhizn' i tvorchestvo.* Moscow, 1949.

Vinogradov, V. "Iazyk i stil' basen Krylova." *Izvestiia AN. Otdelenie literatury i iazyka* (1945), 1.

Wilteben, F. "La Fontaine und Krylov." *WSJ* I (1950).

CHAPTER VII

Section 1: *Intellectual Development*

Billington, J. *The Icon and The Axe.* Princeton: Princeton University Press, 1965.

Florovskii, G. *Puti russkogo bogosloviia.* Belgrad-Paris, 1937.

Tschizhevskii, D. *Russische Geistgeschichte.* Vol. II. *Russland zwischen Ost und West.* Hamburg, 1961.

Zen'kovskii, V. *Istoriia russkoi filosofii.* Vols. I–II. Paris, 1948–50.

Zenkovsky, V. *A History of Russian Philosophy.* English edition. Vols. I–II. New York: Columbia University Press, 1953.

In the following books can also be found important material on Russian intellectual life.

Barsukov, N. *Zhizn' Pogodina.* Vol. I. St. Petersburg, 1888.

Miliukov, P. *Iz istorii russkoi intelligentsii.* St. Petersburg. 1902, 1903.

Sakulin, P. *Odoevskii. Iz istorii russkogo idealizma.* Vol. I. Moscow, 1913.

See also bibliography in Chapter VI, section 1.

ON THE DECEMBRISTS

Alekseev, M. editor and B. Meilakh. *Dekabristy i ikh vremia.* Moscow-Leningrad, 1951.

Chentsov, N. *Vostanie dekabristov.* Bibliografiia. Moscow-Leningrad. 1929.

Kazhmenko, K. *Otzvuki vosstaniia dekabristov v zarubezhnoi literature. Sbornik istoriko-filologicheskogo fakul'teta Stavropol'skogo PI* 13 (1958). *LN* 60 (1956), 1–2.

Nechkina, M. *Dvizhenie dekabristov.* Vols. I–II. Moscow, 1955.

Volk, S. "Dekabristy." In *Sovetskaia istoricheskaia entsiklopedia,* vol. 46. 1964.

Vosstanie dekabristov. Materialy i dokumenty. Moscow-Leningrad, 1925–58.

Section 3:

Brodskii, N., editor. *Literaturnye salony i kruzhki. Pervaia polovina 19 veka.* Moscow, 1930.

Eikhenbaum, B., M. Aronson, and S. Reiser. *Literaturnye salony.* Leningrad, 1929.

Gershenzon, M. *Istoriia molodoi Rossii.* Moscow, 1908.

———. *Istoricheskie zapiski.* Moscow, 1910. 2nd edition, Berlin, 1923.

Kovalevskii, M. "Filosofskoe ponimanie . . . russkogo proshlogo." *VE* (1915), 12.

Maksimovich, G. *Uchenie pervykh slavianofilov.* Kiev, 1907. Also in *KUI* (1907).

Mochul'skii, K. *Vladimir Soloviev.* Paris, 1959.

Nelidov, F. *Zapadniki 40-kh godov.* Moscow, 1910. (Texts.)

Quenet, C. *Tchaadaev et les Letters Philosophiques.* Paris, 1931.

Riazanovskii, N. *Russia and the West.* Berkeley: University of California Press, 1957.

Shakhovskoi, D. "Chaadaev." *LN* 22–24. (1935). (Russian translations of Chaadaev's French letters.)

Tschizewskij, D., and D. D. Groh. *Europa und Russland.* Darmstadt, 1959.

Zenkovskij, V. *Russkie mysliteli i Evropa.* Paris, 1930. 2nd edition Paris, 1955. English edition: *Russian Thinkers and Europe.* Ann Arbor, Michigan: University of Michigan Press, 1950.

Section 4:

Kovalevskii, M. "Shellingianstvo i gegel'ianstvo v Rossii." *VE* (1915), 11; *RM* (1916), 12.

Setchkarev, V. *Schellings Einfluss in der russischen Literatur der Zwanziger und Dreissigerjahre des 19 Jahrhunderts.* Leipzig, 1938.

Tschizewskij, D. *Gegel v Rossii.* Paris, 1938 (reprint).

———. *Schellings Philosophie bei den Slaven.* (In preparation.)

———. Review, *ZfsP* XVI (1940), 3–4.

Tschizewskij, D., editior. *Hegel bei den Slaven.* Reichenberg i B., 1934. 2nd edition, Darmstadt, 1961.

See also literature under Chapter VII, section 1.

Index